"Joni Carley tells a clear and practical story of the potency of alchemical leadership in mission success and life success. Whether you are just beginning the leadership journey or have led for years, Joni's insights inspire and remind us all to connect to our metaphysical power—our *mojo*. I have been honored to know Joni for many years. She is a force of nature—brilliant, compassionate, and filled with the spiritual vitality she writes about in her book. Joni leads with both 'head and heart' competencies, revealing a path all can aspire to. The power of her alchemical leadership *transforms* mundane resources into *gold* results!"

—Rhonda Fabian, CEO, Immediacy
Learning and Editor, *Kosmos Journal*

"Joni Carley offers a clear, inspiring, and unique guidebook to harnessing the mysteries of alchemy to access the power within. *The Alchemy of Power* will give you the deep insights and practical advice you need to bring new dimensions of success into your life, your work, and our world."

—Rev. Deborah Moldow, Founder, The Garden of Light

"This book goes beyond most leadership books: it tells you how to tap into the metaphysical forces of power. A transformational read for any leader wanting to move beyond the status quo."

—Richard Barrett, President of the Academy
for the Advancement of Human Values

DR. JONI CARLEY

THE ALCHEMY OF POWER

MASTERING THE INVISIBLE FACTORS OF LEADERSHIP

Post Hill
PRESS

A POST HILL PRESS BOOK
ISBN: 978-1-68261-623-9
ISBN (eBook): 978-1-68261-624-6

The Alchemy of Power:
Mastering the Invisible Factors of Leadership

Post Hill Press
New York • Nashville
posthillpress.com

Published in the United States of America

With deep gratitude for the hundreds of academic, philosophical, and spiritual teachers who have lit my path of many paths around the world, for my business and nonprofit executive clients who have taught me so much, and for my UN colleagues who always inspire me.

CONTENTS

PREFACE

The Alchemy of Power "ties rocks to clouds" by connecting everyday decision-making and action-taking with:

- philosophical, social and scientific principles
- extensive research on leadership
- timeless global wisdom drawn from many cultures.

Most of what happens at work and in the world happens in the realm of the intangible—we cannot see, taste, touch, hear it, or feel it with our hands. What we can see and touch is a minuscule fraction of reality. Being in full command of what is going on around you requires being conscious of the intangible factors that are affecting everything and everyone at every moment. The intangible aspects of our lives make up our metaphysical reality. Alchemy is the capacity to consciously develop, harness, and unleash the metaphysical forces that are always available but usually overlooked.

The concept of alchemy dates back to medieval times when it referred to the efforts to transform base metals, like tin, into precious ones, like gold. This book uses a broader definition of alchemy: *a transformation of resources into something more than the sum of parts which takes place in a way that is not obvious.* Although we may think of alchemy as a sort of magical process, in many ways it has turned out not to be magical at all as one generation's alchemy has many times become the next generation's chemistry or physics. Although alchemy may seem to be mystical and magical, it can be developed and used in practical ways.

Alchemy happens every day. Alchemical leadership is the capacity to consciously cause it. This book explores how leaders practice alchemy whenever they cause "base" resources, like skills, time, and materials, to produce "gold" results, like brand distinction, stakeholder loyalty, sustained profitability, organizational vitality, and civic contribution; instead of "tin" results from the same resources, like poor quality, infighting, bad reputation, high turnover, toxic work conditions, and financial weakness. Both results can derive from the exact same resources. The differential between them is alchemical capacity.

Whereas physics is the science of things, metaphysics is the science of causality, or what causes things to happen and/or exist. In a world that has largely forgotten, even denied, its fundamental importance and meaning, there's great competitive advantage to recognizing that metaphysics holds keys to a formidable power source that is at the heart of what causes what. The metaphysical domain is generative, creative, infinite, dynamic, and accessible. *Alchemy, meaning the art of consciously using metaphysical principles to cause things to happen, is a grossly overlooked power source for leaders.*

Every successful person has a story about the profound impact of metaphysical experiences, like inklings, inspiration, vision, vibes, and impulses, that commonly play big roles in careers but get little attention and even less accountancy for. Metaphysical principles are always in operation. Ignoring them exposes you to problems that appear to show up "out of the blue" when, in reality, they show up out of the metaphysical field. *Alchemical leaders are causal in the matter of what comes from "out of nowhere," and they are adept with metaphysical elements that are part of everyone's day, every day.*

As a consultant, coach, and adviser to leaders for over twenty-five years, as a news junky who also works on leadership and cultural development at the United Nations, and as a globe-trekking soul searcher, I have always been curious about how intangibilities, like values and volition, impact tangible things like profits and innovation. This book is a deep dive into the essence and meaning of power, how to develop it, and into how it causes things to happen. The pages ahead bring together a world of inspiration and information collected on a far and long path of many paths. *The Alchemy of Power* connects the dots between ancient wisdom, cutting-edge best practices, your inner knowing, and what's on your desktop.

I learned a lot about how alchemical capacity is critical for leaders while trekking the world looking for keys to human potential—from staying with the shamans of the Shuar, a tribe of headhunters in the Ecuadorian rainforest; to Buddhist monasteries and Hindu and Shinto shrines in Asia; to churches, synagogues, temples, and spiritual centers throughout the US; to attending and teaching for universities and cutting-edge leadership and personal development programs; to meeting with tribal chiefs in the African bush; to ceremonies and teachings with Native American elders and religious leaders. I've also had the privilege of learning from the many business and nonprofit leaders, and from departmental leaders in and around the United Nations, whom I have spent my career with, many of whom are not just great leaders but also extraordinary visionaries.

The Alchemy of Power brings ageless wisdom, consummate research, and cutting-edge best practices together for seasoned and emerging leaders. Although the role of invisible factors like metaphysics and alchemy on success may seem complicated, it is really just as simple as an iceberg's structure—the stronger the unseen fundamentals are, the higher it reaches and the more stability it has.

The Pages Ahead

This book is about expanding leadership consciousness because *good leaders evolve, but great leaders consciously evolve.*

- Part One explores the mechanics of some of the invisibilities going on around you.
- Part Two is about using those mechanics to develop personal power and organizational vitality.
- The third, and last, section explores the bigger picture of who we are and what we might want to do about it. Part Three frames leadership in the context of an emergent international shift toward new ways of defining success, a shift that is redefining social and market norms—a shift that is already blindsiding a lot of leaders.
- There are three appendixes at the end:
  - The first is Barrett Values Centre's Leadership Self-Assessment Tool, which will give you a snapshot of your personal leadership profile.
  - The second is *The Ten Principles of the United Nations Global Compact*, which lays out a foundation for leadership in the twenty-first century.
  - The third is a list of values, which serves as a general resource.

Because of the depth and breadth of the contents, flow is especially important. So references, along with many related sources, are at the end rather than footnoted. Since *The Alchemy of Power* covers such a wide range of concepts, there is also a Glossary.

The pages ahead are an exploration of the invisible factors that drive what shows up in the world. Theorist George Box said, *"Essentially, all models are inaccurate, but some can be useful."* That is especially true in such mysterious domains as metaphysics, alchemy, and power because language starts to fail at the edge of the unknown and models can never encapsulate the whole truth. *The Alchemy of Power* summarizes my international journey toward finding words for that which can never be fully known, and it reveals practical and replicable ways to work with invisible causative forces in real-world situations.

I invite you to suspend your professional title as you read, and instead play the role of Head Alchemist, whose job description is to transform your resources into more than the sum of parts. To that end, the Leadership Reflections at the end of each chapter are aimed at helping you consciously cause results worth having. The questions are designed to apply what is in the book to what's on your mind and computer screen, and to what's going on around you. The Leadership Reflections are evergreen and can be revisited over the course of your career. Keeping a journal with your answers will support your insights and your results.

PART ONE

ELEMENTS OF POWER

CHAPTER 1

METAPHYSICS, ALCHEMY, AND POWER

The Intangibles

A group of fit, adventurous, top-of-their-game geologists prepared for a year to summit an Asian mountain peak. They secured a healthy budget for gear and technology, adhered to workout routines with professional trainers, stocked supplies, hired the best-rated local guides, and were given paid time to prepare themselves and to engage in advanced research through their institutions. Their trek was planned and executed with the help of an excellent support team and cutting-edge technological capacity.

On their way up the mountain, they crossed paths with a descending group of professional athletes and climbers who, despite also being exceptionally well prepared, were forced by circumstances to turn around before reaching the top. When the scientists finally summited, their exhaustion and depletion vanished, not just with the exhilaration of summiting, but also with their astonishment at finding a thin man sitting there in an *amudaya*, a kind of Hindu loin-covering. The yogi made a welcoming gesture and asked, "What took you so long?"

The yogi represents the indomitable human spirit that is capable of surmounting boundaries by means of metaphysical capacities. He arrived at the same death-defying destination with a tiny fraction of the geologists' resources and yet he still had the presence of mind to anticipate their arrival. The scientists relied on physics, the science of things, to manage tangibles, including temperature-tested fabrics, altitude-tested gear, and weather apparatus for determining best climbing conditions. While their sophisticated handling of the tangibles gave them a powerful advantage, the yogi's adeptness with the intangibles reveals a different kind of power.

Metaphysics

Metaphysics is the field of study that pursues scientific, philosophical, and spiritual understandings of causality. It is the field of inquiry into what causes what. Metaphysics is the exploration of the nature of being and beings, of existence, time, and space. While physics focuses on things that already exist, metaphysics is the science behind what causes things to exist. While physical laws describe the finite, metaphysical principles describe the infinite. The metaphysical field spans across time and disciplines to explore the:

- invisible fundamental drivers of the human experience
- nature of existence
- mechanisms of causality, that is, of causing things to happen.

Metaphysical principles get at the root of existence and of causation itself. While the elements of physics, things like iron, carbon, and oxygen, are accessible through our five senses, the elements of metaphysics, like empathy, ethics, and will, are only accessible through consciousness. Consciousness is awareness by the mind of itself and the world. *Adeptness with alchemy, that is, the ability to cause unexpected outcomes, starts with tending to your own consciousness.*

The metaphysical domain is generative, creative, infinite, and inherently powerful. Current norms in industrialized cultures mostly disregard, even disparage metaphysics, even though it is fundamental to science, the workplace, and life itself. However, there is no longer doubt about the gains made by companies that consciously manage metaphysical elements like values, culture, and goodwill.

Consider Facebook's initial public offering flop when almost everybody in the company lost money because their compensation included shares of the stock. It happened right around the time that Mark Zuckerberg was voted the top boss in the US by 96 percent of his employees. His invisible cultural context was strong at a time when not only were his financial losses the worst they had ever been, but so were those of the employees who had voted for him, because most of them were vested in the stock that was tanking at the time. Zuckerberg built organizational resilience that ran far deeper than the company's stock price because he had invested heavily in Facebook's values for employees to "be bold with risk-taking" and to "stay fluid and transparent with information." Values are primal metaphysical drivers and Zuckerberg, like many of his tech contemporaries, capitalized on prioritizing them. Over time, though, Facebook's values did get compromised and losses ensued.

Mastery with metaphysics is the differential between two leaders, both with comparable resources and training, who produce vastly different results. Metaphysics is elemental and primary to any process: Before action happens, there must be motivation in the form of vision, values, principles, ideals, justifications, desires, objectives, convictions, beliefs, aims, or purposes. These key causal factors are invisible and mostly ignored. But recognized or not, metaphysical principles are always at play, including in everyday moments of interconnectivity, serendipity, intuition, inklings, creativity, good and bad vibes, déjà vu, "aha," and "wow." Those metaphysical moments cause change, sometimes barely perceptible, sometimes profound.

Although it is common to regard what we cannot see as inconsequential, decades of studies done around the world demonstrate that nothing could be further from the truth because, statistically, there is no doubt that intangibles, like values and culture, are primary determinants of outcomes (see Meglino, Barrett, Miethe, Schwartz, Henderson). Just like it was the yogi's understanding of, accountability for, and facility with metaphysical factors that gave him the edge, leaders who consciously manage the intangibles have a strong advantage over those who do not. Some intangibles, like culture, are measurable. Some aren't. In either case, metaphysical influences can be accounted for, which we'll explore further in later chapters.

Much of what our ancestors construed to be magic is now understood as basic physics, cosmology, biology, and chemistry—sciences that emerged from prior metascientific explorations. Contrary to popular cultural messaging, *there is no reason to believe that hard sciences have dominion over metaphysics. If that were so, there would be no meta-field from which to dream science forward.* Standard economic metrics account well for physical things, but we are now rediscovering what sages through the ages have always known: having command of the metaphysics, the invisible causal factors, is where the real power, which is sometimes called "magic," happens. As many researchers are concluding now, developing the intangible aspects of leadership produces significant quantifiable gains (see Liu, Collins, Flamholtz).

Alchemy

Metaphysics is a blend of science and philosophy, and alchemy is the art of applying metaphysical principles to everyday life. Alchemy is the art of causing unexpected transformation, creation, or combination. While alchemy is mostly portrayed as attempts to turn base metals into gold, that's a limited definition because it is actually the practice of producing more than the sum of parts by way of adeptness with unseen elements. While metaphysics is the study of what causes what, leadership alchemy is the conscious application of metaphysical principles for the purpose of causing specific outcomes. Alchemy is the way that leaders mine metaphysical gold. *Alchemy is what transforms things like methodologies, strategies, and best practices into outcomes that exceed expectations about goals and benchmarks. It is the domain of excellence and extraordinary results.*

Alchemy in leadership can be understood as a means for making the intangible tangible. Alchemy happens every day in every competent leader's life, yet it is rarely consciously capitalized on. But that's changing as companies like Starbucks, Zappos, Ikea, Google, and many more, as well as governmental and nonprofit organizations around the world, are demonstrating how paying attention to intangibles adds significant value to the sum of parts and labor. Western culture's typical definition of alchemy as a mythological art relating to metals is dangerously narrow because alchemy is one of humanity's most formidable capacities.

It is almost beyond comprehension that scientists agree that everything we experience only constitutes 5 percent of reality, with dark energy making up around 70 percent and dark matter being the remaining 25 percent. In other words, 95 percent of what exists is invisible and beyond our current understanding. Alchemy is a metaphysical dynamism that occurs in the space beyond the 5 percent that we understand, yet it is something that can be developed and consciously applied.

We all experience alchemy every day, like when two people follow the same recipe yet one's dish tastes better. Alchemy is the domain of "green thumbs," healers, intuitives, artists, inspirers, and people who just have "good vibes"—all of which are invisible and transformative capacities. In terms of leadership, it is the "magic touch" that surpasses expectations. The impact of metaphysical factors, although they do not slot directly into standard spreadsheets and reports, can be measured, developed, and taken to the bank. Alchemical artfulness with metaphysical principles absolutely does show up in the bottom line, but because it can be hard to see direct correlation, the impact of alchemy is often overlooked. Alchemical leadership creates results that are more than the sum of parts and labor, so it necessarily cannot be accounted for by math alone. But that's no excuse for ignoring it.

Human capacities cover a vast spectrum, ranging from spectacular physical accomplishments to complex invisible experiences like imagination, and from our technological capabilities to the mind-blowing faculties that metaphysical adepts have used for centuries to mysteriously thrive in challenging conditions, to have prescience of others, and to produce results that exceed expectations. The story about the yogi and the climbers is a metaphor for how leadership mastery is an ever-unfolding journey that has always transcended our beliefs about what's possible. It illustrates what quantum physicists claim—that everything is, first and foremost, a matter of consciousness. The degree to which you are conscious of intangible factors is the degree to which you can master them. That mastery is alchemical capacity.

Most successful people would probably object to the idea that their work is alchemical, but few deny that pivotal career moments have come in inexplicable game-changing flashes of transformation, creation, or combination. Quantum physicists have proven that the theory that alchemy is too esoteric to matter is deeply, unequivocally flawed by exposing the link between consciousness and being, and between the observer and the observed. Scientists now confirm what has been articulated forever on cave walls and in hallowed halls: *consciousness and intentionality matter in that they are causal of matter itself.* Alchemy happens in a range of consciousness that yogis and saints have always called our attention to. While much about that range of consciousness may always be mysterious to us, we know plenty about how we access it and about the benefits of tapping in to it.

Metaphysics defines the principles by which alchemy operates, and you can use those intangible factors to your advantage. Leadership studies consistently demonstrate that intangible drivers, like values and volition, outperform tangible rulebooks and strategic plans every time. Still, modern success models typically disparage alchemy and marginalize metaphysics by disregarding both concepts as inconsequential, mythological, fluffy stuff.

The Fluffy Myth

The largest portion of an iceberg, about 90 percent, is beneath the surface. What can't be seen determines the size and stability of what can be. Likewise, invisible workplace factors, like culture, for example, have far more impact on processes and outcomes than the factors that can be seen and measured with standard metrics. (see Barrett) It is not that intangibles cannot be measured. They can. It's that relatively few companies are bothering to adopt new metrics that account for metaphysical realities, despite what we know about their enormous impact on outcomes. That's because there is endemic cultural buy-in to what I call the "fluffy myth," which is the mistaken belief that intangibles are inconsequential.

Fluff mythology reflects systemic disregard for the evidence that intangibles have a far greater impact on success than tangibles. Today, the fluffy myth still prevails in the business world despite the strong verification for how undeniably risky it is to ignore the so-called "soft" indicators, and to neglect the metaphysical factors that are causal in making things happen, which although invisible, are as real as real can be. A lack of accountancy for intangibles constitutes leadership malpractice because, contrary to fluff mythology, investing in metaphysicalities yields high returns, while ignoring them can result in financial and organizational losses (see Barrett).

When we categorize metaphysical realities as fluff, we are, in effect, disregarding the "bottom of the iceberg." But just like denying the reality of the base of an iceberg is even riskier than just ignoring it, actively denying the value of unseen causal factors has the effect of further inflating risk. Put another way, disregarding intangibles is dangerous enough. Unconsciously deflating the value of their influence compounds the risk.

Raising your capacity to cause outcomes requires overcoming social prejudices that disregard metaphysics as fluff. *Accessing ageless keys to causality requires breaking through myopic cultural lenses that are blind to profound intangible influences.* Using the filter of metaphysics will help dilate and then more finely focus your leadership lens. That dilation and refocus, that expanded consciousness, gives you greater capacity for causing alchemy. The power of alchemy has two components:

- Metaphysical awareness of the underlying forces that cause things to happen
- Alchemical adeptness, which is the personal capacity to consciously cause things to happen.

Power

We are all familiar with the power of words, the power of concentration, power in a decision-making process, the power of rank or position, power of influence over other people's emotions or thinking, and supernatural powers like precognition. Physics teaches us that *power is both a cohesive and a disruptive force.* It is cohesive when it holds things together in specific patterns, like when it travels through the walls in just the right mix of positive and negative charges to light a lamp. And change occurs whenever power is used to disrupt patterns of coherence. When power is disruptive, it makes elements scatter in chaos until they cohere again into new, changed patterns. The yogi's power over extreme conditions was a result of body, mind, and spirit cohering together in a pattern of well-being.

Power, like all forces, ebbs and flows—as the Bible says, "to everything, there is a season...a time to build up, a time to break down..." Alchemical leadership engages in ever-evolving inquiry with self and team about when to hold 'em and when to fold 'em, when to move and when to rest, when to gather and when to disperse, and when to reap, to sow, or to allow for fallow fields so fertility can regenerate.

Alchemy is the art of being consciously causal with the metaphysical forces that create disruption and/or coherence. Unconsciousness of the metaphysics of power, of the laws of power that cause things to cohere or to disperse, can lead to complete breakdowns coming "out of nowhere." In reality, there is no such thing as "nowhere." Yet how often do we all buy into disempowering fairy tales about nowhere being the source of a problem? The theory of there being a nowhere and fluff mythology go together—the only way to maintain the belief that there is a magical nowhere from which people's circumstances arise is to buy into the myth that the metaphysical part of our reality is just fluffy stuff. Believing in the myth that "nowhere" causes things to happen leaves believers with nowhere to go to fix things.

To believe that "nowhere" is accountable for your situation is to award your power to a fantasy place, and thereby deny your own access to the field of causality. The nowhere that is often accepted as a dead-end truth is a metaphysical field of potential. We are undergoing an evolution in leadership consciousness today as we're gaining better means of accounting for the "somewhere" that is occupied by metaphysical factors. The invisible field where power lives is accessed by consciousness and is fueled by mojo.

Mojo

I have trekked the world looking for keys to accessing power. What I've learned is that, across cultures, disciplines, and belief systems, there is a *common recognition of a spark of life that is unique in each of us and common to all.* That uniquely common spark of life is a metaphysical power that makes the difference between us being a collection of atoms and us being people who love, dance, laugh, self-reflect, and give toward the well-being of others. Pierre Teilhard de Chardin, a Jesuit philosopher in the early 1900s, wrote a lot about the essential nature of our invisible lives. He, like many theologians and philosophers, concluded that the primal spark of humanity is love, and he said that, when humanity *truly* discovers it, we "will have discovered fire for the second time."

Given all its connotations, love may not be the best word to describe that primal spark for Westerners but de Chardin was referring to a universal phenomenon and not to romantic love. I wrote a doctoral dissertation on that spark, have been all over the globe exploring it, and have given many talks about it. The more I learn about it, though, the more there seems to be to learn and the clearer it gets to me that it can never be adequately named. Eastern religions, as well as indigenous, pagan, and spiritual disciplines, all have words and practices for articulating, harnessing, growing, and unleashing the mysterious, metaphysical spark of the human spirit. There will probably never be a conceptual model that fully encompasses it, but most cultures seem to have tried. Chinese philosophy calls it *chi*; in Japanese, it's *ki*; and the idea of invisible, primal energetics relates to the Hindu concepts of *prana* and *shakti.* I call it "mojo." *Mojo is the power of the fire in your belly, the spark that's there even when you're not feeling it. Mojo is the primordial driving force for what is happening on your watch. Organizational mojo is the collective flame that fuels productivity.*

We can put all the elements that make up a grape into a lab dish, but we cannot make a grape because we do not have the metaphysical capacity to ignite the spark that makes life live. That primal spark in living beings is the essence of what I'm calling mojo. There is not much mojo in a grape, but as life forms become more sophisticated, their mojo increases.

Mojo is an invisible thing, a visceral experience of a metaphysical charge. It is the life-throb that pulses through us as zest, dynamism, drive, passion, zeal, zip, zing, pizzazz, bounce, spirit, oomph, moxie, get-up-and-go, pep, and feistiness. Mojo is the metaphysical fire that de Chardin was talking about. We experience the metaphysics of mojo in moments of everyday magic, like when people just click and that invisible sense of alignment causes us to want to do more with each other, or when we somehow inexplicably know we are onto something and it causes us to pursue further, even when the pursuit doesn't make any logical sense.

Wise ones of every era have sought to understand the phenomenon of *chi/ki/shakti*/mojo and most conclude that it is not a fully knowable thing. Taoists probably got the closest in their teaching from the *Tao Te Ching* that that which can be named cannot be the tao. The word "tao" refers to the way of the universe, to its essential principles, the metaphysics, that underlie our experiences. In recognizing that it is unnameable, the Taoists are teaching that the nature of the universe, and all the power within it, is an ever-unfolding mystery; and also, that the mysteries of the universe are no less real just because we haven't figured them out.

The Taoist reluctance to nail down our deepest truths is resonant with the words of statistician George Box, who warned that "all models are inaccurate, yet some are useful." The truth is that, in congruence with Taoist teachings, none of the models that religions, philosophies, sciences, or leadership theories come up with will probably ever be able to accurately depict the powers that cause things. Suffice it to say that, throughout all of history, there is testimony to an invisible inner fire that is causal.

Mojo is a concept that attempts to distinguish that very real, yet ever mysterious, component of life that is both energy and power. *Mojo is the capacity for making things happen, which is energy, and, at the same time, mojo is the power to convert energy from one form into another and to cohere or disrupt existential patterns.* Mojo is a noun, but it isn't linear or fixed. It is a primal, invisible, energetic flow—sometimes mojo waxes, sometimes it wanes, sometimes it moves, sometimes it rests, sometimes it's raucous, and sometimes it's so subtle as to seem imperceptible. A leader's power comes with the capacity to convert collective energies into actions that fulfill a mission. That power is dependent on management of personal and collective mojo.

In traveling a spiritual and intellectual path of many paths—encountering academia, human potential technologies, interfaith seminary, Amazonian shamans, African bush tribes, American indigenous spiritual leaders, and countless Asian and Western religious and spiritual traditions, I've come to understand a few key things about mojo:

- Access to power correlates with a person's command of personal and group mojo.
- Mojo must be sourced.
- The quality of the sourcing matters.

Moving Mojo

Mojo is both a personal and transpersonal energetic flow that is unique in each of us and common to all. *Your mojo is your means for alchemy. Your group's mojo is an energetic source of your power. Alchemical leadership is the capacity for stoking, harnessing, and unleashing everyone's mojo.*

Mojo fuels your intentions. Think about the difference between an intention you have that you know you will never go for, and an intention that gets your mojo flowing so powerfully that you know there is no way it can't happen. Passion is an indicator of mojo and a good example of how it works. The power in bringing passion to a career is well recognized. However, passion that is unleashed in a culture that can't manage it is often either wasted or turned into destructive energy. Just like passion without consciousness often leads to drama and crises, unconsciousness of individual and collective mojo also causes problems. Passion, like all expressions of mojo, is metaphysical energy that can be consciously channeled or not. Unconsciousness of mojo means that energy is less likely to be effectively transformed into power.

Your capacity for mojo management determines how power flows around and through you. Your mojo, that is, your internal power supply, can be consciously managed such that it flows in accordance with your intention. Or not. With good mojo management, leaders can cause things to happen without bullying or manipulating anyone and without resorting to questionable politics. Those behaviors diminish the leader's own mojo as well as that of the people who endure them. Manipulation and controlling behaviors cause people to spend their mojo elsewhere, when we're lucky, or to spend their energy in defiance of a leader's power, when we're not so lucky. Either way, the leader loses the energetic resource. The better you manage the sourcing and expending of your mojo, the more you can intentionally create the patterns of coherence that you want, the better ensured you can be that disruptions will be productive, and the better you can capitalize on inevitable unexpected coherences and disruptions.

Depending on how much fluff mythology indoctrination you have received, the idea of bringing your mojo to work might seem ridiculous, until you realize that it shows up as qualities like team spirit, cooperation, satisfaction, clarity, and innovation. Behaviors such as bullying, berating, and dishing out other indignities are all signs of diminished mojo, because those actions are low mojo to begin with and they drain energy out of people and organizations.

Unconsciousness of mojo management can result in energy getting wasted on counterproductive behaviors, and in disruptive incidents that provoke fear, spite, and other forms of backlash. When there is a metaphysical drain due to negativity, power needs to be exerted just to keep things together as they are, leaving less power available for organizational growth or proactive change. *Mojo goes retro in the presence of, and unresolved history of, bad behavior.*

Mojo in the Body

Mojo is not sourced by food, money, fame, success, poverty, or suffering. It's sourced by feeding your soul—whether that means carving out some time for contemplation, exploring new paths or diving deeper into a path you already love, reading or listening to something inspirational, writing, singing, creating, dancing, yoga, going to a religious place or service, meditating, or finding solitude in nature. It is also sourced by taking time to really feel things like satisfaction, happiness, and intrigue. Taking time to consciously develop your own internal sparks, your mojo/*chi*/inner fire, gives you access to the metaphysical field of causality that lies beyond everyday awareness. *Mojo is like a metaphysical muscle in that the more you exercise it, the stronger it gets.*

The concept of mojo links our inner, outer, and supra worlds—supra meaning that which is above, beyond, and before. Sufi sages, who are Islamic mystics, including Rumi and Hafiz, taught that we should eat, pray, move, relate, change, and love so that the instrument of our being stays open and tuned for metaphysical winds to play through. They analogize body, mind, and spirit as the flute through which the mysterious force of life expresses.

Your instrument matters. It goes without saying, but our cultural reality is such that almost all of us need reminding, that if you are not eating, sleeping, and exercising adequately, make it a priority. The jury is in on that. Many of us have been conditioned to believe that our bodies are somehow external to our lives, but physical vitality is integral with everything else in your life, including your work. There's a computer programming term that applies well to our bodies, especially our brains: GIGO—Garbage In, Garbage Out. Your mind/body is your leadership instrument. Cultivating mojo starts with cultivating your vitality. To reach optimum mojo management capacity, keep your instrument tuned with high quality, preferably organic food, fresh air, exercise, strong relationships, and regular rejuvenation of your spirit.

Most of all, pursue joy. Book time to stoke your inner fire and to evolve your personal capacity for playing with fire. Whatever that means to you. No matter what you are doing, whether you're conscious of it or not, you are constantly managing the energy of your personal power, which is your mojo. Managing your own mojo is the key to being adept with the collective mojo of your team. It is important to keep in mind that mojo management is paradoxical in that, while mojo may be a dynamic power source, it takes a kind of stillness within oneself to be able to access it. Alchemical leadership includes a personal, dynamic, ever-present, ever-evolving inquiry into your own being and into your personal capacity to cause results. *Leadership alchemy comes down to being able to:*

- *Charge up mojo in yourself and everyone else*
- *Direct that charge toward outcomes that exceed expectations.*

Gandhi said to "be the change you wish to see...." Alchemical leadership modifies that to, "Be the charge you want to see." *Success with being in charge relies on a leader's capacity for charging the charge.*

Alchemical Leadership

Making things happen "out of thin air" is a matter of reconciling the formed with the formless. In order to transform combinations of parts and labor into something more valuable than the sum of both, alchemical leaders attend to personal and collective mojo. Alchemical leadership requires adeptness with the metaphysical factors that underlie decision-making and that drive behaviors. *Alchemy is the art of recognizing, developing, harnessing, and consciously unleashing the richness of the metaphysical reality around and within you.*

Although alchemical leadership is a valuable capacity to have, it is rarely afforded due diligence. Despite a plethora of research that demonstrates the power of the so-called "softer" aspects of success, many organizations still do not yet account for the most fundamental drivers of outcomes, the metaphysical ones. And that's costly.

Leadership Reflections

1. Take stock. What is working and not working for you now? Get in a quiet place and/or with someone you can speak your deepest truths with.

2. What are your assets? Think as broadly as possible. Considering the ratio of tangibles to intangibles, 5:95 percent, most of your assets are intangible. What qualities show up when you do? In other words, no matter how good or bad you feel, what do you usually bring to the table? Make a list of the positives you bring and keep adding—you will likely be surprised by how long the list becomes!

3. What commitments feel burdensome, unnecessary, or annoying? What is most important to you personally and professionally?

4. What makes you happy?

5. On a scale of 1–10, how charged is your inner spark right now?

6. On a scale of 1–10, how is the mojo flowing in your world?

7. Name a few people who you think have great mojo. How does mojo express through him/her? What do you notice about their authority? What do you like about their mojo? How is it the same and/or different from yours?

CHAPTER 2

THE METAPHYSICS OF MOJO

Mojo Flow: Generating, Harnessing, and Unleashing Power

We are surrounded by a world of power—the power of the economy; the power of brand; the power of consumers, boards, and stockholders; the power of government; and the power of family needs and social pressures. And by the insidious power of "never enough." We know the power of oil and of the dollar, yen, and euro, and the power of strong profits yet we usually overlook the most formidable power. Just like a cell's nucleus is one of the greatest power sources on the planet, the concept of mojo attempts to get at the primal power sources that lie in invisible depths of personal and organizational consciousness. Mojo is personal and organizational "nuclear" power.

Just like the power in the nucleus of a cell lies deep within its structure, mojo is situated deep in the consciousness of individuals and collectives. Mojo is neutral energy and we have choice in how our mojo flows. Mojo management is a matter of volition. When there is no consciousness of how it is flowing, mojo can be degenerative or destructive. The culture to which people bring their mojo is the most significant determinant of whether, and how much, of that mojo gets invested toward fulfilling mission and goals. Culture and mojo are inextricably linked.

Mojo is a qualitative thing. Even though it's invisible, there are ways to account for mojo, including through cultural assessments. When mojo is brought into an organizational culture that is wired for its expression, it is generative. When the culture disrupts it, mojo breaks down, or goes around whatever the obstruction is. Mojo disruption can manifest as things like unwelcome drama, distractions, and apathy. *Alchemical leadership includes the capacity to channel individual and collective mojo through your organization in the most effective way possible.*

Mojo is an aspect of the metaphysical field that is often erroneously dismissed as being nothing from nowhere. But there is no such thing as nowhere, there is only mysterious territory. The domain of metaphysics lies in this mysterious space, and it is literally everywhere. Alchemical leadership taps into the inexplicable domain where mojo lives. Wise ones and saints have been telling us for eons that the territory of the invisible, where we experience things like ethics, compassion, and desire, is the most effective realm for impacting outcomes. The metaphysical spectrum holds profound keys to on-the-ground outcomes as demonstrated by aha moments that have transformed science and society, and by the complex range of values, needs and wants that drive most actions and decisions.

Any coherent group is always more than the sum of the individuals that make it up because coherence is a multiplying factor. The concept of mojo is a way to account for that metaphysical multiplication factor in that it describes an energetic charge that can cause coherence to occur among people. The quality and results of your leadership depend on how consciously you can cultivate, cohere, and unleash the collective charge of all stakeholders—your organizational mojo. Alchemical leadership includes the capacity to do mojo multiplication.

We are so conditioned toward materiality that the larger and more generative metaphysical field can seem too unfathomable to concern ourselves with. Metaphysics and alchemy lie beyond the territory of everyday consciousness and within an infinite spectrum of possibility that is both larger and more generative than the "reality" we tend to focus on. The full spectrum of power includes a magnanimous range of meta-physicalities that are rarely accounted for. To the small degree they are ever even recognized, metaphysical influences are often disregarded as fluff. Ongoing, conscious expansion of your own and your organization's metaphysical awareness is the best way to gain access to your full range of options and attentiveness to mojo is a good starting place. Alchemical leadership not only accesses organizational mojo, it directs that energy source toward most effectively, efficiently, and humanely bringing vision and mission to fruition.

When you are leading others, your power is multiplied by the energy of the group. Or not. The equation is simple: when people are stoked up, tapped in, and turned on, there's more energy to be harnessed and unleashed toward mission fulfillment. When leaders are conscious of mojo development and flow, they can function in a metaphysical zone that is, by definition, limitless.

Yin and Yang

Change is the only constant of the human condition. *Your leadership power is reflected in your personal capacity to cause and manage change.* Adeptness with managing change is a critical leadership capacity. When change is managed at surface levels, leaders find themselves chasing symptoms, putting out fires, and struggling to move beyond problem-solving. When change is navigated at more primal levels, leaders experience a sense of grounded flexibility that makes them better at managing surprises and better able to implement core solutions. *Being alchemical with the power vested in you depends on your capacity for understanding and managing the full spectrum of that power.*

The Taoist philosophical principle of dualism, which is denoted by the concepts of yin and yang, provides a useful model for understanding and affecting the universal constancy of change, and for discovering a fuller spectrum of possibilities. (Yin rhymes with in, yang rhymes with gong, not hang.) Yin-yang philosophy offers a time-tested framework for exploring the metaphysical realm of causality, and for articulating the mysterious powers of change. As an ancient, nontheistic philosophy, Taoist teachings on the polarities of yin and yang are especially helpful because the concepts are so metaphysically primal that they carry little cultural or religious baggage. Because yin-yang is gender-, values-, and deity-neutral, it's an uncommonly universal lens, a relatively clear filter, for grappling with the unseen elements of power. Using the yin-yang lens provides a metaphysical means for moving beyond emotional charge, personality biases, gender issues, cultural influences, and limited ideations about success. As a tool for examining the forces of change, the dualistic lens of yin and yang offers an elegantly simple key to unlocking complexities.

Yang is considered more positive, yin more negative—not in the sense of judgment but in the sense of equal and opposite energetics, for example, the positive and negative poles of a magnet. Taoism teaches that light is yang, darkness is yin; fullness is yang, emptiness is yin; demanding is yang, accepting is yin. Yang speaks out, yin listens; yang is firm, yin is flexible; yang is hard, yin is soft. Doing is yang, being is yin. Intention is yin, manifestation is yang. When things are contracting, they are getting more yang. When expanding, they're getting more yin.

Things are never just yin or just yang. Taoists teach that the physical universe is a constant multilevel movement between yin and yang, kind of like an infinite dimensional chess board. Our multidimensional life experiences simultaneously span between vast yin-yang spectrums—from microscopic to cosmic levels of activity, from the vibrational to the physical, from the visible to the invisible. The principles of yin and yang are applicable at all levels at all times.

It is entirely likely that you may have too much yin expression in one area of your work, like too much theorizing (yin) and not enough action (yang), while there's excess yang in another, like too much criticism (yang) and not enough trust (yin). People on the receiving end might compensate for being bullied (excessive yang) by crying (excessive yin). Even at rest, a yin state, our hearts and lungs are pumping, a yang activity. The yin-yang symbol has a circle of white in the black area and black in the white area to demonstrate that there is no such thing as pure yin or pure yang. It's not only possible, it is inevitable that infinite interplays of yin and yang are always going on in and around each of us.

Yin is considered the more feminine principle, yang more masculine, but the terms describe qualities, not sexuality. In fact, yin-yang theory helps to transcend gender issues because gender traits span an enormous yin-yang spectrum. Although yin is more feminine and yang more masculine, no matter how strongly someone identifies with gender, s/he can't just be yin or just yang. For example, a woman (yin) who is very logical, factually and competitively oriented, and who understands setbacks as absolute losses (yang tendencies) is still female (yin). But she is more yang than another female who expresses more creatively, is inclined toward partnership-oriented relationships, leans toward broader vision, and sees setbacks as growth opportunities that are a natural part of the cycle of success (yin tendencies). Relative to one another, the former woman is more yang, the latter more yin. Relative to a burly guy who has limited capacity to adapt to change, and who is unable to understand anything but concrete concepts (big yang), both of those women are yin. You might be more yin (kinder, gentler) than your co-worker but more yang (goal and fact oriented) than your friend. Yin and yang are always relative and never fixed.

Taoists teach that all of existence is nothing but the constant changing from yin to yang and back again. Ancient teachings about yin and yang provide a simple yet profound way of wrapping our minds around the interplay of ever-changing elements—an interplay that is constantly happening within an unfathomable spectrum of possibilities. The concepts of yin and yang help to expose the dynamics between ideas and reality, subtle energies and physicality, between fate and causation.

The concepts of yin and yang are especially helpful with reconciling the physical and metaphysical worlds. The yin-yang lens accounts for the reality that power is an ever-morphing expression of ever-changing atoms and energy. Using yin and yang helps reconcile visible end results (yang) with the role of invisible forces that cause results to happen (yin). Given that life is a constant shifting from yin to yang and back again, the degree of consciousness with which you navigate those shifts has a lot to do with how things go in your world.

Just like positive (yang) and negative (yin) charges create sparks of electrical energy, mojo sparks when yin and yang come together just right. And just like positive and negative currents in an electrical circuit, yin and yang represent unseen energetic flows that can yield power that is as formidable as it is neutral. We understand a lot about how to cause things to happen with electricity and much less about being causal with metaphysical currents. Using the distinctions of yin and yang helps to expose the unique and complex mix of intangibilities that make up each of us and every situation we find ourselves in.

Dualism

Physical formation of anything is evidence of the dualistic nature of our reality in that objects and beings necessarily have a back and a front, top and bottom, and an inside and outside. Whether you think of it scientifically, or philosophically, or not at all, it is undeniable that the human experience is dualistic: we have to know hot to know cold, have to experience the negative to understand the positive, be able to distinguish the visible to conceive of the invisible, and we have to know darkness in order to know light.

Yin and yang describe the inherent dualism of life, but they are not fixed opposites. They are dynamic, relativistic terms that describe polarities. The reason that the yin-yang symbol has a dark circle in the light area and a light circle in the dark one is not just because there is always at least a little yin in the yang and vice versa, but also because they are not static concepts.

There is no such thing as absolute yin or yang. In fact, different schools of Eastern thought reverse their meanings and it hardly matters because the representation of polarities is the same. Because yin and yang describe relativity, and not two permanent states, and because everything is always changing, it is important to keep in mind that *yin and yang describe energetic polarities, not fixed points*. The fluidity between yin and yang is what makes them so helpful in describing metaphysical and alchemical factors, which are inherently more variable than physical factors.

Equanimity

There are times that call for more yin responses and times that require more yang ones, times to lean yin-ward and times to lean yang-ward, times to press on (yang) and times to let go (yin). Although yin and yang are often thought of in terms of balance, it is more accurate to think of them in terms of "equanimity" because balance implies a static state. If you breathe in, you are more yang, breathe out, you're more yin. If you were to reach an absolute balance point of homeostasis, you would have to somehow freeze right then and there to maintain it.

The point of using the yin-yang lens is not to find balance. Absolute balance is delusional because it is fixed, and no entity can exist when the universal dance of yin turning to yang and back again stops—not even for a nanosecond. *Equanimity implies having stability and composure, no matter how your situation happens to be rocking and rolling.* In terms of leadership, equanimity implies the discernment and facility to steer more yin-ward or yang-ward in accordance with present conditions and best outcomes.

Metaphysics is the domain of causality and potentiality (yin), whereas physical manifestations are in the realm of what has already been caused to exist (yang). The hard science of physics is more yang—quantifiable, contractive, ordered, and fixed—because it deals with condensing ideas into numbers, laws, systems, products, and other finite parameters. Metaphysics is more yin given its more expansive elements like creativity, relativity, intentionality, and other intangibles. The meta-domain from which physics arises, which is metaphysics, is more infinite (yin), while the domain of physics is more finite (yang). The amorphous meta-field of all possibility and the precise laws of physics are not mutually exclusive, they are interdependent, and they exist in dynamic equanimity with one another.

Systemization is yang, transformation is yin. Yang impulses want results now, yin proclivities want to expand the horizons. Yang thinking wants to be clear on what is happening, while yin inclinations avail us to the fuzzy realm where creativity and out-of-the box potential live. We experience time itself sometimes in more yin and sometimes in more yang ways. Yang time is more quantitative in that it is scheduled in pursuit of concrete events and results. More yin time is qualitative to the point where we can actually lose track of it, like when we're caught up in music, or having good times with friends, or become fully immersed in satisfying work. When life swings yang-ward, we experience time as a linear past, present, and future, and as a marker for when we will do what. In the yin zone, time feels more amorphous and we are usually not so aware of the time. Yin time is more likely to have us feeling "in the now," that is, for us to be fully immersed in the present, with little to no sense of what has come before and what lies ahead.

Current cultural norms reflect yang-dominant concepts of time, and that makes it hard to wrap our minds around the timelessness of the yin zone. Because it can be hard to account for, we often think of yin time as wasted, but if we do not make enough yin time, we become stressed and unhealthy. Equanimity of yin-yang time doesn't depend on an hour-for-hour balance of activities, it depends on a quality of being. Sometimes it takes a long time just to get to the edge of the yin zone, and other times we can be at the far end of it in a single breath. Yin develops most easily when you immerse yourself in aesthetics that support good vibes—like in nature, religious sanctuaries, meditation rooms, and other feel-good places.

There is a time and place for both yin and yang approaches to everything, but our cultural norms hold higher valuation for systematizing and concretizing (yang), and relatively little for the zone of formlessness and blue-sky thinking (yin). There is no right and wrong about yin or yang, but there is the possibility for subconsciously allowing one to dominate the other in your worldview and in your decision-making. In fact, Western acculturation pretty much assures a yang-dominant worldview because our culture holds tremendous valuation for our yang-ward inclinations and limited valuation for our yin-ward ones. The first step to being able to make use of these principles is to start becoming aware of when and how your own leanings tend to be more yin or more yang.

Swinging Both Ways

Think of it as a pendulum spiraling between two poles: When our work is on a healthy swing yin-ward, we experience expansiveness, creativity, satisfaction, and joy. When we are swinging healthily yang-ward, we tend to experience orderliness, focus, productivity, and efficiency. We are at our best when we find equanimity between both. For example, discipline (yang) in harmony with flexibility (yin), is a healthy equation for success. The yin of joy can easily exist simultaneously with the yang of orderliness—yin traits and yang traits are never exclusive of one another but, left unchecked, they can obfuscate one another. Saying that yin or yang is better than its opposite is like saying it is better to have either a negative or positive charge going through the wiring in your wall. If you chose one over the other, you would have to give up your electrical service.

Leadership plays out in the dynamic tension between yin and yang. *Leadership alchemy is the capacity to manage when and how far the pendulum spirals in both directions on your watch.* It is also having the agility to swing things before you find yourself feeling trapped in a state of disequilibrium. "There is a time to reap and a time to sow, a time to build up and a time to break down," a time to hold firm to goals and projections, and a time to release them for the sake of greater good—a time to lean yin-ward and a time to lean yang-ward. The nature of the human condition is that the yin-yang cycles of negativity and positivity are never-ending. What goes up always goes down, and it is foolish to operate from assumptions that things could or should be otherwise.

Alchemical leadership is the artfulness of guiding your organization to lean yin-ward or yang-ward and back again as it surfs the tides of change. It is having surfer-like agility as options, challenges, and visions constantly evolve, often just outside the field of vision that most leaders are trained to keep their eyes on. *Capacity for conscious causality is not a fixed skill level but more the art of finding personal and professional equanimity with an ever-evolving world, one present moment at a time.*

Alchemical leadership is the art of consciously navigating the ever-shifting waves between intangibles (yin) and what is manifested by your organization (yang), between when it is time to expand outward (yang) or time to develop what is within (yin), when it's time to pare down (yang) or time to expand (yin). If the current that flows in your electrical circuits were to function without equanimity, your electrical power would be compromised. If there is too much or too little of a positive or negative charge, you would rewire to accommodate that inequity. Likewise, outdated leadership models that prioritize yang functionality, like hierarchy, and that ignore the yin, like culture, cannot fire effectively on all cylinders. Using the lens of yin and yang is a means for gaining command over the energetic cycles we are all a part of. By developing greater consciousness of those cycles and better facility with them, you can gain greater capacity for influencing them.

The pendulum of life inevitably swings both ways. Whenever there is a force, there is an equal opposite force. Where there is a front, there's a back. Big front, big back. Power comes with recognizing the laws of symmetry in our proverbial swinging pendulum—as far as life swings one way is as far as it will be swinging the other. Because there is no absolute balance point, and because the dance of yin and yang is going on at many levels at the same time, the Taoists teach that the objective is to develop mastery with how the proverbial pendulum swings both ways.

Alchemical leadership comes with recognizing, and being causal in, how the swinging in your world goes. Your capacity for alchemy has everything to do with your ability to maintain your equanimity/composure when the pendulum feels out of control. On a personal level, it requires squaring movement (yang) with rest (yin), goals (yang) with intuition (yin), productivity (yang) with creativity (yin), and work (yang) with rest (yin). On an organizational level, it means recognizing when it is time to build up (yang) or time to break down (yin); time to expand (yin) or time to contract (yang); time to move (yang) or time to retreat (yin); time to manage what you can see in front of you, like a spreadsheet or payroll (yang), or time to manage the intangibles, like satisfaction and vision (yin).

It is not an either/or proposition—most of the time, leaders are simultaneously juggling yang things like goals, rules, systems, and productivity, with yin things, like brainstorming, professional development, open-ended targets, anecdotal input, commitment, and co-creative processes. Equanimity between striving for workplace excellence and productivity (yang) and supporting innovation and revitalization (yin) is a constantly moving target.

Sparks fly when yin intangibles, like values, are maintained in conscious equanimity with yang tangibles like profits. If your organization is too yin, it is likely that there is a lack of focus and productivity and/or that the bottom line is floundering. If it's too yang, it may not have the cultural vitality to produce at optimum levels, no matter how good the strategic plan is or how efficient operations may be.

Yang-dominant companies can become too rigid, constrained, and inhospitable to stakeholders, including customers, employees, and suppliers. Yin-dominant companies can err toward too much optimism and can be at risk of making ungrounded decisions. More yang thinkers might err on the side of keeping the ball rolling at the expense of compromising fundamental needs, while their more yin colleagues might be inclined to spend too much time at the drawing board, thereby compromising productivity. When there is equanimity, yin reflection time can save precious resources from the more yang problem of premature dissemination.

Common standards of high valuation for yang indicators, like quarterly financial reports, can obscure more yin cultural indicators, like shared purpose and civility. More yin thinkers need yang-oriented colleagues to help bring vision to fruition, while more yang, get-it-done thinkers benefit from more yin-oriented colleagues who tend toward open-mindedness and relationship-building. *The yang drive toward action can help yin dreamers realize what they might never manifest on their own, and yin vision can set an extraordinary course for yang activity.* Allowing the yin to express more fully has the effect of dilating the range of possible outcomes for more yang-inclined team members.

Alchemical leadership is about managing the dynamic equanimity between yin factors, like intentionality, theorization, inner strength, and imagination, and yang factors, like rigor, methodology, data, infrastructure, outer strength, and rationalism. Dynamic tensions naturally arise between yin and yang polarities. To lead well is to be masterful with those energetic dynamics. A leader's job is to establish proportionality, or equanimity, between yang data, rules, and rationalism and yin vision, wisdom, and caring.

Just like we need strong positive and negative currents flowing through our electrical systems, conscious management of yin-yang dynamics sparks vitality in the workplace. Depletion or excessiveness of either yin or yang compromises mojo, because the spark of mojo is fueled by the dynamic equanimity between both.

Pandemic Yang-itis

The pervasiveness of fluff mythology has clouded the validity and value of intangibles (yin). Consequently, our norms tend to be yang dominant. We have placed inordinately high valuation on the yang aspects of the workplace, like profits, and little, often even negative, valuation on the yin aspects, like culture, that are just as real but harder to track. The idea that we have been in a multi-millennial yang-ward spiral is evidenced by predominantly male religious, business, and political leaders, ever-expansive militarism, and a profit-at-any-cost mentality that have resulted in a poisoned planet, millions of starving children, and a level of violence that drains an outrageous percentage of our resources while ending countless lives too early. Our unconscious acceptance of yang-dominant cultural biases has resulted in planetary emergencies at every level of the human experience. What is missing is valuation for our more yin, more compassionate, and more cooperation-oriented sensibilities.

We have "yang-itis," an inflated valuation for yang, combined with a deflated valuation for yin. Evidence of yang-itis can be seen in the lack of women in leadership positions throughout all economic, religious, and governmental sectors; environmental degradation; economic systems that overlook breaches of compassion and justice; and the normalization of violence, hunger, wage discrimination, and sexual harassment. Yang-itis limits potential because its devaluation of intangibles, like free-spiritedness and artistry, means that what can be seen ends up setting very low bars for what is possible.

Rampant yang-itis makes it hard to wrap our minds around the fact that a fully empowered self includes a sensitive self. Yin tendencies toward kindness and caring in the workplace are often negatively valued, but there is plenty of evidence that such devaluation of yin expression isn't good for human survival. And despite cultural mythology to the contrary, we now know that devaluation of yin tendencies is not good for organizational well-being, including profitability.

An antidote for yang-itis is to swing yin-ward. The Me Too movement and the rush of female political candidates in 2018 were yin indicators that may signify a resituating of our cultural fundamentals more toward the yin. It appears that we may be part of a macro-correctional swing yin-ward away from the historic path of extreme yang dominance. In Part Three, we will explore what seems to be a movement of our cultural center point, or what some are calling a paradigmatic shift.

Valuation for Yin

Institutions throughout the industrialized world have been yang dominant for centuries. However, there now seems to be emerging recognition of the need for a fuller spectrum of operations that includes more yin influences, such as out-of-the-box thinking and more humanistic policies. But because we are all so acculturated to yang-dominant norms, making yin-ward swings can seem extreme. Given the influence that cultural norms for yang dominance have had on leadership standards, finding equanimity may well require yin-ward risks that could feel threatening and downright weird. But as more and more companies compensate for child and elder care, offer flex time, and support personal growth, there is increasing evidence that yin-izing pays off well.

The known is yang; unknown is yin. Our yang-itis, our cultural inflation of yang values and deflation of yin values, has aggrandized the known while, at the same time, devalued the vast metaphysical pool of human consciousness that is unknown and apparently limitless. We have lived with yang-dominant norms for so long that we've lost sight of where our authentic equilibrium is. Because we are all fish in the water of the cultures we inhabit, it can be very hard just to see macro problems like yang-itis, and even harder to imagine ourselves healed from it. Nonetheless, emerging leadership development technologies are helping to evolve yang-dominant cultures by giving leaders the tools to consciously manage invisible core drivers (yin), that we know to be causal—drivers like values, and our innate quests for interconnectedness and well-being.

Yang dominance necessarily limits the range of potential behaviors because it countermands the yin zone of potentiality. Yang-dominant companies, by far the norm, often penalize their most insightful and visionary team members because those more yin-inclined folks can seem to threaten the status quo. Despite how much money is often made by breaking through old behavioral patterns, people who instigate those breakthroughs are often scapegoated as troublemakers, and there is no question that their input can be disruptive. Transformation disrupts. As obvious as that is, it is astounding how often leaders desire deep systemic change while remaining averse to disruption of the status quo. The inability to allow for the inevitable cycles of change, along with antipathy toward the inherent chaos of the creative process, are symptoms of yang-itis.

Transformative agents disrupt systems with their knack for uncovering overlooked strengths and weaknesses and for revealing faulty assumptions. Their input often triggers breakdowns, which are usually necessary for breakthroughs. Input from agents of transformation can trigger chaos, which is a critical part of the creative process but is nonetheless staunchly avoided by yang-dominant cultures. Too often, the very people who risk sparking change by challenging norms end up being blamed and shamed for instigating necessary development. Much to their discomfort, and often to their demise, the yin knack for transformation just shows up where certain people show up, often in their asking of hard questions or in their inability to be contained by limited thinking. Yin-ward leaning folks are often victimized by cultures that are afflicted with yang-itis.

But more and more leaders are embracing yin aspects of power that have been ignored, dismissed, and downright trashed as fuzzy, touchy-feely, and irrelevant. Values-driven companies like Zappos, Google, and Starbucks, as well as a plethora of academic studies, are proving that disregard for the yin aspects of success constitutes a competitive disadvantage. Leaders need the vision and fortitude to move beyond yang-dominant principles like "Might makes right"; "If it makes dollars, it makes sense"; "Profit at any cost"; "Domination is a viable strategy"; and "Get over on the next guy before he gets over on me."

There are yin and yang ways of unleashing power—both have capacity for good and bad. Yang unleashing of power is usually more overt, while yin unleashing impacts in the way that a well-planted whisper might. Yang-dominant unleashing happens in the form of concrete goals, numeric benchmarks, and well-defined performance indicators. Yin unleashing is less formulaic, more intuitive, innovative, and more emergent in nature. Our assumptions about the ideal yin-yang equation are changing quickly as we are recognizing that the spectrum of success is wider than we've been acknowledging. *To stay at the cutting edge, today's leaders must embrace a broader understanding of power.* In most cases, that means embracing yin factors in new ways and reexamining yang-dominant assumptions.

Leadership Reflections

1. Get your mojo rising!

   Continue doing three things every week that give you joy, energy, soul sourcing.... Any three things will do; what matters is what they spark in you.

   - Now up the ante by adding a "wild" factor of ten—imagine the wildest possibilities for all three things.
   - Schedule in some of those wild factors. Choose little or big actions that make you feel vibrant, engaged, connected, alive, at-risk, in chaos, free-spirited...

2. Every day, ask yourself: *How's my mojo today? What is going on with the mojo around me?*

3. What would change if your job title included Chief Mojo Officer, or if its description included "the one who is in charge of sparks"?

4. Consider how the dynamics of yin and yang are playing out in your world. *Don't get caught up in being right or wrong about which is which—this isn't an exercise in becoming a Taoist philosopher, it is a way of getting fresh perspective on your leadership.*

- Yin—What makes you feel expansive, joyful, and/ or creative? Does anything feel like too much of a "good" thing in your life? What do you crave? What needs to be released and/or relaxed?
- Yang—In what ways do you feel fit, fired, and ready to go? Where do things feel constricted? What's wound too tightly? In what areas of your work and life are you saying something like, "That's the only way it can be done," or, "I'm the only one who can do this"?

5. Play around with the concepts of yin and yang as you observe the world around you. Imagine making a yin case and a yang case about a situation that concerns you. For example, yin responses include ignoring something, seeking higher ground, or entering into deeper dialogues. Yang responses include shutting something or someone down, confrontation, firming up a position, and/or instituting a new rule.

   Consider journaling about how yin and yang play out in your world. Remember, there is always yin in the yang, and vice versa. Insights will come as yin naturally morphs into yang and back again around your concern.

6. Choose one issue you are concerned with and make two columns on a page—one for yin, one for yang. The point of this exercise is to play with reconciling yin-yang aspects of your world. Put keywords in each column to help map out yin-yang interplay in the situation you're working with. Because these are not fixed

points, it is likely that you will see reasons to put some things in both columns.

If, for example, your problem is in finding and/or retaining talent, the yin column might have entries like "unfulfilled," while the yang column might say "long hours." You might put "high turnover" in your yang column and "lack of clarity" in your yin column. Or, if you are focusing on a team's performance, you might put words in the yang column for every result, number, or efficiency issue you are experiencing and put words in the yin column for how the group is communicative, in breakdown, and/or working from shared vision. Put descriptive words or short phrases in the yin column when people are uncooperative, things aren't flowing, motivation is lagging...and in the yang column when there are dominator behaviors, silo mentality, power-mongering, intimidation...

- What is the overall picture that emerges from both columns? What does that picture inspire in you?

7. List five questions, aspirations, professional objectives, and/or visions. Which require more investment in yang elements? Yin elements?

8. What behaviors or thought patterns can you change, stop, or start so that you can spark a more dynamic equanimity between yin and yang?

9. Create some undisturbed space and time to follow an inkling, a nagging thought, or a persistent concern that feels disruptive. Determine the places and

spaces that best amplify the wisdom voice in you and be diligent about booking time in those places on your calendar. Obviously, deep reflection is easier in nature than it is in a supermarket. Likewise, following through on thoughts that you have not been able to give adequate attention to isn't likely to happen in all your usual places.

Give yourself time to let the issue rise up in your psyche. Check in with body, mind, and spirit on how you are personally triggered by it, where it's landing in you physically, mentally, emotionally, and spiritually. When you discover a nagging truth, follow through on it with a consultant, a trusted mentor, or at least a notepad or recording device. Follow it as deep as it takes you, again and again. Identify how that truth contrasts with your desires.

Keep bringing your consciousness back to the contrast until you know what it will take to experience peace with whatever or whoever is involved. And then act accordingly.

10. On a scale of 1–10, how high is your organizational mojo? Look around you. What is the vibe like? What do people want?

CHAPTER 3

MECHANICS

**Particles, Waves, Quarks, and
Making Things Happen**

According to cosmology, a field of physics, a Big Bang birthed a cosmic emergence that began unfolding 13.8 billion years ago. Everything and everybody who ever existed is, was, and will be part of that ever-emerging cosmic moment. There are no new materials in our universe since that bang—literally everything we know about came forth then. All that has ever happened since the Big Bang is the constant changing of those original particles. That's how we got the old adage: The only constant is change. And the newer one: We are stardust. The truth is we are stardust in a state of constant change. At this moment in time, we are uniquely conglomerated stardust with historically unprecedented means and opportunities to consciously determine how we want the inevitability of change to play out.

Cosmologists tell us that the universe consists of a kind of space-time "foam" that bubbles into and out of existence as it morphs back and forth between an energetic unified field and materiality. (see Swimme) Matter (yang) and non-matter, or energy (yin) happen as particles constantly turn to waves and back again throughout infinity. Taoists and physicists seem to concur.

Everything we currently know and see constitutes about 5 percent of the universe and 95 percent of our reality is a mystery, but all 100 percent is always in the dynamic state of cosmic emergence that began with the Bang. We understand a lot about how the 5 percent unfolds by way of various branches of physics. Because so much of our reality falls into the unknown, it is important to remind ourselves that:

a) *ignoring 95 percent of our reality is a risky and meaningful oversight; and*

b) *consciously tapping into that field affords a strategic advantage.*

Operating from the mindset that the 5 percent of reality that is known to us is the "whole enchilada" is a severely restricted worldview that unnecessarily limits our sense of purpose and possibility. *Alchemy, that is, the power to create "out of thin air," is more accurately understood as the capacity to tap in to the 95 percent.* Alchemical leadership is the ability to see beyond what exists within the 5 percent and to thereby tap in to the 95 percent of the universe that is mostly a mystery to us. Situating leadership power in its metaphysical context affords leaders access to a larger field of potentiality.

From a cosmological perspective, achievements and failures are not just completions, they're also new beginnings in a universe that is infinitely unfolding. Likewise, alchemical leadership isn't a fixed point of power, but rather a fluid alignment with people and situations as you move through the inevitable changes that come with time, and as you preside over the coherence and disruptions that happen as your leadership unfolds. Staying conscious of metaphysical dynamics requires staying attuned to your physical, mental, emotional, and spiritual awareness, which is a lifetime discipline. Because the nature of consciousness is a great mystery that is forever unfolding, every level of awareness gained is a breakthrough into expanded potential.

From Potential to Reality

Physicists, theologians, and philosophers say the same thing in different ways—that the manifestation of people, places, and things starts from a unified field of pure potential. Most say that unified field differentiates first into two and then ad infinitum. Creation myths throughout cultures, religions, and time tell us various versions of the same theme: that we came from One, from One came two, and then came everything else. Some refer to the ultimate Oneness as "God" while others don't think of it in terms of a deity.

Across cultures and disciplines, there are consistent references to a unified field of all things and no thing, or an invisible field of infinite potential, out of which our lives emerge. Whatever it might be named, or however it may be framed by any particular disciplinary lens, there is widespread agreement on a meta-domain that is an infinite field of all possibility. This metaphysical perspective is consistent with cosmologists who say that, ever since the Big Bang caused its massive vibration, the universe continues to unfold in particles and waves through space and time. *Our lives move forward in ever-rolling yin waves of consciousness and yang waves of manifestation.*

There is no such thing as a fixed state at the level of causality. Natural law dictates that all that we see and know is in a state of constant transformation. Solid things, like rocks (yang), transform much more slowly while gases, like oxygen (yin), transform quickly. The concept of yin always changing to yang and back again is a way of articulating the constancy of change. Yin-yang theory offers a framework for thinking about the ever-evolving frontiers of the human condition.

The practice of alchemy is hindered when we think of success only in terms of end goals rather than seeing it in terms of the reality of the infinite possibilities that make up our universe. Some of the principles of alchemy may seem annoying if you are someone who tends to be more naturally yang in their thinking, because from that perspective, things appear more finite. From a more yin, metaphysical perspective, *the more we develop our consciousness, the more the meta-domain itself seems to expand.* Alchemical leaders seek equanimity with both ways of thinking.

Success boils down to what you manifest physically, emotionally, mentally, and spiritually. What you manifest is, in part, a result of your adeptness with the metaphysical field of possibility, whether you are conscious of it or not. More yang thinking may be necessary to complete a specific task while more yin thinking may be helpful when it's time to explore new possibilities. The process of moving between more yin and more yang consciousness is similar to the flow between waves and particles.

Particles and Waves

In the wave-particle, space-time meta-movement that underlies our day-to-day experience, change is always happening
as waves of energy cohere into particles, then those particles
are sooner or later dispersed back into waves, until they manifest again as particles that are cohered in new ways. The relatively recent discovery of atomic particles called bosons helps
to bridge the gap between physical and metaphysical expla-
nations of how power plays out in cohering and dispersing
waves and particles.

Atomic particles are recognized by quantum physics as
the building blocks of matter. There are two types, bosons
and fermions. Bosons are a type of particle that carry force,
versus their better-understood counterparts, fermion particles, which comprise matter. Bosons are vibrational, more yin
because they are tied to energetic transformation; fermions are
more yang in that they are materialized. Given our yang-ward
leanings toward materialism, fermions have been our focus.
While we still understand relatively little about what constitutes so much of our universe, the more recent discovery of
bosons has helped us see that there is an energetic component
of everything. We now understand some of the mechanisms
for how physicality isn't the whole picture, or even the most
powerful element of what we see.

The Higgs boson is of particular interest in the practice of
alchemy. To understand it, we have to start with the Higgs field,
which is everywhere, in all spaces. It is a ubiquitous quantum
field that gives particles their masses in much the same way
that a popular movie star who moves through a party would
attract more and more people until there was a substantive
mass in one part of the room. (see CNN) In a sense, Higgs

bosons function like a sort of atomic gravity because they have the effect of triggering energetic interactions between things. While Higgs bosons are an attracting energy, Gauge bosons provide a driving force. Both bosons work by way of mediating the energetic fields that exist around and between fermions or matter. As particles get closer to one another, the Higgs force becomes greater, just like the movie star's mojo magnifies as the crowd around him/her grows, while, at the same time, the whole group's mojo rises in its collective excitement.

The discovery of bosons gives us a glimpse into the intangible factors that drive our lives. Boson activity happens in the nucleus of cells, making it nuclear energy. The scientific confirmation of Higgs and Gauge bosons gives us relatively new access to the invisible realm of energetics, and it provides some basis for alchemical leadership. As field-mediating particles, these bosons help locate the yin intangibles by demonstrating that what comes "out of nowhere" is a consequence of an energetic, and less understood, somewhere. It is not important to understand particle theory, but it is important to know that there is strong scientific basis for the energetic transformations that are at the heart of how our universe works. The way to tap in to this primal reality is to consciously open ourselves to seeing, feeling, and managing the flow of the energy around us. Tapping into energetics is the domain of metaphysics. Using them is the domain of alchemy.

Energetics

Our yang-itis reflects a fermion-centered worldview in that we have given 100 percent credence to what we can see while disregarding what we can't see. Western thinking has almost exclusively focused on fermion activity, like visible outcomes, and physical manifestations of the particles of life. We've not just been ignoring the boson forces by which fermions get organized into matter, but actively discounting those forces as fluffy stuff. We have disregarded the power of bosons by overlooking energetic realities. *But we ignore energetics at the expense of losing influence over them. Alchemical leaders capitalize on boson activity by creating a Higgs-like pull, as well as a Gauge-like driving force, for people to come together toward fulfilling a shared mission.* While there is a lot that we do and don't understand about why, we know unequivocally that our intention has a huge impact on which particles do what.

The discovery of bosons means that we cannot go forward thinking that only fermions (materialization) are important. We can no longer pretend that what we see is all there is. If the only power lines you're accounting for are on the fermion-yang spectrum, you simply aren't in command of all of your power. It takes courage to dabble in the 95 percent of the pie that fluff mythology has relegated as out of bounds. We think easily about being intentional with fermions (matter), but we're much less intellectually diligent with how we manage energetic elements, which makes no sense since the energetic realm is exactly where our influence has the most impact. *Our human consciousness appears to play a big part in how, where, and when bosons do their thing.*

The transformative power of bosons provides a helpful analogy for why working from the inside out of an organization pays off so well. Alchemical leadership is the capacity for harnessing and transforming energy at the nuclear level of an organization, which, though invisible, is highly determinate of outcomes. In leadership, as in science, religion, and politics, our history of putting far higher valuation on external manifestation (yang) has obscured the power available to us in the yin domain of energetics. To distinguish leadership merely by yang-centric metrics of materialization is to disregard the yin power that causes coherence between people and that sets the trajectory of their work together. Unlike more yang elements that can literally hit us in the face, yin elements require far more diligence just to recognize, let alone to address them.

Leadership alchemy is adeptness with the cycles of causality that bounce back and forth between wave and particle, between boson and fermion, between energy and physicality, between intention and results. Part of that adeptness comes with being in ongoing inquiry about what causes what. Even though we may never find satisfactory answers, it is to every leader's advantage to keep asking questions like: What sources the Higgs boson's energetic pull? Who or what drives how and why Gauge bosons mediate the forces they carry? What determines how Higgs boson energy brings masses into coherence in the same way that the movie star brings partygoers into a coherent group? And who or what determines which particles are impacted by Gauge boson forces? Pondering these kinds of questions is not for the purpose of gaining expertise on particles, but rather for accessing the realm where the power to cohere or disperse actually plays out.

Bump Up Your Boson Bodacious-ness

Alchemical leaders exercise power by taking bold, bodacious action in the realm of energy transformation. Being bodacious means being audacious, but in a way that is seen as admirable. Whereas audaciousness implies being impudent, cocky, reckless, disrespectful, and brazen, bodacious-ness implies a boldness and a striving for excellence that is attractive to others. Audaciousness is more yang in that it's a more superficial and individualistic expression, whereas bodacious-ness is more yin because it involves deeper, more inclusive processing.

Audacious leaders operate on the flawed premise that power over people is more powerful than holding power with them. Bodacious-ness, on the other hand, demonstrates a higher, more attractive and holistic stage of consciousness. Audacious people are often off-putting and have a hard time getting enrollment in their efforts, while, like the star at a party, bodacious leaders create coherence. What makes bodacious people attractive is their resonance with universal driving forces like values. Positive values, like respect and honesty, provide boson-like forces that invisibly bring people together and that also energize behaviors that are consistent with those values.

Values expression can be thought of as the pulse of an organization, as an indicator of its life force. Negative values, like selfishness or deceit, slow the pulse. The degree to which positive values drive systems is the degree to which an organization's human energy is available and engaged. (see Barrett) Positive values expression means an organization's pulse is strong and that its collective mojo is ready, willing, and able to engage.

There is a meta-field that sources big, bold, bodacious action. It is accessed by the pursuit of wisdom, and it is operationalized by values fulfillment.

Metaphysical Awareness

Boson research offers insight into how profound the intangibles are. Using a quantum perspective helps substantiate the value of subtle energetic drivers like intention, attraction, coherence, and other long-neglected yin aspects of success. Whether we use the lens of metaphysics or physics, power is enhanced exponentially by consciousness of nuclear, internal, invisible energy. We're coming through an era in which valuation for metaphysical principles might have hit an all-time low. But valued or not, fathomable and unfathomable metaphysical influences are always operative. Metaphysical awareness is surging as increasing numbers of leaders, seekers, and scholars are identifying the economic and social value of intangible truths.

The metaphysical nuclear power, the dynamic force, of a collective can be thought of as a sort of corporate boson. Leadership alchemy comes down to mastery of that power. Applying quantum intelligence to organizational best practices may seem obtuse, but it is a way of accounting for invisible vibrational realities and there is no denying that good vibes make good workplaces—deeply good vibes, not just pleasantries or the absence of bad vibes. Conscious vibe-setting is alchemy. In the next chapter, we'll explore how and why to build good vibe cultures.

The metaphysical domain is so powerful because it is the meta-field from which things can be caused to happen. Attuning to metaphysics is a task of consciousness. Vibes, bodacious-ness, and all other energetics are experienced at the level of consciousness, which is at the root of all leadership practices. Quantum physics has only begun to be unraveled. As it progresses, it will no doubt bring greater understanding of the connections between particles, consciousness, the 95 percent of the universe we don't know about, and the manifestation of results.

Consciousness

One of the greatest pioneers of quantum theory, Max Planck, winner of the Nobel Prize in Science, said in 1931, "I regard consciousness as fundamental. I regard matter as derivative from consciousness." Planck confirms what spiritual masters have always taught: what's going on within you and what's manifesting around you reflect the mutual interdependencies between consciousness and reality, between metaphysics and physics. In short, *consciousness is causal.*

Consciousness is a multilevel awareness of self in the world. Leadership consciousness is awareness with a purpose, the purpose being mission and vision fulfillment. Being conscious of your consciousness is a way to deeply stake your composure as you surf the inevitable tides of change. Consciousness is key to how your mojo moves through the ever-unfolding big and little waves of yin turning to yang and back again. Your level of consciousness has everything to do with how your own cycles go and with how you ride the waves in your world.

Consciousness gives you access to mojo, which is energy that is potentially available to you for accomplishing your mission. Your consciousness determines how well you manage your personal and collective mojo, the ever-evolving essence of being that fuels everyone's work. The more conscious you are of what is causing the results around you, the more adept you'll be at causing the things you want to happen. Your consciousness ultimately determines who you are being while you're leading. It has to constantly evolve in order to maintain your equanimity throughout the full spectrum of what is playing out around you.

Consciousness is awareness of the gestalt of physiological, cultural, emotional, and energetic patterns that make up your life and that make up the matrix of your organization. Degrees of consciousness can be thought of as degrees not just of awareness, but also of responsiveness, sensitivity, focus, and intentionality. The rights and responsibilities to control outcomes might be in a job description, but authentic power is an inside job. Power is accessed by paying attention to the many levels of consciousness within yourself and everyone else, that is, by being conscious of consciousness itself—which isn't as hard as it might sound.

Consciousness is the capacity that mystics have always told us about and that visionary leaders are changing the world with. As we've evolved to become more and more conscious of our consciousness, we have become increasingly aware of how primal intangible drivers, like values and desires, determine what we make tangible. *Outcomes depend on the catalyst that consciousness is for everything everywhere.* The level of your consciousness is your level of capacity for causing things to happen the way you want them to. *The consciousness with which you negotiate your circumstances is highly determinant of outcomes.*

Consciousness is a metaphysical field that is accessed through personal and systemic self-awareness, that is, through intentional development of consciousness itself—something that leaders often mistakenly believe they can't justify devoting time to. Even though exercising the invisible "muscles" of consciousness yields insights and develops capacities that pay off unequivocally well, fluff mythology has obscured the value of consciousness development. However, cutting-edge leadership theory is confirming what metaphysicians have always said, and what quantum scientists now confirm: *consciousness doesn't just determine whether and how we get up the proverbial mountain, it is determinate of the mountain itself.*

Given widespread cultural prejudices, it's understandable to mistake the development of leadership consciousness as an expense that takes time and money away from mission fulfillment. But it is not accurate to post it in the expense column, because development of leadership consciousness is a capital investment in something that sources all results. Sourcing your source is a good investment. Taking it for granted is risky.

Developing metaphysical consciousness is the path to authority. Consciousness building is capacity building. Building consciousness builds mojo. Mojo is metaphysical capital. Building metaphysical capital is fundamental to building and sustaining physical capital.

Locating Power

It is a common trap for people in high places to believe that their power is in their positions, despite that we've known for centuries that *the most formidable power is an internal situation, a state of being.* Research confirms that every leader's authority is superseded by anyone on the team who is further along in his/her values development—no matter what their job titles say. Values development is part of consciousness development. *Developing your consciousness increases your moral authority, which supersedes all other forms of authority, in terms of people's natural responses to you* (see Hall).

Since moral authority is a result of personal development, and moral authority is more powerful than rank in terms of ability to cohere or disrupt, if your consciousness is stagnant or devolving, so is your leadership standing, regardless of your position. Many leaders are jeopardized by this reality because their understanding of leadership is prejudiced by cultural norms that relegate consciousness as inconsequential fluffy stuff. When you develop your yin "muscles" by investing in consciousness-raising activities, there is high statistical likelihood that you will receive big returns on those investments, starting with an increase in authority. A Metrix Global study identified a 689 percent return on investments in leadership coaching, which is a method for raising leadership consciousness, because it correlates with that much gain in annualized benefits. The higher your level of awareness, the more capacity you will have for managing whatever is in front of you.

Consciousness may seem like an unfathomable thing but, in many ways, it is no more than the interplay of yin and yang. The key to alchemical adeptness is to develop your internal equanimity such that you can gracefully move yin-ward or yang-ward in response to any given situation. Your consciousness determines whether and how you act, react, and/or respond to the ever-changing cycles of the human condition. There are times to paddle hard (yang) and times to relax and ride the wave (yin); times to surf the edge of a huge wave (yang) and times to wait a wave out (yin). Surfing the unique complexity and intensity of the intangible waves that flow through a leader's day requires a kind of internal equanimity that is not unlike a surfer's adeptness with the ocean's waves.

Multiple meditation studies, including those of Ruedy and Schweitzer, as well as Desbordes, Gard, et al., have demonstrated that navigating any given situation with the equanimity of consciousness that comes with regular meditation practice tends to result in better outcomes. The underlying principle is pretty simple—regularly sitting with the intention of being in a state of equanimity helps establish more stable ground for good decision-making. Meditating helps clarify awareness of the pushes of fear, doubt, and worry and the pulls of wishing and hoping. It also has the effect of tuning us in to the voice of inner wisdom that tends to be highly accurate when we can hear it clearly. *Meditation, like self-reflection, develops consciousness.*

It also leads to greater contentment. *Contentment demonstrates authority and it supports adeptness in causing things to happen the way you want them to. Paying attention to qualities like contentment, and to how and why you think about what you think about, pays off.* But paying attention to aspects of your own consciousness is hard to do in isolation. Sifting your personal issues out from what you face in the workplace can be almost impossible without objective insight. Professional surfers invest in coaches not to fix bruised ribs, but rather for support for staying at their ever-present best. Likewise, *spending time with paid or unpaid wise counsel is a capital investment in maintaining your metaphysical edge.*

Values

The interface between consciousness and the concrete is values. More specifically, it is how you play out your own values and those of the people you lead. *Schwartz and others have demonstrated that, by far, our primary motivation is our pursuit of values and so values are metaphysical in that they are causal of behavior.* The degree to which your behavior reflects your personal values and supports the values of the people around you is the degree to which people will naturally follow you. *Values are such primal motivators that it makes no sense to assume that people will trust your leadership if you are not accounting for what is most important to them.*

Values are our ideals, principles, morals, and standards—our rules for living. Values are the metaphysical links between the tangible and the intangible in that people are most likely to make things happen if they value something about the doing of those things. Our primordial drive toward fulfillment of values is hardwired into the human psyche. Actions taken in pursuit of values have practical, psychological, biological, and social consequences. (see Schwartz)

Everybody wants to feel good, usually through fulfillment of values like achievement, family time, and humor. When we feel good, we tend to be more productive, generous, and innovative. On the other hand, studies are clear that sound decision-making and productive work habits are handicapped when values like dignity and truthfulness are compromised. *The metaphysical bottom line is that personal and organizational mojo move in accordance with values fulfillment and development.*

Leadership alchemy depends on personal capacity to capitalize on values being the energetic drivers of human behavior and to consciously catalyze those energetics. People naturally respond best to whoever treats them the best. Team members will put their better efforts toward supporting leaders who make them feel good at the core, that place in gut, heart, and mind where mojo lives. Good feelings are usually a result of fulfillment on values like respect and appreciation. If you are not apprising yourself of exactly which values are motivating your team, which you cannot figure out by guessing, you are not availing yourself of your full cultural capital, nor of the corporate momentum, you've got at your fingertips.

Mojo Grows as Values Flow

People naturally behave in ways that optimize fulfillment of their values. According to Koivula, Barrett, and other values researchers, values are the primal drivers of behaviors. They have been demonstrated over centuries and throughout cultures to be fundamental to decision-making regardless of age, race, shared interests, and other delineating factors. Values are even more primary determinants of behaviors than genetics, according to twins studies (see Whitney and Schmitt). Values are like social bosons because they are the energetic mechanisms that bring people into coherence with one another, that drive them apart, and that motivate them to do things.

Study after study on the role of values in success have demonstrated that a leader's adeptness with values has a strong correlation to outcomes. The amount of mojo that's available in any given situation is highly influenced by the degree to which personal values are being fulfilled. When people's values are aligned with organizational mission, they mutually pursue positive outcomes. *That mutuality is a source of alchemical power in that it creates ease and confluence in a system, meaning less likelihood of disruption and more likelihood of efficiency. Since, when it comes to people, one plus one can equal so much more than two, the mutuality that comes with values alignment is an alchemical factor.*

Values are alchemical mechanisms. If you think of alignment between your values and those of everyone around you as a pipeline, it makes sense that when values are aligned, just like when sections of a pipe are aligned, mojo flows smoothly. When values for caring are held in equanimity with values for productivity, workers align more sustainably and more wholeheartedly toward getting the job done well. For example, when an entire organizational culture systemically values customer care and employees are empowered to go the extra mile to keep buyers coming back, even if it means temporarily ignoring something else that's important, there is coherence in the flow of mojo toward shared objectives. When the culture is well aligned around customer satisfaction, whether the boss is in the building or not, s/he can usually count on having happy clients or customers.

On the other hand, if cultural norms are such that higher value is placed on internal competition, employees will spend their mojo on competing, or avoiding competing, and may not even have customer care on their radars, despite what handbooks, mission statements, and wall plaques say. Even when the same words are said to the same customer, the difference in that customer's experience can be radical depending on the cultural platform on which an employee's words stand.

The fluffy myth supports the premise that people will always try to dominate one another and will always choose to slack off if given the chance. However, there is comparatively little substantiation for the notion that most people value domination and laziness. Research from all over the world, including by the government of Bhutan and Whitby, is extremely clear that what people value most is feeling interconnected with one another, feeling well and happy, and feeling fulfilled. When those basic human values are operational, competitive politics diminish and cooperative dynamics flourish.

Values fulfillment is an operational advantage. Strong and happy team members, who make good choices most of the time, can be developed by way of making investments in values for physical, emotional, soul, and social well-being. *Alchemical leadership includes accountancy for the metaphysical reality that values are a primal factor in outcomes.* For example, when gender and generational concerns are managed in the domain of values, the ground is laid for honoring and transcending differences. Values alignment creates common ground.

When negative values are operative, the loss is not just in the energy that gets spent on nonproductive activity, there is also a more general loss of mojo because people simply don't bring their whole selves to any situation where negative values prevail over positive ones. We are naturally reluctant to spend our energy on anything that doesn't feel right. When cultures reward things that limit people, for example, control-centered behaviors, a lot of invisible resources are spent on things like managing the fear and indignity of being controlled. That results in behaviors like gossip, avoidance, and political gamesmanship superseding behaviors aimed toward keeping customers happy or toward improving performance. The more dedicated people are, the more upset they will feel when their values are compromised. Negative values contribute to turnover of some of the best people because their choices are to tamp down their caring, which results in apathy, or to seek employment in a culture that can better accommodate their dedication.

Values are the metaphysical means for tapping into mojo. They function as boson-like energetic mechanisms that determine why, if, and how people get things done. *Values are the bridge between your consciousness and the demands of your position.*

Leadership Reflections

1. Jot down a list of things that are mysterious to you. The purpose of this exercise is to get in touch with just how much of our lives is unknown and seemingly out of reach.

2. On a scale of 1–10, how conscious are you of your consciousness?

   a) 10 = I regularly self-examine and take time to tune in to a deeper sense of who I am, and I seek opportunities to self-develop.
   b) 1 = I never think about anything that isn't sitting right in front of me.

3. List ten values that matter most to you and ten that you think matter most to the people who work around you. (There is a list of values in Appendix 3)

   • Ask the people who work around you to confirm what their values are.
   • Identify five action steps you can take to fulfill your own values aspirations and five actions steps you can take to help fulfill other people's values.

4. Take a good hard look at your level of personal values development. Do you naturally find higher ground by leaning toward greater good? Do you naturally seek the lowest common denominator of self-preservation?

a) Chances are, like most people, you fall somewhere in between and that you lean one way or the other according to circumstances. What would it look like if you made a personal leap toward the next level of expressing the values that matter most to you?

b) *Take time to gauge how you are expressing your personal values, because that's the starting place for raising your consciousness of your own causality.*

5. Take the Barrett Leadership Self-Assessment Tool (Appendix 1) to clarify your values profile. After you record your scores on the histogram at the end, note your strengths and gaps and consider how you might work with them.

CHAPTER 4

CULTURE, CAPITAL, AND ENTROPY

What I Learned about Culture from a Tribe of Head-Hunters

Culture is determined by the values, beliefs, and behaviors that underpin the policies, systems, and structures of a collective entity. Like the air we breathe, culture is so ubiquitous that most of us don't think about it at all. But to the extent that we are conscious of it, culture usually boils down to being "just the way things are." Culture is the metaphysical ground of an organization. The primary elements, or building blocks, of any culture are its values.

An organization's culture is a way of being that represents the intellectual, emotional, and aesthetic development of the group, whether it be a company, nongovernmental organization, or a whole society. Values serve as an intersection between individuals and the social, professional, and cultural circles they are part of. They function as common denominators between people, regardless of how conscious the population is of their operative values.

Culture is the most studied workplace intangible. In their article in the *Journal of Management*, researchers Meglino and Ravlin conclude it has "been proven over and over again: Culture is captured by the significant conversation in the organization and through its management and policy documents, which in turn reflect the values priorities held by the organization." According to Kotter and Heskett's *Corporate Culture and Performance Study*, conducted over eleven years, companies with strong adaptive cultures that are based on shared values outperform other companies with

- 400 percent faster growth
- 700 percent higher job creation rates
- 12 percent faster stock price gains
- 750 percent higher profit performance.

In their classic, *Built to Last: Successful Habits of Visionary Companies*, Collins and Porras noted that organizations that consistently focused on building strong values-driven cultures over a period of several decades outperformed:

- companies that did not prioritize values by a factor of six
- the general stock market by a factor of fifteen.

Progressive companies are topping the stock exchanges as they place high priority, which translates as high valuation, on employee and community well-being while prioritizing respect for the individual. For example, Barrett Values Centre's studies of *Forbes' 500 Best Companies to Work For*, which, by definition, invest in satisfying employees' core values, found that those companies' share prices beat the Standard & Poor's 500 averages by 600 percent. Barrett has demonstrated that, compared to industry standards, values-driven companies experience higher profits, share prices, stakeholder loyalty, innovation, and team coherence.

It's a leader's job to identify, and then create coherence around, common values so that everyone is working from the same basis, toward the same ends, and with trust in one another and in the processes that are in place. There will always be problems. Your choice is to create a culture that does or doesn't feed into them and that is resilient enough to weather them when they arise.

The Shuar

I learned a lot about culture when I stayed with the Shuar, a tribe in the Amazon jungle who are known for their fierce warriors and their head-hunting tradition, which they say is rarely or no longer practiced, depending on who you ask. Their ferocity is legendary, but their world revolves around quality family time, autonomy, laughter, and community. They are fun and joyful people to hang out with. As far as the head-shrinking, the Shuar consider us to be far more barbaric because our warfare causes the death of non-warriors and kills entire opposing units for the sake of determining an outcome. To them, the horrific effects of bombs and big guns are far more brutal than taking the head of a leader or two, which was always done in the spirit of respect for someone powerful enough to be a threat.

Shuar warfare nowadays is mostly only in service to the Ecuadorian government, which comes into the jungle to recruit them when the toughest of the tough are needed. On the battlefront, they bring their indigenous ethics to government-led combat by demonstrating unwavering personal stability and support for fellow soldiers, by using their extraordinarily clear presence of mind, as well as their better than average intuition, and by mending bodies and souls with traditional healing methods. Shuar warriors are strategically minded, sharply focused, team-oriented, physically strong, and highly discriminate about whom they harm. It is incomprehensible to them that any non-warrior, much less a child, would be displaced, injured, or killed in the practice of war, because they never harm, much less kill, indiscriminately. Not even plants. The Shuar traditionally use deadly power only between and among warriors, and only in the face of imminent threat to their village, or when they feel aligned with their government's military objectives.

It is reprehensible to them that anyone would allow children to die, not only in warfare, but also by way of social and commercial practices that expose them to poisoned water, systemic hunger, and rampant violence. Many of our most fundamental assumptions about progress are too ruthless to fit into the Shuar worldview. There is absolutely no place in their ethical framework, that is, in their cultural paradigm, to even consider harming a nonthreatening being. And *because they are so strong physically, emotionally, and spiritually, they are not threatened easily.*

The Shuar worldview literally cannot accommodate the concept of "collateral" damage. They see all life as interdependent, and so inflicting harm at any juncture in the circle of life is inflicting harm on all life, including one's own. *The Shuar ontology, that is, their very ground of being, simply does not provide any foundation for comprehending how a living person, plant, or animal could possibly be collateral to anything, or why well-being should be subject to negotiations with anyone but their shamans.*

The cycle of life churns very quickly in the wet, warm jungle where prolific bacterial and fungal activity break down materials almost before your eyes. In their worldview, material items have inconsequential value compared to their connections to one another and to the land. Shuar cultural norms are such that material acquisition just does not hold enough value to risk a relationship for. They know that the quality of their interrelationships determines whether or not they will be able to count on one another in the face of the jungle's challenges.

It astounds the Shuar that so-called civilized ontological frameworks place any life as secondary to any other. They've suffered an increase in deaths as a result of companies coming in and bulldozing the resources that have always fueled their survival. In my time at the United Nations, I have witnessed multiple indigenous leaders from all over the world report on the torching of huts, the poisoning of water, the strip mining of land, and the killing of their people for the sake of profiteering. The horrific injustices they encounter are all the more striking when you realize that the stories are coming from people who live in extraordinary integrity with nature and one another. Although aid usually flows from governments and from the UN to tribes, I often wonder about how much good would come if governmental bodies could accept the aid to consciousness that indigenous wisdom has to offer in return. Having more indigenous wisdom in the mix would likely alleviate the need for so much aid.

The Shuar hold much deeper systemic valuation for well-being in their social fabric than Western cultures hold in theirs. While the sanctity of life is espoused by pretty much every culture, many policies and practices do not conform with that espoused value. *For the Shuar, as for many indigenous cultures, valuation for the sanctity and interdependence of all life rises above all else. That high valuation is core to their cultural makeup and is embedded in their fundamental concepts of reality.* Western culture, while it also espouses the sanctity of life, nevertheless accommodates many conditions that are not aligned with it, for example, contaminated water supplies, systemic poverty, and collateral deaths in the name of "progress." For the Shuar, valuation for the full circle of life is a cultural pillar in a way that it is not for most people living in westernized cultures.

The Shuar have a profound respect for, and a very conscious relationship with, power. Warriors are seen as having a particular type of power, not in the sense of being violent power-mongers or warlords, but more in the sense that they serve as a particular link in the chain of a powerful people. They choose adversaries in terms of power matches, believing that no warrior worth his title would use power against someone who has much less power because that would demonstrate cowardice. In other words, they only "pick on someone their own size."

The Shuar ethic for respecting power carries forward from their ancestral headhunting days. Headhunters only went after the most powerful leader or leaders and removed what they consider to be the container of the enemy's power, their heads. By tradition they do not slaughter all of the opposing warriors because, for them and for the opposing indigenous tribes, mass slaughter is diametrically opposed to their values. Their rules of warfare included believing that the minds of leaders got them into the problems and, therefore, removing the leaders' heads was the way out.

When the victorious warriors got back to their village, they conducted a head-shrinking ceremony that was deeply respectful of the power of the opponent. The Shuar, like many indigenous groups, understand power to be existential. That is, they believe that power exists in and of itself and that it, therefore, doesn't necessarily stay contained in any one person or thing. The Shuar word for this invisible force is *arutum*, which I equate with mojo. They believed that, through spiritual ritual, the *arutum* had to be extracted and redirected toward the tribe's well-being and that the warrior who captured the head was entitled to assimilate some of that power into his own power reserve. They believed that any remaining remnants of the opponent's power needed to be contained by way of shrinking the skull around it and sewing it up in sacred ceremony so that the enemy's *arutum* could not escape and threaten their community. The post-warfare ceremony ritualizes the channeling of the *arutum* (mojo) away from control of enemies and toward the tribe's greatest good.

It's not Utopia, but the Shuar are remarkably happy and healthy, they have robust spirits, and they literally have zero problems with theft. There are also low theft rates among people living under violent dictators. But in the case of the Shuar, they are not motivated by fear, but rather by their ontological reality of knowing their interdependency with one another and with nature. They have no inherent need to steal because their fundamental, shared values for truth, along with their high valuation for their interdependency, mean each tribal member gets what s/he needs, and that trust prevails. Also, there isn't much to take because, in a non-monetized culture located hundreds of dense jungle miles away from more developed areas of Ecuador, material things don't tend to accumulate. Once a Shuar family knows they can be fed, which can take from a few hours a day to a weeklong hunt, they focus on enjoying life. They think first in terms of familial well-being and secondly of communal strength. Personal profiteering is not part of their cultural norms and does not fit into their worldview.

Westerners' propensity to dream of material gain, often dreamt about with little regard for its social and environmental costs, is considered delusional by the Shuar because they are experiencing demise as a result of those dreams and they strongly believe we are setting ourselves up for the same. What constitutes value in our world, like beef and fossil fuels, creates life-threatening deficits in theirs. From an indigenous perspective, we all live on one interdependent planet—if you harm others, you harm yourself. Where we tend to see "the other," the indigenous mind sees individual branches on the common tree of life. The Shuar welcomed me, as they do others, with the intention of helping to recalibrate our Western acculturated beliefs about what success really is. They hoped to change our dreams so that we could better accommodate the sanctity and interdependency of life.

The Shuar have cultural moorings that have kept them strong in the face of harsh jungle challenges and have kept them alive as they negotiate lethal corporate intrusions. I saw in them a physical and spiritual vitality unlike anything I've witnessed in my lifelong journey of seeking keys to transformational wisdom throughout the world. The Shuar's remarkably vibrant mojo appeared to be inextricably linked to the strong communal weave that is their culture. Experiencing such a stark cultural contrast to my own world brought much insight into the role that culture plays in everything every day.

Ontology

Ontology is the branch of metaphysics that deals with the very nature of being. A culture's ontology is its ground of being, its existential nature, the basis on which it exists. Every culture is grounded in a matrix of unique concepts and categories with particular properties and relations between them. A culture's ontology is the ground on which it sits and from which it views the world. Whether it defines an organizational culture or a nation's culture, a cultural ontology is the subconscious, intangible scaffolding of shared language, norms, worldview, customs, and expression. Our ontology is the proverbial water we swim in.

In 1921, Albert Einstein, Nobel Prize winner and legendary genius, was referring to the need for ontological awareness when he said, "We can't solve problems by using the same kind of thinking we used when we created them," meaning real-world breakthroughs cannot happen on the same old ground of ontological assumptions. Ontology is the figurative box that people talk about stepping out of. The more aware you are of your ontological box, the more aware you can be of whether and how you are in or out of it.

Alchemy is not all that magical when you think of it in terms of transforming or transcending cultural constraints. Alchemical leadership requires developing one's consciousness to see beyond common beliefs about what is so, and beyond words and behaviors that reinforce ontological patterns. *Alchemical leadership requires the courage to consciously expand beyond what is known, beyond the ontological boundaries within which you exist.*

Ontological awareness, that is, consciousness of deep, underlying assumptions, values, and norms, gives you access to the ground from which things can be caused. The more conscious you are of personal and cultural assumptions, the more adept you can be with knowing when and how to maintain your ground of being and when to disrupt or shift away from your ontological ground so that new things can happen.

Organizational Culture

We are all fish in the water of the cultures we live and work in because our ontological assumptions are so ubiquitous, we rarely consider them on their own terms. It makes sense that so many studies are confirming that culture is by far the best indicator for success because culture is the metaphysical ground of being from which things happen. Culture is fundamental to organizational mechanics because culture is the basis from which any given group operates. When a culture is fertile, both productivity and vitality increase. Vitality always works its way to the bottom line, often by way of unpredictable yin-ward pathways. Being a metaphysical as well as a physical phenomenon, vitality comes not just from having good health and some spunk, it also comes from feeling like you are participating in something good. A cultural ontology that holds high valuation for vitality provides the basis for thriving.

The high valuation for *arutum* (mojo) within the Shuar culture results in a mostly happy and healthy population that is safe within itself, despite the extraordinary pressures on its safety that are imposed by commercial interests and by the wildness of the jungle. Safety is a relative thing and is never ensured—things can go horribly wrong anywhere at any time. We all want and need to feel emotionally and physically safe and we need to believe that our cultural container is resilient enough to thrive when our safety gets breached.

The Shuar face safety issues that are unimaginable to us, including poisonous insects and snakes, food insecurity, electric eels that can kill during a bath in the river, and even the possibility of a jaguar eating a child. While there is good argument that they should feel less safe than we do, the Shuar are not nearly as fear-driven as we are. Their culture is cohered around the ontological basis of high valuation for each and every being's vitality and that provides them a deep, systemic safety net that doesn't have the holes that our politicized and patched-together social safety nets do. That is because the Shuar social safety net is built around primal values for the sanctity of all life. Western political parties espouse those values, but statistics on bigotry, hunger, and violence make it clear that we have not figured out how to live out those values. All safety nets can be breached, but what the Shuar have is the contentment of knowing that when theirs is, they are unequivocally in it together.

While the lessons of tribal life are not fully applicable to organizations, borrowing some Shuar distinctions can help shed light on organizational vitality. The Shuar do not only recognize the *arutum* (mojo) within each being, they understand that when each is powerful, all are powerful, and that collective power is strongest when everyone is thriving. Their social structures are built around an ethic of supporting individual and group *arutum* so all are fed, relational, and powerfully strong bodied. They share well-realized values for family time, nature, and spirituality, and they appear remarkably content. The Shuar culture holds high valuation for joy.

Part of our fluffy myth conditioning is believing that productivity and joyfulness are mutually exclusive or, at the very least, that doing work and being joyful are unrelated. The Shuar place much more value on keeping equanimity between the two than we do. The Shuar cultural ontology spans a much fuller spectrum of human beingness compared to our hyper focus on human doing-ness. They make their living on muddy jungle soil that grows very little human food, mostly a starchy root vegetable called manioc. They hunt with blowguns that were almost too long and heavy for me to even pick up, let alone blow a dart through. There is no electricity and so no refrigeration in their tropical habitat. Productivity is literally a matter of life and death every single day.

The immediacy of the jungle, its unabated churning of elements, and its natural challenges, demand hard work under the toughest conditions. Yet the Shuar spend more of their time enjoying nature and one another than they do working. The Shuar culture holds inherently higher valuation for happiness and well-being than ours does. They have always lived what "leading-edge" Western organizations are now finding out—that the more an organization invests in its cultural vitality, the better it does with profits, productivity, customer and employee loyalty, and market share. As data on the impact of cultural strength on productivity has been pouring in over the last few decades, there is stronger and stronger ground for questioning whether Western or Shuar culture has the most to teach the other.

Thanks to companies like Zappos, Ikea, REI, and Google, we now know that the world's most remarkable success stories reflect organizations with cultures that are coherent around shared ethics for common good and stakeholder well-being. Because culture is the most impactful factor in a leader's ability to cause results, it pays to be vigilant with it. The most successful systems place high valuation on the presence of, and partnership between, healthy and happy human beings who trade, work, and live within the company's reach. For people to bring their whole bodies, minds, and spirits to work, they need to believe that it's in their best interest to do so. *It is futile to expect people you are working with to do their best for the organization if the organization disregards how much good it is doing for those individuals and their community.*

You cannot override people's values, no matter how stringent the rules or how strongly they are enforced. Cultures can be developed so that they do not accommodate the desire or need to break rules, and, at the same time, a lot of rule-making isn't needed when cultures are strong. *People can and do self-regulate toward best outcomes when the culture makes it safe and satisfying for them to do so, that is, when leaders ensure that there is alignment between individual and organizational well-being.*

Cultural Coherence

Cultural coherence refers to the degree of personal alignment between the stakeholders of an organization as well as the degree of their collective alignment with the vision and mission of that organization. Whether they are clearly stated or unconsciously assumed, cultures are the expression of a particular set of collective values. It doesn't matter whether it's in the jungle, a business, governmental or nonprofit organization, or an ad hoc group, prioritizing cultural coherence by paying attention to values pays off. Alchemical leadership includes the art of building cultural alignment so that the organization is functioning like a stream. *The degree to which there is nonalignment is the degree to which your full cultural stream isn't flowing with your direction.*

The more conscious you are about intangibles like values alignment, interconnectivity, and integrity, the more access you get to the metaphysical field from which alchemy is practiced.

Cultural coherence can be thought of as integrity in the sense that when something is integrated, it is part of an undivided, internally consistent whole. Since values are the fundamental building blocks of cultures, just like the pillars that hold up buildings need to be made of material that holds together well, cultural pillars get their strength from coherence around shared values. Just like building pillars require material integrity, cultural pillars have a sort of metaphysical integrity based on coherence around positive values expression.

Integrity also refers to people standing on strong moral ground. The absence of lying and theft in the Shuar culture is integral with their worldview of their interdependence with everyone and everything. In their coherence around that worldview, they maintain a cultural ontology, a fundamental ground of being, that simply is not capable of sustaining motivations for immoral behaviors like stealing, harming, or compromising one another. It's not that they have to try to be truthful or to restrain themselves from stealing; it doesn't come up for them because those behaviors don't fit into their social container, their cultural paradigm. Because the Shuar paradigm, meaning their worldview or ontological reality, holds all of life as deeply integrated, they value every member of the tribe equally—a consistent concept with the original teachings of Christ, Buddha, Mohammed, and other prophets and mystics.

The Shuar are happy and healthy individuals who actively support one another in being the same. While the Shuar norm is for everyone being of equal value, they still have leaders and their own systems of hierarchies and duties. As in other indigenous cultures, Shuar leaders are always in counsel with other tribal members to ensure that the community's priorities are coherent with the leaders' decisions. Their leadership infrastructure is flatter than a typical organization's in that the people who have been awarded the most power see themselves as part of a more circular, rather than vertical, system. Applying indigenous wisdom to organizational cultures, it behooves a leader to find ways to flatten vertical infrastructures because *mojo flows better when it is going around than when it's going up and down.*

The immediacy of a jungle tribe's circumstances means that they pretty much need to get each present moment right or risk death. There's not much wiggle room. An organization, though, can withstand a steady drip of resources for a long time and not even sense the loss because *our acculturation to norms often blinds us to problems that are inherent in those norms.* One issue I encounter in consulting and coaching is that, because leaders are acculturated to their own proverbial jungles, it can be easy for them to overlook, even perpetuate, problems and fail to recognize solutions.

The Power of Partnership

Cultural historian Riane Eisler says there are only two types of leadership styles: partnership and dominator. Those who lead by means of dominating can't possibly build the cultural coherence that partnership-oriented leaders do. Domination fractures coherence. Partnership builds it. Partnership-oriented approaches work out so well because they enable people to leverage their relationships and commitments so that they can achieve more together than they could as individuals doing the same amount of work.

A strong partnership ethic is an essential metaphysical mechanism for cohering collective mojo. Coherence aggregates energy. And just like love and many other metaphysical phenomena, human energy multiplies when it aggregates. Leadership power, which is the transforming of energy into desired outcomes, is therefore multiplied according to how energy is aggregated. That is why there is so much correlation between a leader's facility with managing the coherence of the collective and the results s/he achieves.

Shared vision is a basis for partnership. Shared vision creates a metaphysical funnel for mojo movement. Taking time to develop shared vision is a good way to harness collective mojo. Without aligned vision, mojo is more likely to move in a helter-skelter way. The best way to know if your culture's vision and values are coherent is to measure them with data-based cultural assessment tools.

The Golden Rule

The energy of mojo yields optimum outcomes when it is channeled not just in accordance with vision, but also in accordance with commitments to treating others as we ourselves want to be treated. That is, in accordance with the Golden Rule, a universally recognized precept for living in the world together. Every major religion has a version of it. Here are a few:

Do unto others as you would have them do unto you.

—Christianity

Hurt not others in ways that you yourself would find hurtful.

—Buddhism

**What is hateful to you, do not to your fellow man.
That is the entire Law; all the rest is commentary.**

—Judaism

**No one of you is a believer until he desires for his
brother that which he desires for himself.**

—Islam

Blessed is he who prefereth his brother before himself.

—Baha'i Faith

Golden Rule compliance generates and circulates mojo, which is a key reason why it is accepted across religions, cultures, languages, and time. Alchemical leaders wield the power they have over the flow of mojo in accordance with the Golden Rule because, as it turns out, the Golden Rule rules even when it comes to creating riches. Actually, especially then. A leader's power expands when everyone's mojo is in dynamic equanimity with everyone else's, and treating others the way we want to be treated is a great way to establish equanimity.

It stands to reason that nobody is going to wholeheartedly follow you if your exercise of power is out of alignment with how s/he wants to be treated. Expression of negative values, like condemnation, is inherently less powerful than expression of positive values, like curiosity, because negativity naturally repels people. When negative values prevail, people are more likely to react to challenges out of fear than respond out of sound thinking. Sound thinking beats reactive impulses pretty much every time.

When fear-based values are endemic in a culture, mojo flows away from that system. That's because when people are afraid of one another, they don't partner with one another. They either passively or aggressively conflict, which is unproductive. Or, to greater or lesser degrees, they flee, which removes greater or lesser amounts of their mojo from your power grid. The collective energy of your team, your organizational mojo, is your cultural capital. In terms of developing it, *the Golden Rule rules!*

Cultural Capital

Cultural capital is the value that can be placed on the energy or mojo in your organization. Cultural capital is intangible, but investing in it, and prudent management of it, yields tangible returns. Cultural coherence is a good indicator of cultural capital because, just like you'd have less ability to light your office if the electricity in the wall were shooting in different directions, there is more organizational capacity when people's mojo is flowing in sync with one another.

Values are primal drivers that trigger the releasing or withholding of energy. When values align within a group, that alignment is evidence of the kind of cultural integrity that is necessary to produce more than the sum of parts and labor. Values alignment is cultural coherence and that coherence can be thought of as your cultural capital. The degree of alignment determines how efficiently and effectively collective resources get harnessed and unleashed. Cultural capital can be captured by measuring and managing values alignment. Conscious development of cultural capital increases satisfaction, ease of operations, and returns on investment in and of human resources (see Barrett).

According to values and culture expert Richard Barrett, "Cultural capital is a measure of the value that can be placed on the way of being, or the nature of a collective." Weak and rigid cultures reflect diminished cultural capital, whereas, strong and adaptable cultures reflect robust cultural capital. *Just like tangible monetary currency is a means for getting things done, cultural capital is the energetic currency of your leadership power.* Cultural capital is your leadership currency in that it represents the sum of the intangible energy that is at your discretion. Even though cultural capital is a metaphysical concept, it can be measured and managed through annual cultural assessments with instruments like Barrett's Cultural Transformation Tools. Taking data-based accountability for cultural capital increases capacity to consciously cause what happens within your culture. Measuring and tracking cultural capital connects yang data with yin factors—a solid basis for alchemical sparks.

Alchemical leadership is both the science and art of cultural capitalization. Alchemical leaders produce extraordinary results because they capitalize on their intangible resources to stoke, harness, and unleash collective energy most effectively. How well you develop and deploy cultural capital depends not only on your professional skills, but also on your capacity for managing the metaphysics of cultural capitalization. Cultural accountancy, that is, accounting for your culture, is a means for tracking mojo and thereby providing a basis for alchemy, for producing more than the sum of parts and labor.

Using data-based instruments to quantify your culture is a good means for identifying the full spectrum of collective potential. In fact, the repeated findings on the impact of culture on success are so compelling, and assessment tools in the marketplace are so well tested, that stockholders could easily make a winning case against a CEO and board of directors who are not accounting for culture. Studies overwhelmingly confirm the advantage gained by taking cultural accountability (see Miethe, Barrett, Liu, Collins, Flamholtz, Hall, Kotter).

Measuring your cultural capital is a way to account for the fundamental energy that's driving you and everybody else. Power comes down to the capacity to convert energy from one form to another, like for example, a worker's personal energy converting into work productivity. If you do not account for the energy that falls within your leadership, it is hard to exercise your full power. Cultural assessments provide both qualitative and quantitative data on an organization's energy, as well as on the effectiveness with which a leader exercises his/her power to transform collective energy into results. Assessment data clarifies:

- strengths, needs, blind spots, growing edges, as identified by the whole
- where mojo is and isn't flowing
- where and how energy is draining out of the system.

Assessing your cultural alignment can give you a good picture of your collective mojo profile as well as data-based insight into how to manage it. Cultural accountability is a capital investment in strengthening invisible organizational scaffolding in the same way that investing in the physical infrastructure of a building sustains it.

There are a number of software/data-based instruments for quantifying culture. I use Cultural Transformation Tools (CTTs) because they have proven themselves worldwide in situations from three-person offices to whole countries and in every size and type of organization in between. CTTs work by taking three values measurements, that of each individual, of what people see as the current cultural values, and what they see as the values the organization should be aspiring toward. The sophisticated technology on the back end breaks those values measurements into seven levels of organizational consciousness that correlate with Maslow's hierarchy of needs: survival, relationship, self-esteem, transformation, internal cohesion, making a difference, and service.

I especially like using Barrett's Cultural Transformation Tools because they not only provide data on seven levels of cultural capital, they also situate pressing concerns in the vernacular of values. That means the issues that are identified are automatically contextualized in terms of the underlying values development that needs to happen rather than in terms of the politics and personal dynamics that are symptomatic of values divergences. When problems are situated in the causal domain of values, they can more easily be resolved in ways that actually change behaviors and the culture is then better positioned to sustain those behavioral changes.

Our current economic norms hold high valuation for tangible things, like buildings and battles, while holding low to no valuation for intangible factors, like satisfaction and happiness, even though that makes no statistical sense, because companies that account for intangible factors perform so well. *Intangible breakthroughs and breakdowns precede the tangible ones.* If you have been acculturated, or conditioned by cultural norms, to believe that you can disregard the metaphysics of cultural capital, your oversight is understandable, but it leaves you and your organization extremely vulnerable. When you have data on your cultural capital, it not only helps you identify ontological norms that aren't working for you, it also enables you to manage your culture without having to guess. Quantifying cultural capital is a way to establish a clear baseline for gauging energetic capacity, which is the fuel of any leader's power.

Energy that is not consciously managed can drain out of a system and/or be systemically disruptive. Say, for the sake of illustrating this point, that your team represents one hundred units of mojo and forty of those units are being spent complaining, gossiping, power playing, and withholding information. You might have 100 percent attendance, but the mojo you have to work with is only sixty units strong because it is either being consumed from within by negativity or it is being kept out of the workplace entirely by people who are motivated to spend their energy elsewhere. On the other hand, if everyone brings their whole selves to work and their mojo is aligned with one another's toward getting the job done, you'll be powered up at 100 percent capacity.

Although mojo cannot be contained or measured in units, or described by math, that illustration demonstrates that cultural capital pays dividends when whole people come to work with common purpose. When your team is engaged to its fullest capacity and all that capacity is aligned toward the same results, your cultural capital is well positioned. Cultural capital is diminished when people are not aligned with one another and/or a leader's attitudes and behaviors. Alchemical leadership happens naturally when people are aligned with one another and with organizational mission because that means their leader's power is automatically sourced with the collective's full energy which, in turn, is metaphysically multiplied by its coherence.

Like cutting-edge corporate, governmental, and nonprofit leaders, the Shuar cohere around common-good centered decision-making. Common good can only be determined by being in dynamic relationship with one another. That's why the Shuar are always in the process of discovering and enhancing their alignment with one another by making plenty of time for connectivity, mostly in the form of hanging out and laughing together. That connectivity translates into a powerful, multilevel social coherence.

Most Shuar have never heard of human rights—it would be hard for them to conceive of needing to articulate human rights as something to aspire to because the concept of a human who doesn't live in fulfillment of basic inalienable rights does not fit into their cultural ontology. The Shuar prioritize living in integrity with common values, while we often struggle with the cost of how much our systems have devaluated what humans value most. Our systems prioritize financial capital while theirs prioritize cultural capital. Our acculturations might lead us to believe that there is an inverse relationship between profits and people having a good time together, but that is not the case. We know that stronger cultural capital leads to greater financial strength (see Barrett, Wheatley).

Entropy

When cultural capital is weak, it indicates values digressions and it is tough to maintain momentum because energy naturally flows away from situations where values are compromised. Energy that drains away from mission fulfillment is cultural entropy, a concept borrowed from physics, where it refers to thermodynamic energy that is not available for conversion into mechanical work. In terms of organizational culture, entropy is the measure of energy not being spent on getting the job done. In other words, it is energy falling through the proverbial cracks of incoherence in a culture. *Entropy can be thought of as the degree of dysfunction in an organization.*

Entropy expresses as negative values like complacency, information hoarding, and greed. Entropy looks like people being mentally checked out even though they're clocked in, or worse, functioning in a way that forces other people to check out or otherwise dysfunction. People pull their mojo out of a system to the extent that they feel like their values are compromised. Their bodies may be at their work stations, but the energy they invest in making things happen is diminished to the degree that values are compromised. That energetic diminishment is entropy.

High entropy equals low cultural capital. Low entropy equals high cultural capital. Entropy means that you are not operating on all the cylinders in your organization. It is the metaphysical means by which your power gets compromised. Barrett Values Centre's studies on cultural entropy confirm that energy is lost in the gaps between positive and limiting values. For example, if values like manipulation and dishonesty are more operative than values like commitment and excellence are, energy will be lost from the system as team members withdraw their mojo rather than risk being manipulated and lied to or about.

Cultural capital is lost as entropy whenever bad will is created through disrespectful language and/or through fear-driven practices and policies that deviate from common values. High-entropy cultures create employees who are fearfully watching their backs; who have to distance themselves from their own bodies and hearts to make it through the day; whose creative urges are suppressed; and whose jobs feel like imprisonment. Too many leaders unconsciously rule by fear and that compromises the values they would be happier and more successful living by. Head-hunting was part of warring for the Shuar, but no head-hunting was ever involved in keeping tribal members in line. Even something so egregious as head-hunting does not lead to entropy when it's not used as a weapon for controlling interpersonal behaviors. On the other hand, small things, like hoarding information to keep someone subservient or otherwise disadvantaged, can create significant entropy over time.

CTT reports include quantification of entropy, which is helpful because the costs of entropy are not always apparent. Once there is entropy data, it is a matter of applying simple math to determine its cost. Let's take silo mentality or information hoarding, for example. For every minute someone has to do work to compensate for information that is not shared, that time can be multiplied by their pay rate. The result of that equation will give you insight into how much the entropy costs, but it would still not account for coffee-break conversations filled with gossip and negative interactions versus talk about how those same people might overcome a mutual problem or innovate.

Identifying entropy points, which are expressions of negative values, helps to expose problems and to raise consciousness of the ontological framework, on which your organization runs.

Ontological Shifting

It is almost impossible to generate things like creativity, stability, and vitality from within a stifling ontology. The ontological ground of your culture plays out in what is said and how it is said. Thought influences language and language influences action. Language is the access route to the ontological realm because language is the basis of the stories we tell about what's so. For example, if there is a theme in the stories you tell about others being at cause for your situation, you have given away your power to the people in your story. On the other hand, *if your ontological foundation is expressed by a personal story that stakes claim to your own causation, you will be standing on much more powerful ground.* Your stories contain critical clues about what you are perpetuating and about how you are and are not adept with power. *Realities shift when language does because language expresses the ontological basis on which a person's understanding of his/her reality sits.*

Let's take failure for example. A yang-dominant ontology tells failure stories through language about bad endings, victimization, disempowerment, and blame. A more yang-oriented ontology produces dualistic stories with clear good guys and bad guys and with win-lose scenarios. A more yin ontology tends to produce stories about lessons learned, appreciation for risk, and framing of failed efforts as growth opportunities. A more yin ontology tends to treat failure as a trigger for self-reflection and for letting go of the past. Stories of failures are told without negative judgment of those who made mistakes. *As more organizations are reaping the benefits of yin-ing out their perspectives, we are seeing an ontological shift away from failure being a shameful endgame and toward it being understood as an opportunity to mine the vein of gold that runs through every wound.*

Yang-dominant leadership models are more likely to respond to interpersonal tensions by silencing the squeaky wheel, squeaking being big yin and squelching big yang. Yang-dominant decision-making tends to passively or aggressively avoid the kind of tension that naturally arises in work-places. More yin-inclusive methods wholeheartedly dive into dynamic tensions and use them to progress toward uncharted results that emerge as the path of authenticity is followed. *When the ontological ground is set for attending to, and accounting for, the fuzzy yin stuff, there is a stronger basis for managing the concrete yang stuff.*

A healthy ontology, or ground of being, has the range for swinging yang-ward when losses need to be cut and yin-ward when time needs to be taken. There are times when failure needs to be a resting place (yin) and times when it needs to be a catalyst (yang). The benefit of looking at leadership through the lens of yin and yang is that it helps in both comprehending and transcending ontological polarizations of right/wrong, good/bad, too much/not enough, and even male/female issues. Using the dualistic lens of yin and yang helps to articulate the dialectical grounds for a both/and, win/win ontology.

The uptick in organizations that are recognizing extraordinary gains from making the workplace a good place to be reflects an ontological shift from understanding the workplace as strictly a place of human *doing*, to recognizing that happy and well human *beings* do productive things, like cooperate and go the extra mile. Consciousness of your organizational ontology gives you greater awareness of invisible fundamentals. That heightened awareness is critical to being able to cause things to happen at fundamental, metaphysical levels—alchemy.

Culture-building is accomplished by a leader's deepest drivers aligning with those of his/her stakeholders. No matter how exotic or commonplace a particular organization's culture is, it is subject to the universal will for people to be happy and well. *Creating an organizational ontology, a ground of being, that includes happiness and well-being yields tremendous return on cultural capital.*

Leadership Reflections

1. If you could wave a magic wand to change one thing about your culture, what would it be? Why that? What would be different if your wish came true? What are three action steps you could take to make it be so?

2. Describe your workplace culture. What is working in your culture? What is not working?

   - What values stand out? What specific values could be better expressed?
   - Are there negative values? How do they play out? Do people you work with have to check their values at the door to get through the day?
   - What values are people most aligned on?

3. Where does your culture seem particularly dull or negative? When, where and how does fear play out? On a scale of 1–10, with 1 being no fear and 10 being fully motivated by fear-based concerns, how big of a factor is fear in your operations?

4. Describe your culture's underlying norms and assumptions. List concepts, properties, and categories that define your work and describe the relationships between them.

5. Ask what's most important to the people on your team and then try to make sure their values are fulfilled. Where do everyone's values converge and diverge? Consider getting a professional cultural assessment so you can work with real data.

6. Think of a situation that's got you stymied and apply the Golden Rule to it—no matter what.

7. On a scale of 1–10, 1 being chaos and 10 indicating full alignment between team members and organizational mission, rate your workplace. Also, rate your sense of personal alignment with your team and with your organization.

8. What stories do you tell about your work? What workplace stories are best put to rest? What stories need to be told or told better?

PART TWO

PERSONAL POWER

CHAPTER 5

MOJO EVOLUTION

Personal Stuff

Good leaders evolve. Great leaders consciously evolve. Personal power is not a fixed thing. It is ever-emerging and so, to manage it effectively, your consciousness of it must be ever-evolving. Emotions, needs, fears, desires, unfinished personal business, and other psychological, emotional, and spiritual factors are the stuff of being human. We each have self-limiting hang ups, that is, our "stuff," the baggage of our preconceived notions, unresolved issues, habitual thinking, shortcomings, and vulnerabilities. Strong leadership consciousness includes awareness of personal "stuff."

We've all got our issues. If someone tells you they don't have any baggage, it may indicate a potential lack of self-awareness and a possible tendency to blame things on others. When people don't own their issues, the issues rule, usually when we least expect it. Of course, it's always easier to see other people's issues and, as a leader, you cannot afford to overlook them. *But it is amazing how fast other people's issues stop being problems when we manage our own.* Effective reflection on "stuff" starts in the mirror.

The evolution in consciousness that's necessary for alchemical leadership requires more than just being aware of personal issues. It is also critical to recognize your own causation of effects. We all play a causal role in creating our own circumstances. In addition to their own, leaders create circumstances for their stakeholders. *The greater responsibility you take for being at cause in your personal life, the greater capacity for causality that you will have in your professional life.*

Developing personal consciousness increases your capacity to respond reasonably and creatively to challenges, versus reacting to them from lower level, unresolved triggers. Alchemical capacity requires perpetual vigilance over whether you have your issues, or your issues have you. Lack of accountability for personal issues leaves you vulnerable because people with more self-awareness are automatically functioning at higher levels, and therefore with more authority, no matter what the optics look like. To avoid grappling with personal digressions and pain points is to thereby award power over your vulnerabilities to others.

It can be upsettingly humbling to come to grips with our own stuff. It is always a choice as to whether or not we claim the little flip in our guts or the subtle troubling of our minds and hearts. Tuning into those sorts of internal factors is a worthwhile pursuit because body/mind sensations are reliable signals of growth opportunity ahead. If your issues have you, gut churning can become gut wrenching. *If you own your issues, your inner rumblings can serve as indicators of your next level of personal evolution.*

When it comes to managing personal issues, the only way out is through. That throughway might start with looking at what you are blaming someone else for. The self-reflective ride on that throughway might include speaking, writing, dialoging, apologizing, questioning, internal wrestling, facing, confiding, dis-membering, and/or re-membering pieces of your life.

Capacity

Alchemy means adding value that supersedes the standard value of something. That extra value comes from mojo. Mojo is cultivated by way of physical, mental, and spiritual evolution. It doesn't matter whether you're evolving from listening to recordings of people like Tony Robbins's or Deepak Chopra's thoughts on success, reading sacred literature, or from listening to the sound of a stream, inspirational music, your inner voice, or a child's voice. What matters is that you are constantly, consciously evolving yourself as a human being, because your state of being ultimately determines your capacity.

Embracing anger, shortcomings, blind spots, and upsets as your own is an important part of leadership alchemy. The reason for that is because powerful, and sometimes even seemingly small negative experiences do not usually just disappear. When they are not consciously resolved, they remain, sometimes deeply hidden, sometimes right on the surface, ready to trigger. The result is that these negative influences, usually from past experiences, cause us to make energetic investments in the past, and that pulls mojo away from the present.

Whether we harbor unresolved energy consciously or unconsciously, it is energy not going toward other things. Unresolved stuff causes increased personal entropy as it drains mojo away from what we want. However much personal or collective mojo is being spent on things that hold emotional and/or psychological charge, is how much you do not have available in the present—and cannot invest in the future. While it does require investment of time and energy to get to core resolution, managing personal stuff ultimately both frees up mojo and brings heightened clarity. *Staying rigorous with self-reflection on what you are fueling with your energy is a sure way to raise your leadership capacity.* That's because unresolved issues are necessarily being fueled subliminally, and that fuel is coming from your personal energy supply. *To be human is to have issues. If you are up to speed with your own personal "stuff," you are far less likely to be handicapped by it.*

Alchemical leadership capacity comes down to mojo flow. Yin and yang are simple tools for qualifying that flow. Linear, goal-centered, streamlined thoughts and activities are yang, while more values-centered, process-oriented, or holistic ones are yin. Working toward goals is yang-izing in the sense that striving toward accomplishments releases certain hormones that activate us, enhance confidence, and strengthen our sense of self-worth and contribution. Being in creative flow, releasing preconceived notions and habits, and taking time for fun are yin-izing, because doing those things releases pacifying hormones that make us feel more relaxed, harmonious, and content. More yin activities restore body, mind, and spirit, and enhance our sense of possibility and joy. There are times to lean yin-ward and times to lean yang-ward.

Circuitry

Mojo is a kind of metaphysical energy that defies description, but the analogy of an electrical circuit provides a helpful lens on the circuitry, or infrastructure, of mojo flow. The power going into, for example, your computer, equals the voltage, or electromotive force (yang), combined with the charge (yin) in the circuit. Similarly, *mojo is an energy that flows through interpersonal circuits that lie within and between people. That energy becomes power when it combines with metaphysical charges like vision, will, and pursuit of values-fulfillment.* When relationships with self and others are smooth, it flows smoothly. When things that spark the human spirit are introduced into healthy energetic circuitry, the magic of mojo gets unleashed.

In electronics, charge flows through the current of a circuit, for example, the current flowing in the circuit that runs between the wiring in your wall and your computer. Just like the output of electrical circuitry is where it becomes the power for your computer, your mojo output is where your power manifests. And just like an electrical circuit can be more or less conducive to the flow of energy, and hence power, so is your personal circuitry more or less conducive to the flow of mojo and hence personal power. Mojo management requires accountability for your own internal circuitry and for the circuitry among your team.

Similar to how a charge runs through the currency of electricity, mojo flows through the currency of the cultures it's expressing in. Electricity is a transmission medium for electrical energy in the same way that seawater is a transmission medium for wave energy. In much the same way, humanity is a transmission medium for mojo. Wave energy expresses through the medium of seawater like mojo expresses through the medium of individuals and collectives. How it flows through people depends on personal and group consciousness.

Part of the human experience is that we sometimes have our circuits wired such that our mojo keeps recharging negative historical issues that are not healthy or helpful. Just like diverting energy to a different outlet would change your computer's functionality, using mojo to keep fueling past issues zaps your personal energetic capacity. When personal mojo is leaking out as negative expression of past problems, how much can be at your disposal in any given moment? Alchemical capacity includes the ability to redirect mojo away from fueling upset, which constitutes entropy, and toward sparking the circuitry you really want to juice up.

Mojo is a metaphysical energy that can remain dormant, spark miraculous things, cause horrific pain, and do everything in between. The difference depends on:

- the quality of the mojo
- the quality of the circuitry through which the energy is channeled.

As a leader, it's your job to make sure that people's mojo is not dampened by cultural problems and that circuits/systems are conducive to mojo being directed toward where and how it will do the best good. Power comes not just with making sure that your mojo is in its most usable and productive form, but also with dedication to everyone else's being in peak form, and with ensuring that collective mojo is flowing coherently toward common vision.

Mojo is a resonant phenomenon in that good mojo usually triggers more good mojo. Mojo is charismatic, it attracts. When yours is at full potential, people respond accordingly— just like the people at a party who get energized from being with a star, and who, in turn, energize the star, who, in turn, gets all the more energized by being the object of attraction and so puts out more charismatic energy. You don't need the charisma of a star to be a great leader, but you can capitalize on the same energetics by consciously strengthening mojo and developing the circuitry for it to flow as effectively as possible.

Stoking Your Mojo

The first step toward firing up your mojo is personal accountability. Until we get a grip on personal issues, we can't possibly be in the lane of full potential. As things inevitably change, the constant is your presence. The quality and fullness of your presence determines how much you can consciously influence the situation you are in the presence of. Your presence is the key component of your alchemical capacity. *Bringing full presence to your work requires being 100 percent accountable for your inner landscape—because that inner terrain has everything to do with how things are showing up in your outer world.*

Presence doesn't just mean being in attendance, it means being in attendance with attentiveness, empathy, open-mindedness, and whole heartedness. *Presence is a physical state of location and also a metaphysical state of consciousness.* Being metaphysically present requires not having any emotional, intellectual, or energetic capital tied up in unresolved drama, fear, resentment, bad behavior, or crises of confidence. Full presence is free from the effects of history and future, meaning all circuitry is available. (Michael Brown's *The Presence Process,* listed in References, is a great resource on presencing.)

Presence and mojo are inextricably related. Like the quality of water determines what kind of transmission medium it is for waves, the quality of our presence determines what kind of transmission medium we are for mojo. The capacity for presence is built, in part, by self-reflecting on negative values we may believe and project, and that we may not be conscious of. It pays to take time to identify how negative values are playing out around you. Negative values can appear as many types of behaviors including rigidity, power-mongering, arrogance, emotional blackmailing, hatefulness, vindictiveness, status-seeking, judgment, blaming, territoriality, control, silo mentality, miserliness, information hoarding, corruption, lying, and stealing.

Expression of negative values drains mojo. At the same time, expression of negative values always points toward potential gains. Just like we need negative and positive electrical charges, we need negative values to surface because they are part of the circuitry that moves us forward. However, and this is critical, without commitment to personal evolution and the humility to follow through on it, we are unlikely to manage negative values such that we can capitalize on better options for mojo investment.

Even really nice people play out negative values. We all do from time to time; it is some of the "stuff" that comes with being human. Our challenge is to be able to stand in full presence with internal and external negativity—that is, to move beyond our natural tendencies to deny, deflect, or denounce so that we can simply be present with what is. A person who is fully present has greater capacity to manage a situation than someone who is not. *It is only by being fully present to negativity that we can fully understand and therefore transcend it. Alchemical leadership is somewhat paradoxical in that it always happens in the present, and yet to wield it effectively, it requires transcendence of situational concerns.*

Negative Values

Negative values and the presence of unresolved issues go hand in hand. For example, if someone is upset that they never receive documents on time because the culture includes negative values like information hoarding and control, then that person is more likely to display negative reactions including emotional meltdown, being behind schedule, being afraid to ask for clarification and so prone to mistakes, thinking defensively instead of in forward motion, and/or sending out resumes to put her/himself in a less stressful situation—all of which create entropy.

Part of managing mojo is figuring out how it is leaking from personal and collective circuits. Negative values are usually sources of mojo leakage, which is entropy. The art of effective alchemical leadership includes minimizing the entropy caused by negative values while developing alignment around shared positive values so that, when energy is flowing, it is all going in the same direction.

We all bring our own energy and energetic flow, our mojo, everywhere we go, including to work. If people work in a culture that amplifies negative values, like a culture of distrust, those negative values prevent the cohesive flow of energy in that culture which, in turn, stimulates disruptive behaviors like drama, negligence, avoidance, and gossip. For example, if there is bullying or power playing going on, the people who are on the receiving end of it feel abused and, consequently, risk as little of themselves as they can get away with going forward, which, in turn, tends to provoke more negativity from the aggressor. No matter how hard both parties try to resolve their issues, the disruptive loop will continue because they are simply pushing intractably against the other like two opposing magnets being forced together. On the other hand, when positive values are more operative in a culture, when difficulties arise, they get managed from within an ontology that is geared for effective mojo flow.

Cultures have to accommodate perpetrators of negative values in order for them to stay in operation. Often that accommodation is unconscious and that is why it is so critically important for organizations to make time for systemic self-reflection. Just like people need self-reflection in order to evolve, organizations need systemic self-reflection in order to identify and redirect mismanaged mojo. Here again, Cultural Transformation Tools are especially helpful because they actually quantify entropy by articulating and measuring negative values. At the same time, CTTs reveal exactly how the group is aligned around specific positive values and what its shared vision is, which illuminates the path forward.

You Can Only Evolve What You Claim as Yours to Evolve

The expression of regressive values indicates questionable decision-making capacity. Managing the expression of negative values starts with a kind of personal homework, which, just like school homework, is done away from your desk so that you are better prepared when you get back to it. The quality of your personal reflection and development directly correlates with your capacity to lead in a positive way because clarity around personal "stuff," that is, your challenges and issues, affords you much greater discernment, higher response-ability, and lower reactivity. While there might be plenty of evidence that others are culprits, alchemical leaders always start with themselves. By starting with personal homework, they fundamentally change the dynamics of situations they are dealing with by breaking cycles of blame that disrupt the flow of mojo.

Personal homework entails coming to terms with the fact that you and only you can resolve your issues, no matter how right or wrong you can prove another person to be and no matter how many people agree with you about that person. At one time or another, we are all inclined to avoid, ignore or blame others for what we're experiencing, but we impede our personal evolution when we allow ourselves to stop there. Owning our own issues is the first lesson of personal homework. *You can only evolve what you claim as yours to evolve.* What is yours to evolve is absolutely everything in your life story, which is your personal ontology—your ground of being. Alchemical leaders claim that ground, the good, the bad, and the ugly.

Mojo rises with avowing that you control your issues even if they are in some ways dependent on another. Our upset resides in ourselves, and it always signals an opportunity to evolve toward better ways to manage the situation that is upsetting us. *To blame others is to award our power to whoever we are pointing at. Alchemical power comes from claiming that no one can cause you to do anything you have not compromised your own causality for.*

When we assign others the responsibility for our internal condition, it not only diminishes our own power, it also reduces theirs, because by laying blame on them for our state of being, it reduces them as well—a double mojo loss. *Naming and claiming personal breakdown is much more powerful than blaming and shaming other people for it.* Naming and claiming negativity indicates conscious ownership of personal energy.

Blaming and shaming reduces personal power and results in mojo loss and therefore increased entropy—not just within self, but also in the form of pushback from targets and/or witnesses whose values were violated. Reactionary leadership costs a lot of mojo because it means you are spending mojo from your personal power reserve and using it to shut down the mojo of a team member. Blaming and shaming might make people feel right and/or powerful in the moment, but it ultimately compromises moral authority. And it is deadly for everybody's mojo.

Personal homework doesn't just include resolving the "stuff" that clogs up the flow of mojo. It also includes regenerating your mojo. It's important to carve out adequate time and space for rejuvenation, solo contemplation, and meditation, and also for taking deep dives with wise and trusted counsel. Taking time to reflect can save you from investing too much personal capital in stuff that's going nowhere and that drains mojo away from actualizing vision and mission. But even more importantly, deep reflection sources mojo. And when you take the time to release what is eating up energy and to charge up your positive reserves, you enhance your alchemical capacity to cause sparks in your circuitry.

Generating and Regenerating

Personal homework includes scheduling both regenerative and generative self-care as well as taking reflective time. The most important thing you can do to rev up your mojo is to seek feelings like contentment and joy. *If you want to be your most powerful, take time to do the things that inspire you most.*

Getting work on your body, like any type of massage or pampering, is always good for mojo. Whether you have never tried meditation or have practiced it for years, studies are clear that it is a great investment of time (see Desbordes). It seems somewhat paradoxical, but the more we detach from our issues through activities like meditation, creative expression, and being silent in nature, the clearer we get about those issues. Unlike self-reflection, meditation and retreating into creativity or nature, gives us the opportunity to detach from our concerns. It is kind of like what happens when we lose our keys.

When we stop looking for them, we suddenly know exactly where they are. Whereas we tend to think that looking harder is the best way, it is often in the letting go that we get what we want. Unlike avoidance, which is unhealthy letting go, the detachment that happens through meditation, creativity, and spending time in nature are productive ways of letting go.

Your capacity to bring your full presence to any situation depends on the state of your being before the situation occurs. In other words, *your alchemical capacity depends on the state of your body, mind, and spirit, and on your ability to be fully present with yourself and with others.* No matter what position you are in, self-development is always a good bet. But in the case of leaders, it is only a first step because they are in charge of collective mojo and not just their own.

When people are stoked, that energy feeds back into the organization, creating positive energetic feedback loops that kick the metaphysics into high gear. Little things can go a long way toward stoking collective mojo—I saw one office that turns on music and dances for three minutes at 3:00 p.m. every day! Big things go even further. It's not hard to imagine the energy boost someone gets from a midday check-in with a preschool son/daughter or elderly mom/dad who are accommodated in the same building. The bottom line is that mojo flows well in organizational cultures that are coherent around positive values. *When a team's energy aligns around co-creating results that everyone agrees are worth aiming for, and that vision is fueled by vibrant mojo, alchemy is a natural outcome.*

Time to Yin Out?

Given the yang predominance in Western thought over so many millennia, finding equanimity may well require yin-ward over-compensation. In other words, given that we've set our norms so far to the yang side, it is going to require some yin-ing out for us to realize the full range of our potential. In our centuries of widespread yang-dominant cultural ontologies, we have been prioritizing yang activity. But neurological and psychological sciences could not be clearer about the value of activating yin by engaging in what feeds our inner well-being—our hearts and souls.

Misunderstanding and overlooking the power of yin exposes people to yang-itis, causing symptoms including anger, health issues, sleep problems, mean-spiritedness, addictions, and other cycles of dysfunction. Through a yang-itis-tinted cultural lens, success looks like a series of goals and benchmarks to be attained at all costs. Through a more equanimous lens, success looks more holistic because strong performance metrics are contextualized with personal and cultural considerations. There are times to steer yin-ward and times to steer yang-ward, but given how acculturated we are to yang-dominant norms, finding equanimity is going to involve strong yin-ward correction.

The tendency for people who work hard to also play hard is a good example of the complexity of finding equanimity. *Playing hard is not the opposite of working hard. Resting is.* On one level, there's a healthy yin-yang flow between working and playing at the same intensity. On another level, valuing the hardness of working and the hardness of playing is valuing doing (yang), while disregarding the value of simply being (yin). We, and especially leaders, are so acculturated toward yang dominance that it's easy to make questionable assumptions about what balances what. In our collective yang-itis, we tend to believe that we can somehow do more to balance out the problem of doing too much but that is clearly delusional.

Being balances doing. Alchemical leadership requires keeping doing and being in healthy relationship with one another.

Personal equanimity implies successful negotiation of the dynamic tension between doing and being. Leaders always have plenty of doing-ness going on. Creating time for being-ness could start with just taking a few minutes to wonder about what "being" time might look and feel like. Especially for more yang-ward-leaning leaders, doing is usually their comfort zone. But when we dare to dive into the mysterious abyss of being-ness, our doing-ness improves, often in unpredictable, yet quantifiable, ways.

Breaking through Yang-itis Acculturation

Humans adapt to the cultures within which they are living. Acculturation is the adaptive process of normalizing a particular worldview. We are all acculturated to yang-dominant norms, like gender imbalances in leadership and human suffering being endemic in micro- and macroeconomic policies. *As we have over valued yang cultural components, yin acculturations have been overlooked and undervalued for millennia.*

Since our acculturation reflects yang dominance, the chances are good that accessing the full spectrum of your personal capacity requires some yin-ing out—some broadening of activities and perspective, some relaxation of rules and habits, some proactive self-care, and risk-taking into unknown territory. *Cultivating yin, by recognizing and consciously evolving the metaphysical aspects of leadership, reduces the risks of the ravages of yang-itis.* Symptoms of yang-itis include chronic overwork, uninspired action, burnout, numbness, unhealthy behaviors, overwhelm, frustration, values compromises, physical and/or emotional pain, and undignified communications. It is not possible to maintain a healthy, dynamic equanimity of consciousness when too little attention is given to the yin half of the equation of life.

Workplaces are more yang by nature given that they are in existence to accomplish things effectively and efficiently. So it's logical that people lean more yang-ward when they're at work. It takes yang to get things done and so an extra dose of it can be very appropriate at work. To a degree. Given that we have a cultural bias toward yang and given the propensity for people to be leaning yang-ward in the doing of their work, it is not uncommon for workplaces to yang-out so hard that they become epicenters of yang-itis. Leaders in those places can end up with severe cases of it.

Leaders who are afflicted with yang-itis are more likely to be perceived as domineering, privileged, arrogant, oppressive, tyrannical, and/or disconnected from their teams. It's not their fault—many, if not most of us, are acculturated to yang-dominant leadership models. Still, even when leaders have the best of intentions, unaccounted-for yang-itis hinders the practice of alchemy. In the short run, exerting power over people can be efficient, like in dictatorships where one leader makes all the decisions and so things can happen quickly, and there is a coherence, albeit a forced coherence, to what they dictate. *However, the efficiencies that are gained by hyper yang-dominance are more than made up for when whole people go to work in a culture that accommodates the full range of the human condition.*

So how do you bring in yin? First, understand and acknowledge why it is important and then make time and space for fun, delight, inspiration, and creativity. According to experts, including the journal *Frontiers in Human Neuroscience*, creativity for creativity's sake, even if you throw away the results, creates neurological and psychological changes that are highly conducive to making wise choices.

Energetic Equanimity

The climb to leadership is a more yang endeavor, undertaken most often by those who naturally lean that way. The knack for keeping focus constructively narrowed on success is a yang characteristic compared to, for example, the tendency to reflect on philosophy or to write poetry. There is no right or wrong. Humanity needs both folks who are more yang-driven and folks who are more yin-driven. The problem that many leaders are running into is that their naturally more yang inclinations exist within cultural norms that are highly yang-dominant. Yang plus yang equals excess yang—a state that obliterates critical yin influences.

Most of us are acculturated to a long-standing ontology, an accepted ground of being, that dismisses yin-leaning activities as weak and yin-replenishing activities as unimportant. Our natural sense of what equanimity is has probably been corrupted by cultural norms for yang-dominance. We have been so acculturated to believe that leaning yang-ward is best, and systems are so yang oriented, that we can often be unaware of just how much yin-ing out we might need to do. Think of it in terms of an electrical charge. No one would ever advocate for having just one polarity come through the outlet. But that is exactly what we do when we allow unrelenting yang influences to overpower the yin.

Leaders often complain of having a sense of being squeezed by the pace, responsibilities, expectations, and pressures that come with leading. They can find themselves a long way down the yang-ward stream before they realize that something is off with systems that squeeze the life out of people. Between having natural proclivity to overlook the yin parts of life and living in a cultural stream that drowns out the value of yin, personal equanimity can feel elusive, especially for people who are already yang-wardly inclined and who take on the inherently yang-izing endeavors of leadership.

The more drastic the pendulum swing is between the extreme yang of a brutal workplace and the extreme yin needed to recover from it, the more difficult it is to establish the equanimity that is necessary for optimum productivity. Less dramatic pendulum swings are more productive because less drama indicates that cultural capital is being invested in functionality. It too often takes a crisis to break through yang-dominant norms. For example, it can take a heart attack for someone to realize s/he has to work fewer hours. Crisis is a highly effective, albeit high-entropy, opportunity for expanding consciousness. Depending on the individuals and the culture, workplace crisis can be the leading edge of innovation or it can be symptomatic of a circuitous rut of lurching from problem to problem.

In the absence of higher level cultural accountability, crisis-driven leaders often find themselves in vicious cycles of stumbling over unwanted realities and picking themselves up as though nothing ever happened, thereby setting themselves up for more crisis. Perpetual crisis management can indicate a hyper yang-dominant style of leadership that leads to individual burnout and organizational messes. While most often a symptom of yang-itis, crisis management leadership styles can also be symptomatic of excess yin in that persistent problems can be the result of not taking care of business.

Alchemical leadership entails having facility with the metaphysics that are operative as people's natural inclinations play out. It is also the capacity to flow yin-ward or yang-ward as needed in accordance with metaphysical indicators. Alchemical leaders consciously and productively manage the flow between yin and yang by way of recognizing when one is too dominant or too weak and making corrections accordingly. *Alchemical leadership includes the act of creating dynamic equanimity with organizational energetics.*

The Yin-Yang Pendulum

The nature of yin and yang is that a big swing one way will always cause an equal and opposite effect. For example, due to their natural inclinations toward intensive work focus, leaders often build up a sense of feeling pressured or yang-ized. It is no accident that many are drawn toward the literal wide horizons of golf and boating, horizons being a yin phenomenon because they are expansive. Hyper focus (yang) and the wide horizons of a golf course or ocean (yin) are complimentary polarities that help establish equanimity.

When the proverbial pendulum is not allowed to swing both ways, leaders, because they are often naturally more yang-leaning, can find themselves stuck in cycles of yang-itis that can look like long work hours, stress, lack of empathy, malaise, and a lack of latitude for "smelling the roses." Whenever there is a big back, there's a big front. Unhealthy yang excesses relate to unhealthy yin excesses like addictions, overeating, and unhinged emotions. *It is not unhealthy to be yang-oriented—everybody's gotta be some way! It is unhealthy to be unaccountable for it.* There is no such thing as a balanced person. Everybody leans a little or a lot one way or the other. The point is that, especially for more yang-leaning people, it is all the more important to be aware that the culture around us naturally leans yang-ward and that can disorient our very sense of what equanimity is and of what constitutes normality.

Although it is less prevalent among leaders, excess yin is as big of a problem as excess yang. When there is too much yin going on, there can be a lack of focus, purposelessness, excess emotiveness, inattentiveness to financial realities, and unclear directives. Because yin and yang play out on multiple levels, there can simultaneously be too much yin and too much yang. For example, there can be inattention to details, a yin problem, and overly aggressive leadership, a yang problem, happening at the same time.

Swinging Yin-ward

Yin-ing out happens in creative, heartwarming, body-pleasuring, soul-satisfying time. Diving deep into body/mind/spirit is always good, but even shallow diving will do. Depending on the situation, you can go a long way toward resetting your equanimity by taking a few minutes to sing a song, to be grateful, to pick up an instrument or paintbrush, play with a child, read or listen to something inspiring, or just take a walk. Appreciation, creative process, healthy relating, and taking time to feel good on the inside yin-izes us in the sense that those things release endorphins while supporting our primal desire for connectivity, a yin factor. Quality yin experiences include wholesome recreation, spending time with loved ones, self-reflection, spiritual engagement, time in nature, and immersing in cultural experiences. Taoism suggests that the quality of yin activities indicates the quality of yang ones, like competent delegation, clear decision-making, high productivity, and impeccable accountability.

Just like you wouldn't try to run your office from a yoga retreat center because such a yin environment would not naturally support such a yang task, it is hard, and often inappropriate, to yin out at work. But sometimes, yin-ing out is the thing you need to do most at work. A quick walk, or a simple well-timed trip to a restroom, can yin you out just fine for the moment. Though not aesthetically conducive to deep soul diving, the stall can offer sanctuary for triage yin restoration!

The best preparation you can do for maintaining your equanimity throughout your day is to establish a regular "being" routine, preferably first thing in the morning for ten to twenty minutes of writing, meditating, visioning, praying, or affirming. Consider it as a sort of mental, emotional, and spiritual hygiene. If you want to explore meditation, there are plenty of guided meditations on YouTube, many community centers offer classes, and there are extraordinary meditation teachers everywhere as people are discovering more and more value in yin-ing out. Experiment until you find what works for you but book something regularly that accesses your "being zone."

In our pandemic yang-itis, we often clearly establish the goals and endpoints in the yang zone while disregarding that there is always an equal and opposite yin zone. Given our yang dominant acculturations, we all need to consider whether our personal fulcrum, or balance point from which our lives move yin-ward or yang-ward, is truly centered. In the absence of accountability for yin, it's easy to establish unrealistic and unhealthy expectations and habits. Consciousness makes all the difference between swinging your pendulum yin-ward when you need to or having it "hit you upside the head" when it inevitably swings that way.

Leadership Reflections

1. Write a list of alchemical leadership practices for you personally and for your organization, and note possible advantages to instituting those practices.

2. Take a moment at the start of every day to look around and find things to appreciate—the warm bed you're getting out of, a room or sofa color you like, a person who influenced you, an inspiring thought, someone you love, a situation around you, the potential of your work, the morning sky, ocean, desert...

   Milk this exercise—go on a rampage of appreciation for the big and little things that work in your life, and about the things you especially love about yourself and others. This simple exercise will give you an energetic set point that can make a profound change, especially when practiced regularly over time. *Appreciation stokes mojo.* (see Hicks)

3. How is the equanimity between doing and being in your life? What needs to happen to strengthen the harmony between the two?

   How can you add more regular being time into your week?

4. Take stock of the words you choose. Identify limiting and undignified words and note what's going on inside your mind, body, and spirit when you get sloppy with language. Ask someone you trust to give you feedback on how and when your words tend not to work in your best interest.

5. List five things you are sure you're right about. Write down three questions that challenge each of those opinions.

CHAPTER 6

CORE WORK

Beginner's Mind

Buddhists say, "If you meet the Buddha on the road, kill him." That's because they believe that any human being who claims to have reached an endpoint of personal development has to be a fake. The truly enlightened mind understands that everything is always evolving, including mind, heart, and soul—even those of the greatest teachers. Buddhists use the concept of beginner's mind as a discipline for bringing fresh eyes and open-mindedness to the present moment. To access beginner's mind, one must release past beliefs, prejudices, and understandings. Beginner's mind means being present in each moment with openness to all learning, unattached to history, unafraid of future, and unencumbered by established norms. The beginner's mind is neither fearful nor hopeful, neither full of its own expertise nor devoid of it. It is neutral and so open to all possibility.

Masters throughout most traditions have been deemed that by others but never called themselves masters because they understood it to be a trap. They believed that claiming to have reached the highest rung would limit their ability to access rungs they had not perceived of. It makes sense, because how could the mindset of knowing it all be the precursor for knowing more? The advantage of beginner's mind is that, because it is always open to expansion, it can access a much broader spectrum of information and power than a mind that believes it has reached its highest level of expertise.

It seems like an oxymoron, but higher levels of consciousness come with practicing beginner's mind because stopping at even a highly evolved fixed point necessarily limits the ability to further expand. That's why so many so-called gurus go down in disgrace. Even if they have truly attained advanced spiritual levels, once they latch on to the premise that they have "arrived" at an endpoint, a kind of spiritual arrogance can set in and lead to bad behavior.

A true master's mind is a beginner's mind. Many masters have spoken of being humbled by how there is really no such thing as being done with the process of enlightenment. *In that sense, mastery is simply being fully present to the ongoing enlightening experience of living life.*

Expertise

Beginner's mind is the open slate of all possibility, while expertise is a declaration of a kind of fullness of mind. Studies on creativity, including some cited in NPR's *Hidden Brain* program "The Edge Effect," have shown that the more we know about a subject, the more likely we are to ignore evidence that contradicts our knowledge, and the less likely we are to be creative in our approach to that evidence. In other words, the more we know, the less likely we are to be able to innovate new solutions.

The mantle of expertise, combined with the hierarchy of position, can become an invisible, internal ceiling, even a trap. Being in a position of power can make it especially tough to break through the constraints of expertise and that can blind you to options. Although it might seem contradictory, the higher profile that your job description gives you, the more important it is to seek beginner's mind, that is, to suspend your expertise and positioning so that you can make way for what you don't know that you don't know. *Beginner's mind is an especially meaningful concept when it comes to our areas of expertise because assuming that we have attained our upper limits can diminish our capacity for expanding them.*

Beginner's mind means never claiming full expertise, never claiming to be the "Buddha" in your world. The more expertise you have, the more important it is to play with adopting a beginner's mind. Otherwise, expertise can have the effect of closing you down to new information and that can leave you functioning in a range of consciousness that is unnecessarily limited. As consciousness goes, so goes reality—you cannot hold on to the belief that you've reached the top and then see beyond where you are. *Adopting a beginner's mind allows you to see things that others don't.*

Beginner's mind recognizes that it is not possible to maintain attachment to preconceptions, no matter how accurate and productive they might be, and to expand your options at the same time. Beginner's mind is a subtle but profound distinction that determines your capacity for alchemy because alchemy entails discovery. It takes humility to suspend what you know so that you can discover what you don't know. It also takes a leap of faith because our acculturation helps us believe that power comes with being the know-it-all. Having the humility to bring a beginner's mind to what you know most about positions you to move beyond where you would be if you stayed bound by what you already knew. *You simply cannot hold fast to the boundaries of your expertise and break new ground at the same time.*

Beginner's mind is an access route to the metaphysical field of all possibility. Adopting a beginner's mind is risky business because it requires letting go of what got you this far. It takes a lot to step into the domain of not knowing, but the rewards are the stuff of legends. Letting go of "expert" consciousness is a journey in and of itself that can lead to questioning one's own identity and authority—existential questions that leaders often believe they have no time to deal with. The vulnerability that comes with the authenticity of not knowing it all can cause awkward moments, maybe some rumors, and possibly worse. But ultimately, openness to seeing things in new ways is the best way to stay on top of your game and to bring about transformation.

A beginner's mind is a curious mind. The nature of metaphysics is that its frontiers are always expanding and so staying curious is critical to alchemical leadership. Intelligence levels correlate with curiosity because the inquisitive mind is an adept mind. That's why curiosity is a hallmark of greatness and why questioning is part of the language of success. Curiosity is also an excellent indicator in personal relationships because love always wants to go deeper, it always wants to know more and more of the beloved. *At work and elsewhere, consider ramping up your question quotient.*

Awesomeness

Beginner's mind is more than open-mindedness. It also includes the ability to be awed, to experience a kind of reverential wonder. Mojo is fueled by the willingness to be awestruck and to stay curious. Awe arises naturally in kids but there is nothing immature about it. Approaching an issue with the wonder of a child enables us to see with fresh eyes, with beginner's mind—with an open, unbiased, unprejudiced mind that is geared toward being delighted by discovery. Experiencing awe creates internal shifts that widen and sharpen your field of vision and your range of options. Awe powers up mojo—it juices us. Just like it is easy to be delighted by seeing through the eyes of a child, when someone is awed, it tends to trigger positive responses from the people around him/her. Revving up your own sense of awe will spark the collective mojo you are working with.

Awe is a great feeling to aspire toward because it means you are in the power-filled territory of inspiration. Inspiration has dual meanings. It means to be stimulated in a particular way by a person, experience, or idea that is brilliant, creative, or timely. And inspiration also refers to the act of physically taking an in-breath. The word "inspiration" is derived from a Latin word meaning to sense divine guidance. In terms of alchemical leadership capacity, inspiration involves the taking in of collective mojo and being brilliant, creative, or timely with how you guide it. Taking time to be personally inspired empowers you to better guide collective mojo.

Beginner's mind is a key to inspiration because it is hard to be inspired by things you already know all about. Often, two different people walk away from the same inspiring talk and one reports a life-altering experience while the other can barely remember what was said. The talk is the same, but the receivers were tuned in differently, that is, they were present to the words in different ways. The person who was moved had the presence to let inspiration in—an openness to teachings and to awe. That is not to say that there is something necessarily wrong with the person who was not inspired, because the talk may have included nothing new or needed for that person at that time. It is to say that without an openness of spirit, there is diminished possibility.

Accessing Beginner's Mind

One way to access beginners mind is to take a moment every day to look around and find things to be grateful for, maybe for a nice office or bedroom, for what you love about your lifestyle, or your family or friends. Taking a few minutes as part of your morning routine to just focus on what you are grateful for opens up metaphysical floodgates because it establishes a trajectory of consciousness for the rest of your day. It sets you up to be awed and it gets your mojo rising as soon as you rise. *An attitude of gratitude opens our psyches to all that's in front of us.*

The easiest and hardest way to source your mojo is to do something so wild that it threatens who you think you are—something at which you are unquestionably a beginner. Risks taken in the spirit of growth are rewarded by breakthroughs in the status quo, even when there does not appear to be any direct correlation between the risk and the breakthrough. Breaking new personal ground lays strong foundations for breaking professional ground, even when personal risks seem unrelated to professional situations.

Cultivating beginner's mind transforms vicious cycles of having the same-old-same-old and wanting something different. No one can keep beginner's mind running all day every day, but accessing it is as simple as consciously releasing your knowingness with an out-breath and inviting in what's new and/or awesome with an in-breath.

Take a Breath

Simple as it seems, taking a conscious breath of air can be a transformative act, whether it happens by taking a moment to consciously breathe in and out once, or by sitting in a breathing meditation for hours on end. When you look through wisdom teachings from religious and spiritual traditions throughout time, a pattern emerges: the most profound teachings are usually the simplest. *Taking a conscious breath is one of life's profound simplicities.*

Mindfulness and other popular meditation techniques are shedding new light on the power of staying mindful of, or present to, your breath. Scientists have documented the positive effects of conscious breathing, including improvement in memory, decision-making capacity, mental acuity, and the ability to remain calm in a crisis. Conscious breathing is one of many ways to unclog your metaphysical pipes, one that is demonstrably effective and undeniably time tested.

There is a subconscious satisfaction that comes with a deep, full breath. But getting that full breath is not so easy when we're stuck in negativity because, during states of frustration, anger, or fear, our breathing becomes shallow. If we are conscious of it at all, we might have the sense of it feeling stuck or being cut off when we think about things that drag our consciousness down. That's normal. That stuck-ness manifests as held breath, uneven breathing, and/or shallow breathing. It also manifests in distractions or feeling like you want to get away. That's also normal. Just bringing your attention back to your breath, and following it to the deepest place you can imagine, is a transformative act.

Conscious breathing gives you access to the point where things get choked off. It is also a metaphysical means for moving through the energy that's stuck. Mojo follows breath. When your breath catches in your throat, chest, or gut, it is giving you metaphysical information on how you are about what you're concerned with. When you imagine that you are breathing into whatever charge or discomfort you're feeling, you will bring a heightened state of awareness to that discomfort. That awareness avails you to a new level of consciousness that cannot be attained while under the influence of an unconscious charge.

Breathing links the physical sensation of the flow of your breath with the metaphysical indicators of unresolved issues or of energetic misalignment. Staying present to the flow of breath reveals metaphysical gateways for locating and resolving problems. Conscious breathing accesses options. Here is one way of doing it:

- Mindfully follow a deep in-breath and notice any sensations of discomfort—maybe a sense of your gut flipping, a sense that the breath gets stuck somewhere, or that your mind is alerting, or your emotions are triggering.
- Imagine your breath going directly to wherever/however you feel the unease. Direct it beyond the words you might use to describe your upset and into the pure energetics of it. Just allow the breath to connect with the emotional charge, and when thoughts come up, release them.

- On the out-breath, allow the charged-up energy to discharge by expelling as forcefully as you need to, which might include making a sound.
- Stay with the inhale into the charge and the exhale of the pent-up energy until your breath is settled and even. Allow thoughts about solutions, or about people or factors of the upset, to come and to go as you keep bringing your attention back to your breath.

It may seem crazy that we would have to practice one of our most basic instincts, but mindful breathing does take practice. If you make it a habit, you will become very aware of how well your breathing time pays off, and you may even miss it when you don't do it.

Simple breathing can be a powerful antidote to problems, but breathing is all the more powerful in the absence of upset because your breath can take you to the absolute source of mojo within you. When it is unimpeded by issues, a deep, steady, conscious inflow and outflow of air can elevate your vantage point and thereby recontextualize your world when you get back to it. If you cannot focus on two breaths in a row, that is metaphysical data on your state of consciousness. Even advanced meditators' minds wander, but as you practice, you'll experience less of the chatter that yogis call "monkey mind" and more of the focused mind from which wise decisions arise. Steady, unconstricted breaths are a key physical indicator that your mojo is flowing.

No matter how well or bad things are going, it is normal to lose concentration on your breath. No problem. Conscious breathing is a process of continual release of thoughts by way of bringing your awareness back to your breath. It is imperative to keep reminding yourself that it is no problem that your mind wandered, otherwise self-judgement over meditation success can overwhelm the process. (see Carreira)

Yogis from various Hindu traditions have told us for millennia that the breath is a key channel for accessing our energy reserves. Hindus teach the concept of *prana*, a kind of vital life force that exists around and through everything and everybody. *Prana* and mojo have a lot in common. Over millennia, Hindus have developed yogic breathing techniques as a means to stoke, harness, and unleash *prana*, which also stokes, harnesses, and unleashes mojo. All of the Hindu yogic breathing exercises and all of the mindfulness techniques, which are mostly rooted in Buddhism, are methodologies for managing mojo in that all of those techniques are ways of opening to, and enhancing, the flow of it.

The data is clear from countless meditation studies being conducted at hospitals and universities worldwide: when you practice conscious breathing on a regular basis, you are not only more likely to maintain personal equanimity in the face of struggles, it is also more likely that you will respond to problems with your most effective answers. *You will be amazed by how many solutions emerge when you stop thinking about what you're thinking about and start thinking about breathing.* The simple act of taking even just a few seconds to breathe with awareness can be a profound game changer. There is literally opportunity for stoking your leadership mojo with every breath you take. The mundane act of a little conscious breathing has the power to reroute your future because connecting with your breath anchors you in your presence.

Conscious breathing is a means of accessing and grounding power. You may be surprised by how much potential opens up when you postpone giving an answer, making a decision, or jumping to a conclusion until you can take at least a couple conscious breaths. In the midst of managing a problem, when you take a moment to concentrate on your breath, it can connect you with that emotional charge that tells us that we are not in an equanimous mindset. Accessing emotional or mental charge, by way of awareness of where your breath leads you, can reveal the path to a more rational approach to whatever it is that's charging your angst.

Conscious breathing helps you discern how your mojo is doing, and it can reveal when and how to redirect energy that is not flowing toward what you want. Sometimes mojo needs stoking, sometimes it needs calming, sometimes redirecting. There is no doubt that conscious breathing not only stokes your mojo, it also helps you discern exactly where, when, and how to direct it. Breathing exercises have been part of many wisdom teachings, and they are becoming more common as Mindfulness is being integrated into more and more professional and health programs. Consider checking out some local classes or some YouTube videos to discover breathing and meditation practices that work for you.

Success guru Tony Robbins does this mojo-pumping morning breathing ritual:

- Inhale while raising both arms up, hands outstretched, palms facing one another above your head
- Strongly exhale while bringing open hands, palms up, back to thighs.
- Repeat the sequence ten times before taking a few regular breaths.
- Repeat the whole cycle of ten dynamic and a few regular breaths three times so that you are taking thirty dynamic breaths broken up by some regular breathing.

- Gradually build up from ten to thirty dynamic breaths in a row, and repeat three times with some regular breathing between each set.

In Hindu terms, Robbins is priming his *prana*, but you could also say that he is juicing his mojo. You can find hundreds, if not thousands, of other techniques for charging your spark and tuning your leadership instrument with breathing. Keep in mind that you will benefit from even one conscious breath.

Integrity

Just like a pipe has to be in full integrity for water to flow through it and not drip out, there is an internal integrity that's necessary in order for mojo to flow in full stream, that is, with no entropy. Integrity is the internal plumbing of alchemical leadership. When your own integrity is diminished for any reason, even for really good reasons, your access to collective mojo is restricted. Reasons are mojo killers. That's because nobody is going to bring his/her full energy to any job where the boss thinks it is reasonable to maintain leaky mojo pipes. Mojo leaks out to the degree that your integrity is not intact. Mojo leakage is entropy.

Integrity implies being honest and having a strong moral sense. Integrity also refers to a state of being whole, unified, and structurally sound. In terms of leadership, the two definitions need to merge because the more honest and moral a leader is, the more honest and moral a culture s/he will build, and the more unified and sound that organization will be. Integrity is both personal and relational. *The more integrity you keep with common values, that is, the more principled you are in decision-making, the more people will entrust their mojo to you.*

Historically, when Quakers represented a much larger proportion of local populations than they do now, especially in the Northeastern US, they were the most successful businesspeople and some of the wealthiest. Their religion holds exceptionally strong values for modesty, simplicity, and ethics so their success was not because they were highly motivated by money, but rather because they were so well known for their integrity that, especially before there were many regulatory protections, they were implicitly trusted and so became the preferred people to do business with. Their moral authority acted like Higgs bosons in that it was the unseen energetic that attracted customers in much the same way a star attracts a crowd. Morality is a charismatic trait that contributes to the integrity of a group.

Integrity is the glue that creates a unified whole, whether it be a wholeness of self or the coherence of an organization. Staying vigilant with your own personal integrity, no matter how much of it you and others know/believe that you already have, is critical to being in authority. It can be a very productive discipline to keep bringing beginner's mind to your own integrity. For good and for bad, living the human experience entails kidding or outright lying to ourselves in one way or another and often in multiple layers. No matter how moral or evolved someone is, part of being a human being is making moral mistakes, overlooking personal digressions, and missing things that can seem so obvious in hindsight. That is why unflinching self-examination is an important component of personal integrity.

Having integrity means being fully present to our own inadequacies, fears, and other conscious or unconscious triggers that make us want to compromise ourselves or someone else. Self-reflection is critical to integrity, and it is an area where it can be dangerously lonely at the top. Ironically, it is hard to engage in productive self-reflection in complete isolation, even though isolating yourself from time to time is a highly effective strategy for self-reflecting. As a consultant, I have had more than one client say something to the effect that, "I self-reflected and it turns out everything I think is right," a sign that s/he is probably not listening enough to other people and/or that there is probably significant personal homework to be done.

We sacrifice integrity for all kinds of reasons, most having to do with fear-based beliefs and decisions. We also grow in integrity for all kinds of reasons, like coming to new personal truths after a tragedy, seeing an old problem from beginner's mind, taking 100 percent responsibility for being in an unwanted situation, stopping a habitual reaction, or admitting fallibility. Shifting limiting beliefs is a great way to strengthen integrity. A belief is just a thought that we keep thinking. It is easy to get so attached to limiting beliefs that we can sometimes feel like we're fighting the good fight even when we are not. *Mistaking beliefs for truths is a common cause for sacrificing integrity.*

Integrity includes recognizing your own personal brand of the woundedness that comes with being born, growing up, and occupying adulthood. However, embracing woundedness does not mean wallowing in your own "woundology," the language of excuses for staying stuck in modes of anger, fear, blame, disempowerment, and victimhood. Letting your wounds define you, even for a minute, disrupts the integrity of your mojo pipeline. Staying stuck in woundedness diverts your mojo in ways that lead to extreme personal entropy.

Your diligence with your personal integrity indicates the range of alchemical possibilities available to you, because standing fast in beliefs that want and need to evolve is a mojo disrupter and having your full integrity intact is a mojo accelerator. Integrity comes with owning your issues rather than letting your issues own you—a subtle but big difference. If your issues have you, the power of the subconscious can cause you to react to situations from distinctly disempowered places in your psyche, from places within that are out of integrity with your best instincts.

Personal integrity relates to your capacity to integrate with the whole of what is going on around you, good, bad, or indifferent. Many good, honest, and well-intentioned leaders are perceived as not having integrity simply because they have not integrated the team's values with their strategies. Values are the links in the chain of integrity. When things are not feeling integrated, consider what values are being played out and what values people would rather have playing out.

Your team's integrity, its honesty, its wholeness, its coherence, is your cultural capital. When the values and vision of an organization are coherent, the group's integrity forms a metaphysical pipeline through which mojo flows clearly and cleanly. The equation is simple: *the more integration there is between personal and organizational values, the more cultural capital you have at your disposal.* Just like tangible capital, the more consciously you manage intangible cultural capital, the more power you have with it. Vigilance with your personal integrity, and with how your values and vision integrate with those around you, increases the amount of cultural capital you have to work with.

Truth

It is pretty obvious that malicious lying drains mojo when you think about how deflating it feels to be affected by someone else's lie. It is a lot harder to see the honest mistakes, the subtle delusions, and the unwitting compromises to truth that seem to be part of the human condition. Leaders need to stay especially vigilant with finding and facing truths as they unfold. Integrity, though, is a more complex distinction than truth because some truths change. Also, it is common to mistake temporary conditions for truths. Truth is more than just facts, but even facts as simple as red cars and blue cars can be misconstrued by an honest witness of an accident who is sure that the red car hit the blue one until s/he sees the video.

Some truths are more fixed than others, but there is power in staying curious about all our truths because our limitations get boxed in when we stop inquiring into truths that really need to evolve. That's why integrity is not just truth-telling—it is a never-ending personal integration with what's so in the ever-evolving world around us. For us to stay in integrity, to stay integrated with the constantly changing world, our understandings about what is true must continually evolve. Beginner's mind is a key to maintaining integrity.

The discipline of beginner's mind helps bust through obsolete truths and break through ontological boundaries. Stagnation comes with marrying our own truths because mojo does not flow well in the presence of righteousness. True progress includes a process of integrating new beliefs about what is true. One pitfall of a yang-dominant worldview is that success can be misconstrued as reaching what is, in actuality, just a point of stagnation when limited beliefs and conjecture are mistaken as truth. Alchemical leadership includes an ongoing process of uncovering deeper and deeper truths. *Because the more deeply rooted your truth is, the more powerful its expression can be.*

We naturally experience ease and resonance when we know that truth is being told. Our universal resonance with truthfulness is like a metaphysical drone string on a banjo or sitar. A drone string plays one continuous note. It is constant. It's up to the other strings to resonate with it because the drone, like truth, establishes a vibrational ground of being, the key around which the music is centered. Your word is like the drone string with which your team needs to resonate. When your team can depend on truth-telling as a cultural norm, you've got the basis for making the "music" of coherent team efforts that play out in harmony and off of the same page. Truth-telling is a metaphysical anchor for every other aspect of your leadership.

The drone string analogy falls apart quickly, though, because truth is paradoxical in that it is a constant but, at the same time, it evolves. As the drone string of your truth inevitably retunes throughout your personal evolutionary journey, capacity for alchemical leadership increases with each re-attunement to each evolution of your consciousness. *Authority comes with being impeccable with how your word reflects your best truth in the present moment.* It also comes with personal accountability for misunderstandings you have had, or compromises you've made, with truth. Yang-dominant leadership norms have many people believing that admitting lapses in truth diminishes someone's authority. There is absolutely nothing to substantiate that idea, while there is plenty of evidence that authenticity in the face of digressions facilitates powerful transformation.

Truths are not always easy to tell and can be even harder to hear, especially revelatory truths. We say that truth can set us free, because not only does truth-telling free up mojo that was invested in hiding it, but our deepest truths penetrate ontological barriers, and that can threaten our very idea of what truth is while, at the same time, new truths open up new frontiers.

Authority and Language

Authority, authorship, and authenticity share the same Latin root, *auth*, which comes from *authenticus*, which meant "principal" in the sense of being first or chief. As the root of the words "author," and "authority," it denotes the chief person who determines how the story goes. "Auth" is also the root of "authentic," which means that personal behavior is regarded as genuine, significant, emotionally appropriate, purposive, responsible, and self-directed. Authenticity is a commitment to honesty, to mattering, and to living in accordance with values. Authenticity is rocket fuel for mojo and it is the basis for having actual authority because there is a direct correlation between having command of how things go and being authentic.

Being an authority figure does not make someone the authority in the room, because most of us have a visceral sense of who is being straight and who is not. How you say things telegraphs whether or not you are in authority. Scrupulousness with the dignity and integrity of your words is an important part of that. The speech process is both a physical and a metaphysical phenomenon. Extrapolating from Einstein's wisdom, you cannot use the language of the status quo to define change. In other words, you can't keep saying the same things and expect to manifest different results. Be diligent with words and ideations like, "I always...," "We can't...," "They never...," "Remember what happened before...," and, "That's the way it is." That kind of language is limiting at best, maybe even extremely damaging, because it indicates an ontological basis that may be rigid and likely stuck.

Having authority includes doing due diligence with the consciousness with which your words flow. *Your authority and your authorship with the words you choose are intertwined.* Command of language is an authoritative skill that is so basic that it is easily overlooked. Take stock of your words and the stories you tell. Be impeccable with your word—say what you mean and mean what you say in ways that preserve the dignity of others. Contrary to the way it can feel in the moment, disrespectful words disempower the originator of those words even more than they disempower the person being denigrated—a reality that is often obscured by yang-dominant leadership norms. *Before speaking, consider whether what you are about to say is true, kind, and/or helpful. If what you have to say is not at least two out of those three, consider doing some silent self-reflection on your authorship.*

Alchemical adeptness starts with truth-telling. While our truths can and do morph, it is incumbent on each of us, in the name of basic civility, to tell our most truthful truths at any given moment. Think about it: one of the most universal triggers of upset is when we realize we're being lied to. Lies break down relationships and they disrupt mojo. Always. No matter how small or expedient the lies are, or how much we believe they are "necessary." A lie may ease a short-term condition, but it sows long-term authenticity issues. The authenticity of your words reflects the clarity and integrity of your consciousness and it indicates the degree of authority you actually hold.

Language is such a subliminal phenomenon that we tend to be unconscious about it. And, to a large extent, we need to be unconscious about it because we cannot limit ourselves by thinking about every word we speak. At the same time, language is the currency of cultural capital in that it is the means through which members of a culture interact. Impeccability with how you choose your words is a metaphysical task. The impact of language on outcomes is alchemical in that it can make the difference between a team producing more than it knew it could or producing at a subpar level.

Words can have the effect of leveraging cultural capital and they can have the effect of debiting it. As a leader, your words pretty much define your impact because they can create or destroy possibilities. The more we find out about the impact of values on productivity, innovation, and profitability, the more leaders need to be accountable for how well their language reflects positive values.

It pays off to stop and name the subtle triggers that upset our guts, minds, and hearts because they are disruptions in our being-ness. *Quality of being determines quality of doing, and quality of language is a good indicator of quality of being.* Taking time for deep discernment about the language you choose to use is a good way to find out how you might be investing mojo in woundology, future worries, or entropy-causing behavior. Processes of deep discernment can start with simply breathing into the sensation of how and where we're feeling triggered until we're able to name it and claim it. Sometimes simple triggers seem to take whole lifetimes to dismantle, while seemingly very complex ones can resolve in a flash when they are clearly discerned.

If a situation still triggers or nags at you, even after you've done everything you can think of to manage it head-on, keep working on finding words that reflect your next level of authenticity. If you can feel authentic contentment in the presence of thinking about, or facing, the issue or person that triggered you, you have likely reclaimed the mojo that had been trapped in the problem. Issues sort out as we find new words for them—as we re-author our stories about them. *Evolve your language to resolve your problems.*

Consciously aiming your language toward greater and greater levels of integrity is a powerful strategy for changing your work world.

Dignity

It should go without saying, yet needs to be said in too many workplaces, words that denigrate people are words that are not working to anyone's best advantage. When a leader relies on yang-dominant behaviors like threats, put-downs, yelling, and power plays, it has a similar effect on organizational mojo that allowing an excess of positive (yang) electrical charge into a building would have on electrical currency. *Power flows in accordance with the language you choose.*

Mojo is wasted with words that do not hold the authority of integrity and the dignity of respect. Mojo and dignity go hand in hand. Dignity comes with using words in accordance with the Golden Rule, speaking to and about everybody else how you want to be spoken to and about. A respectful dialog with the person you consider to be the source of your upset gives you the opportunity to reclaim power over your well-being that, at some level, you have awarded to her/him. When problems result in shaming, blaming, blowing up, or other indignities, that's an indicator of compromised leadership capacity. *The quality of your language denotes the quality of the ground of being, the ontology, that your leadership stands on.*

Dignity comes with finding your way to unconditional positive regard for everyone, even the worst mistake-makers. Developing unconditional positive regard for others is never about them. As much as it might feel good to vent, and no matter how right we might be, we lose our authority if we react with venting rather than responding with respect for the dignity of others. Thinking of mojo as a spark, if you reactively "spark off," it means that you've discharged energy you could have put to better use, which is entropy. *When, instead of reacting with a flash of upset, we respond by investing mojo more consciously, we gain stronger authority over the power within and around us.*

The full amount of any organization's cultural capital is only accessible to leaders who maintain the personal authority to access it. Indiscriminate language used in challenging times is extra damaging because it means that when you are in the biggest need for cultural capital, it is getting trashed from within. We often think the opposite—that we somehow get a free pass when the chips are down—but no research on cultural well-being supports that notion. On the contrary, if people know someone is likely to blow when things get tough, they are more likely to choose to make themselves scarce at that time or to engage in dysfunction. Whether they dodge or dysfunction, it creates entropy, which is increased when disgruntled team members send out resumes after uncomfortable encounters.

If people risk humiliation even in sustaining the status quo, what is the likelihood of them risking their time and talent toward exceeding the status quo? Even when the most avoidable mistakes happen out of the worst incompetence, undignified words still diminish cultural capital and they diminish authority. Alchemical capacity is correlative with the personal capacity to manage your own and/or someone else's mistakes without jumping into murky moral territory. Your words matter, so it can be very effective to take a few breaths until the right ones emerge. If necessary, take a few days or maybe just a trip to the restroom. Reacting to failures with language that compromises your own dignity or that of the person being spoken to, squanders cultural capital.

Ignoring issues is not an answer to preserving dignity because if concerns are big enough to trigger upset, they are big enough to warrant paying attention to. The energy that is flowing when emotions get triggered can, when properly channeled, lead to unimagined breakthroughs. Yang-dominant systems dismiss the benefits of managing emotional upsets by asserting that everybody should just buck up, get over past upset, and not be distracted by uncomfortable conversations that might manage problems head-on. Far from it being a distraction, though, taking time to rectify values digressions actually does not waste resources. It pays dividends.

Stories

Your reality is both reflected by, and is a result of, the stories you tell. This cannot be emphasized enough. Our lives and our work are literally defined by the stories we tell. Stressful, harmful, and unfulfilling work-world norms can seem inevitable when an organization's ontology, its fundamental language about what is so, perpetuates the story of a crappy place to work. The story of your work is the out-picturing of subtle language choices you make every day. At the same time, your workplace's story influences daily language choices. Changing *your* story changes *the* story and vice versa. As a leader, you are an author of what stories take place on your watch. Due diligence with the story of your work is a metaphysical task. Conscious authorship of the story is alchemy.

Here is a story told two different ways: A very bright employee at a social media company was charged with coming up with innovative ideas. The nature of the work of innovation is not the same as the nature of other kinds of work, so his day looked very different from that of the administrators and sales professionals in the office. It entailed spending time just thinking, diverting attention often so that he could return to a project with beginner's mind, and triggering his creativity by doing unrelated things. One way of telling his story is that he is lazy, unproductive, distracted, and frittering away his time playing ping-pong and drawing pictures. Another way of telling it is that he transformed his industry with the so-called "flash" of innovation he had, and with his capacity to harness that flash by identifying viable, specific applications. The former story is told from the ontological basis of an organization where innovation is choked off. The latter suggests that there is fertile ontological ground for innovating.

Alchemy happens every time you consciously up-script your stories. The story of your workplace is a powerful mechanism with which to exercise authority. Finding the best words requires diligence. You practice alchemy through language every time you refuse to create and tell stories that proliferate victimhood, shame, blame, judgmentalism, and other fruitless takes on problems. You practice alchemy every time you are mindful with staking your past, present, and/or future on the integrity of your most evolved words about what's going on under your watch. That does not mean sugarcoating. It is a matter of focus, authenticity, and diligence with language.

Standing on Your Best Ground

Leadership development is consciousness development. Your inner being is your personal metaphysical, ontological ground from which you operate. It is causal of how you author the world around you. Consciousness of the ontology in which you stand gives you access to the zone of causality. True greatness comes from beyond the "box" of subconscious norms. Self-reflecting on your particular ontological "box" gives you the wherewithal to step into or out of it at will.

Leadership Reflections

1. To develop beginner's mind, make a list of ten questions about your work. See how much you can wipe your mind clean of all preconceptions by trying to answer your questions from the perspective of someone who has no background in your field.

2. Set a timer for three minutes and just focus on your breath. Notice how it does/doesn't flow.

3. What stories are you perpetuating? Are they about how charged everyone is or could be, or about how wrong they are? Are they about dominating or partnering? Are your stories reactive or responsive? Do your stories indicate inspired action or negative reaction?

4. List five professional issues that you could use some new light on. Who is capable of helping to shed some outside light on those issues? Book time with him/her.

5. Who could you use a good dialog with so that you can move into a more dignified relationship? Take a look at nonviolent communication websites and books for simple steps for raising effectiveness with language (see "nonviolent communication" in Glossary).

- To release unproductive negative thinking, write down those thoughts (and even burn the pages if you'd like); look up anger management techniques; engage in personal growth programs, meditation, and/or prayer; and/or talk with a friend, colleague, coach, therapist, or consultant so that your own personal homework is out of the way before approaching the person you are in conflict with.

6. How might you re-author your language to better protect and grow cultural capital?

7. Stay on the lookout for wise people and for people who seem to have their mojo flowing. Especially look for them in places you might not normally hang out. Take time to connect with at least one of those people and ask questions.

CHAPTER 7

CATALYTIC CONVERTING

Being a Converter

Catalytic converters are devices attached to the exhaust system of a car or other engine to eliminate or substantially reduce emissions that pollute. They work by converting harmful substances into harmless ones. Transforming the harmful into the harmless is an important leadership skill. People will always have problems, and some bring disagreeability into pretty much every situation they enter. A leader's job is to convert cultural pollutants in such a way as to neutralize or transform them into strengths.

Alchemical leadership entails not just identifying positive options, but also discerning how and when to manage negative metaphysical components that can only be converted into productivity to the degree that they are named and claimed. The more accountability there is for negativity, the more likely it is that it can be transformed into positivity. Negativity only becomes entropy to the extent it is not consciously converted.

Two powerful mechanisms through which cultural toxicity can be transformed into cultural fertility are catharsis and epiphany. Catharsis, which is the act of releasing or letting go, can open up space for epiphany, which is a sudden revelation or transformative insight that breaks through the status quo. Catharsis and epiphany, which can occur independently or in conjunction with each other, are metaphorical catalytic converters in that they are mechanisms through which negativity gets converted. Letting go and breaking through are both ways of releasing energy into a system. Alchemical leadership requires the capacity to cause release of energy that is trapped, for example, by holding on to ideas that don't serve. It also requires paving the way for breakthroughs.

Alchemical capacity is dependent on letting go of what does not best serve (catharsis) and on being available to revelatory insight (epiphany). Both catharsis and epiphany are powerful mechanisms for transformation because they both create leaps of consciousness. Great leaders seek both and competent consultants pretty much guarantee them.

Catharsis

A catharsis is a profound shift in beliefs and/or feelings that has the effect of releasing ideological and/or emotional baggage. The word comes from the Greek *kathairein*, which means "to cleanse," and from *katharos*, which means "pure." A catharsis leaves us feeling freed, like a weight has been lifted, like our psyches have been cleansed, such that we feel more pure and open. Cathartic release helps us break through the boundaries of our beliefs, and that frees up the mojo we were spending on maintaining them. Catharsis is an internal mechanism through which entropy is stopped by way letting go of thought and behavior patterns that do not serve.

The cathartic experience is mostly visceral, that is, it is instinctive, gut-seated, deep-rooted, inward, and/or emotional. Catharsis may give you a heightened sense of relief, clarity, satisfaction, or joy, along with a sense of inner relaxation. It might tingle, or make you smile, or cry, or cause you to spontaneously take a deep breath and let it out with a sound. Or it could come as a subtle sense of your gut relaxing, or your heart expanding, as you relieve the burden of ideas and emotions best left behind. A cathartic moment feels like you have turned a corner or like you can see things in a new light. Cathartic moments of release and/or relief move mojo.

Catharsis brings relief from mental and emotional blockages. It can happen by way of drama, by hearing or seeing something that triggers the release, or by intentionally staying attentive to, maybe by breathing into, a negative feeling, a nagging physical sensation, or a strong belief about a person, idea, or situation, until there is a shift in the tension it creates. It can also come by changing your story about someone else's faults or mistakes to one in which you claim full responsibility for what is bothering you. Catharsis lets other people off the hook. Hooks tend to hang heavier and heavier over time. Keeping people on them is an unproductive place for their mojo to be hanging and for yours to be invested. Cathartic release of a hook frees up energy you were investing in that person's wrongness so that you have that energy back in your own reserve and it allows their mojo the freedom it needs to express in healthier ways. *No matter how it gets triggered, the cathartic shift releases old "stuff", and that release opens the space to evolve a situation.*

While many of us have been taught to go around, ignore, or blast through the proverbial stones on our paths, Buddhists say that "the stone on the path is the path." Meaning, the more wholeheartedly you can walk with your pain points, staying present with them rather than dodging, squelching, identifying with, or focusing too much on them, the better able you will be to reach your destination. Catharsis can be brought about by embracing negativity as the next stone on the path rather than trying to resist it as something other than a part of your path.

Acknowledging that the stone is the path is a simple, yet highly impactful way of contextualizing the things that contrast with our ideas of how things should be. Although the stone analogy may be too mild in comparison to the kinds of boulders that show up on leaders' paths, the fastest way to reach cathartic resolution is to clearly name and claim the stone, no matter its size. To whatever degree negativity is showing up on your path, that is the degree to which it needs to be addressed on its own terms. Claiming the negativity on your path affords you the opportunity to consciously convert it into positivity. That conversion frees up mojo that is then available to you in a way that it wasn't before.

In the face of negativity, it is easiest for us to act kind of like the robotic vacuum cleaners that come right up to a wall and turn. But we cannot transform what we do not allow ourselves to bump into. In short, when you're facing negativity, face it! Because avoiding or resisting negativity can become a black hole for mojo. *Power does not come with controlling negativity. It comes with how you negotiate the inevitability of it.* Just as the most challenging part of giving birth is right before the baby crowns, maintaining full presence right to the brink of catharsis can be tough, but the payoff is great. Staying fully present with challenges through the point of catharsis yields far greater gains than we can get from bypassing them. Transformative opportunities reveal themselves when we embrace the negative. *Maintaining presence with the negative is your ticket to a cathartic experience that can blast you beyond it.*

Fear and Failure

There's a Hindu saying: "The farther up a monkey climbs, the more you see its behind." Alchemical leadership is about knowing when to climb anyway, when to perch, and when to get off the tree to thrive in another. Gandhi said that the most inalienable human right is to be entitled to our own failures. Latitude for mistake-making is yin-izing because it supports creative flow. Mistakes, failures, and other cathartic triggers can bring us to greater clarity and better positioning when we are diligent with how we are perceiving them and with our stories about them.

Doing personal homework helps build the metaphysical scaffolding for letting go of sure answers, and for allowing the unraveling that needs to happen (yin) in order for things to ravel up differently (yang). Risking, by definition, invites failure, which is often a trigger for catharsis. The clarity and energetic renewal that come with catharsis can only happen when failure is accurately framed as an inevitable part of personal and/or organizational evolution.

Risk, whether calculated, substantiated, or simply blind, is always a factor in success. But who would want to take a risk when there is fear that it could result in feeling diminished if your risk turns out like many risks do? The part that fear plays in the process of risk-taking is highly determinant of outcomes. *The degree to which decision-making about risk, or any-*

thing else, is based on fear is the degree to which evolution is stunted. Fear is awful ontological ground for success.

The toxicity that fear can bring can be catalytically converted to mojo when it is managed on its own terms. But letting fear dictate is a surefire way to avoid catharsis and to ensure that too much cultural capital gets spent on repressing problems and thereby perpetuating them. The release and relief of catharsis can be obstructed by fear of the negative. Fear of failure is a waste of mojo because failure is always an opportunity for catharsis.

Go Ahead, Fall Apart

Just like a seed has to break apart so that it can come to its fullest fruition, sometimes things have to fall apart so that we can reach ours. Sometimes we need to let go so completely that even our sense of identity may feel threatened. Often, especially right before the cathartic moment, it can feel downright awful, because the thoughts and beliefs that need converting can be muckiest at their breaking points. Catharsis comes most efficiently with taking the risk of diving headlong into dark holes.

We tend to think of success as a series of wins. We are culturally conditioned to believe that positivity and growth are the only viable options for success. But the upside can only ever be half the story of anything anywhere. There is no such thing as a world with flow and no ebb. The nature of life cycles of organisms and organizations is that without some falling apart, there is no thriving. No matter how people choose to perceive it, the nature of reality is that everything cycles between integration and disintegration, yang and yin.

Alchemical leadership is the art of being at conscious cause for timely integrating and disintegrating.

Consciously embracing the reality that things do and will fall apart is the first step to reclaiming power that is lost in the delusion that things could be otherwise. Falling apart is risky business. And it is absolutely necessary from time to time if you want to keep things evolving. Catharsis can be scary stuff. And it pays off. Catalytic catharsis, the kind that transmutes negatives to positives, requires consciously following whatever negative charge you are feeling, sometimes down very dark and difficult tunnels, until the emotion or thought pattern releases its hold.

Cultural norms have been such that we have come to believe that falling apart and leadership are antithetical to each other. They aren't. Western acculturations frame falling apart as bad and wrong, and so our cultural lens helps to prejudice, maybe even blind, us to exactly what is going on during our inevitable spins through our more challenging cycles. *Alchemical leadership entails having the consciousness to fall apart in cathartic ways rather than blow apart in dysfunction.*

Catharsis, in effect, serves to unplug your energy from where it has been charging dysfunction or stagnation. Catharsis breaks energetic circuits, which enables them to be rewired more effectively. The inner release that comes with catharsis frees you from energetically funding perceptions, beliefs, and thought patterns that do not serve. With newly released energy available, new possibilities and new truths show up, sometimes in the form of life-changing revelation (epiphany). Catharsis breaks things open to reveal new levels of consciousness that transcend your current understanding. That newly revealed state of consciousness is a new rung of personal evolution that you can choose to climb or not.

Epiphany

Catharsis may be directly followed by an epiphany that takes you to a whole new place of understanding. Catharsis is a sense of internal release, while epiphany is the aha moment of sudden insight. Both can be as subtle as a whisper or more like fireworks disrupting your whole life. Either way, cathartic experiences and epiphanies, as disruptive as they may be, are signals that your mojo is in gear.

Epiphany is a visceral, felt sense of transcendence to a new level of insight—a new plateau of consciousness from which there is no going back. Epiphany is the revelation of a new normal. An epiphany is a frontier moment in that it is an opening to new grounds of consciousness. When mojo is flowing, epiphanies naturally unfold. They usually show up on people's faces—a tear, a smile, a sigh, a startle.... Epiphany can feel like someone just turned the lights on. Epiphanic moments are transformative in that they always evolve the circumstances in which they arise. Epiphany often leads to innovation.

Even though epiphany is usually a spontaneous experience of mind and heart, organizations can still be geared toward having ongoing epiphanic growth. Good team retreats and planning sessions are engineered for epiphanies because they ground new insights and ideas in the personal and organizational transformation that is necessary to bring them to life. Epiphanic growth can be hardwired into cultures by way of establishing cultural values for discovery, catharsis, transformation, exploration, and risk-taking.

The story of Newton discovering gravity when an apple fell on his head may or may not be true, but it is the story of an epiphany and it illustrates how intelligence evolves by way of epiphanies. Creating a culture that is conducive to epiphanic insights is an alchemical task.

Positivity and Negativity

From ancient Taoist teachings, to the binary codes that make up the internet, to the positive and negative charges that are needed to create an electrical spark, we know that the world is existentially dualistic. Duality is a fundamental law of physics. It is inevitable and it cannot be reconciled with the growth-only economic belief systems that permeate most workplace ontologies.

Positivity (yang) is the opposite pole of negativity (yin), meaning that positivity and negativity define a mutual spectrum of reality. Since negativity and positivity are two ends of the same spectrum, diminishing one necessarily diminishes the other. The nature of the human condition is that we are always swinging between poles. Alchemical leaders are not only conscious of the inherent symmetry in how things swing, they are causal in the swinging. The more intense your power situation is, and the more consciousness with which you manage your capacity for causation, the more radical it is when you make shift happen. That's why personal equanimity is a prerequisite for alchemical leadership.

It is not possible to find the equanimity necessary for alchemical leadership if you only accept half the equation of the human condition. Yet leaders are rarely trained in how to surf when tides are ebbing, or how to mine the gold that inevitably appears when depths are delved into, much less how to purposely swing yin-ward away from more evident yang objectives of profits and accomplishments. Just like trees are strongest when they root as deeply into the dark earth as they reach into the sunshine, so must leaders understand that sustainable growth requires plunging into dark places to meet face-to-face with negativities like self-doubt, worry, upset, bad circumstances, compromised behaviors, and fear.

An ancient Chinese proverb says, "If you are patient in one moment of anger, you will escape a hundred days of sorrow." Widening that wisdom, being patient with negativity can result in options for escaping hundreds of times as much negativity. Patience is the state of holding mojo in escrow, meaning that by not letting it flow toward the problem, we can allow it to be dormant so that it is available for solutions as they become clear. Organizational catalytic conversion is an alchemical skill that sometimes comes with simple acts of patience as things are breaking down. Patience allows us to take an extra minute to breathe, to seek personal accountability, to see things from the other's viewpoint, and to respond rather than react. Finding patience helps to establish your presence, which is a key component in the act of catalytic converting.

We often lose our patience because of unrealistic expectations about the inevitability of hard times. The wisdom gained from losses, restoration gained from powering down, and strength gained through contraction often do not feel wise, restorative, or strong in the moment. Those moments can actually feel more stupid, draining, and weak. Having the courage and fortitude to be fully present with those feelings raises our consciousness.

It is certain that we will cycle through circumstances that contrast with how we think things should go. It is our decision as to whether that contrast will be allowed to impede the flow of mojo or be understood as a marker on the path that shows what we do not want so that we are clearer about what we do. Contrast is an inevitability in the human experience.

Embracing contrast is necessary for metaphysical catalytic conversion. Denying it is mojo malpractice.

The field of positive psychology confirms what spiritual teachers have always said: that a positive approach is the most productive. But without the negative, there would be no positive. So, while it is normal to want to have only positive experiences, true mastery of positivity cannot possibly happen by resisting the negative. That is why so many people have such temporary results with so many positive-thought methods even though there are well-documented psychological, spiritual, and physiological benefits that come with positivity. We are often unconscious of ubiquitous biases that come from mainstream ideations about positivity—starting with the incredulous concept that negativity should never happen.

What is often missing in the positive-thought field is the critical importance of being able to discern between using positivity to dodge negativity or using it toward greater mastery of a situation. Though it may seem counterintuitive, mojo is enhanced by embracing the discomfort of negativity as well as the fear that darkness sometimes brings. At the same time, mojo is drained by attaching to negativity and it can be challenging to discern the subtle, but profound, difference between attaching and embracing. Maintaining your presence with what is falling apart beats dodging or attaching to the emotionality of negativity because, although it can feel like a short-term win, avoidance and hyper-focus are both unconscious strategies for causing the long-term negativity you are trying to avoid in the short term.

It is one thing to train your mind for positivity by being grateful for the simplest things, like even how much you like the color of your sofa. It is another thing entirely to be focusing on a nice sofa when your house is on fire. The mastery it takes to convert negativity to positivity requires the equanimity to embrace all present elements, no matter how dark and dirty some may be. It is only in processing the negative that catharsis can convert it back into available mojo. The only way out of darkness is to go through it. Mustering the fortitude to look and work in dark places, while it can certainly be exhausting in its own way, is good mojo management.

Catharsis comes with the willingness to work out the hard and messy things within yourself, and with whoever else is part of whatever you need to resolve. Owning what you are hanging onto, and daring to let go of it, can be almost impossible to do in a vacuum. Bringing in the voice of an objective third party for the purpose of gaining clarity, and specifically not for the purpose of seeking agreement for any sense of righteousness, can save tremendous amounts of time and money in the long run. Other people's insights are often key to catharsis and epiphanies.

I learned about the Native American medicine wheel from Iroquois oral historian, Paula Underwood, who taught it to corporate leaders as a model for understanding and managing transformation. Different tribes use different versions of the medicine wheel. Underwood divided it into twelve points, just like a clock, with specific transformational processes at each point. The shift at eleven o'clock entails the process of seeking outside counsel. It is at that final spot on the wheel because, once due diligence is done by moving through the previous ten stages, an outside perspective is considered necessary for transcendence into the next cycle of development. The indigenous wisdom that calls for bringing in outside perspective is confirmed by studies like those of Anderson for MetrixGlobal, which have found good consulting pays an average of 600 percent return on investment.

Attachment

Whether we push a coffee mug away or pick it up, we are temporarily attaching our hand to it. If we let go, as long as the cup is the focus of our attention, we still have an attachment to it. Attachment to something means that a certain amount of our physical and/or mental resources are unavailable for other things. In other words, attachment is a mojo expenditure.

Attachment is an easy concept to work with when it comes to tangibles like cups. But even if we focus on avoiding the cup, we are still thinking about the cup and so part of our consciousness is attached to it. That kind of intangible attachment can be deeply disruptive. Avoidance, which is its own form of attachment, leads to fear-driven mojo expenditure, which is never a good strategy. Attachment and avoidance are situational and conditional whereas alchemy happens in the metaphysical realm, which is unencumbered by situations and conditions.

If you literally stay attached to a physical object, it is obvious that you would make a mess of a lot of other things. It is not as easy to recognize our invisible investments in intangible equivalents of the coffee cup. Metaphysical catalytic converting cannot happen in the acts of resisting, avoiding, or attaching to good or bad things. By definition, we cannot convert what we are holding on to yet the chaos that can come from the act of letting go can lure us into staying attached to limiting ideas and habits.

Make Chaos Okay

Historically, chaos was understood as the formless matter that is supposed to have existed before the creation of the universe.

The formlessness of chaos was understood as a fertile metaphysical pool. In the domain of physics, the word "chaos" is used to describe behavior so unpredictable as to appear random, but which behavior is attributable to great sensitivity to small changes in conditions. Alchemy is the art of causing and capitalizing on seemingly imperceptible changes. It is the art of harnessing the power of chaos. Not the chaos of dysfunction, corruption, and ill will, but a more universal kind of chaos.

The chaos of dysfunction is entropy while the universal field of chaos is all possibility. The former keeps the offices of psychologists, politicians, and lawyers busy because it usually involves manipulation, inauthenticity, and other compromises to civility. The more universal understanding of chaos is written about in the *I Ching*, the Taoist book of wisdom, which says that chaos is "where brilliant dreams are born." The kind of chaos from which brilliance is born happens in the crack between the physical and the metaphysical. Comfort with chaos allows us to walk through that crack so we can play in metaphysical pools.

Chaos is a particularly powerful field from which to practice alchemy because, in the breaking apart of systems that ensues with chaos, the components of those systems are in free flow and therefore able to be reformulated into what we want. Just as important as integrity is for keeping things together, is as important as chaos is in the process of organizational evolution. Power, by definition, happens both with cohering and dispersing so avoiding chaos is not advisable. It is a necessary part of creativity because chaos means that mojo and other resources are available for reconfiguring. The chaos that is at the root of all creativity is a critical component of alchemy.

Avoiding chaos creates rigidity and limits innovation. The disorder and confusion that comes with chaos are part of the transformative process. The nature of chaos is that it breaks down barriers to possibilities. Rather than spending resources on the avoidance or shutting down of chaos, it is generally more productive to work with and not against it. *If you do not allow, or maybe even cause, things to break apart into some formlessness once in a while, the rigidity of your form is likely to dysfunction.* Personal homework becomes critical here because it makes the difference between whether you make the unconscious mistake of causing dysfunctional chaos, or you are adept with making positive changes happen in the universal field of all possibility.

Resisting the chaos that comes with transformation can indicate too much attachment to things that need to, and that are probably going to, change. Fear of chaos is an extremely weak position to lead from because it narrows the scope from which you can respond to the inevitability of change. No time is probably ever a good time for chaos to set in, but when you find yourself navigating it by going with the flow and embracing it, you will likely make new discoveries, possibly on frontiers you may not even have known existed. In times of chaos, the yin-yang swings of life feel extreme and erratic. How skillfully you surf the tides of chaos hinges on how much equanimity you have developed by doing personal homework.

The risk that it takes to embrace chaos is undeniable. Even so, alchemical leaders go beyond just embracing it to consciously catalyzing chaos by moving mojo in such a way as to kick up a little of it from time to time. The more tuned up your metaphysical muscles are, the better you can navigate that risk. Chaos is only painful to the degree that it is resisted.

Make chaos your friend by breathing deeply into it. If you can "dance" through chaotic times, that's even better.

Being a Catalyst

To catalyze means to cause or to generate some kind of shift. Catalysts stimulate, spur, spark, incite, and create impetus, all of which are metaphysical processes in that they are causal. As a leader, part of your job is to consciously cause the energetic sparks that will best catalyze your operations. Alchemical leadership is having the capacity for catalytic agency, that is, the ability to catalyze or spark something you intend to happen, the ability to be consciously catalytic. *Your intentions are a catalyzing agent in the act of alchemy.* The quality of your intentions determines the power of the sparks you can set off. *Intentionality is a reflection of consciousness development.* Building shared intention is a formidably powerful force for mission accomplishment.

Catalyzing is very different than controlling. There is a time for each, but in cultures where control is a dominant value, things generally don't catalyze very easily because mojo is dampened by controlling behaviors and atmospherics. Control is a limiting value that indicates that a culture is too yang. It shows up as people feeling stifled, as fear-based decision-making, general disempowerment, dull workplace vibe, and tunnel-visioned leaders, none of which is conducive to catalyzation.

In order to catalyze change, a person or organization facing control issues has to either find a way to shift yin-ward on purpose or allow the pendulum to swing so far yang-ward that there is no choice but to shift the other way. Consciously shifting yin-ward toward the field of chaos is an alchemical move that can prevent control issues from playing out to the point of pain.

The Field of Alchemy

Alchemical leadership is the capacity to be catalytic with primal, metaphysical drivers, like values. Metaphysical principles apply to everything we know in ways that we do and do not know. Alchemy itself can probably never fully be known because the more we discover about it, the more we realize that it entails more than we can ever know. As the universe continually unfolds, alchemy itself is ever evolving.

There is much mystery in the mastery of metaphysics and so there is an elusive quality to alchemy and to the mysterious field from which successes emerge. Still, alchemical leaders who engage in ongoing development of their mastery with metaphysical principles find they are increasingly able to convert negativity and to catalyze the future they want for themselves, for their work, and for the world.

Leadership Reflections

1. List three things that need to be resolved or evolved at work. Note what resolution and/or evolution would feel like. How would resolving these issues affect your mojo and that of your team?

2. Are there toxic aspects of your culture that you would like to convert to a healthier state? What resources are attached to that toxicity? How can those resources be recaptured and redirected?

3. Choose a question or issue that is up for you right now. Take time to clarify it. Keep it present for yourself over time by putting a note to jog your thoughts in your calendar, in your pocket, on your desktop, or on your mirror; by taking time to reflect on it and/ or write about it; or by talking with a trusted adviser about it. Be relentless with the concern until something shifts. Was the shift cathartic? Epiphanic? Both?

- Where could your systems use a catharsis, a release of that which doesn't serve?
- Where could your systems use an epiphany, a new, transformative way of seeing things?

4. What changes need to be catalyzed in your work world? In what ways do you feel you are in a position to do the catalyzing? In what ways do you feel ill equipped to catalyze change? What would it take for you to grow in your capacity to catalyze? How and when can you invest in growing your catalytic capacity?

CHAPTER 8

YOUR INNER GPS

A Global Positioning System that
Isn't Sourced by Satellites

Heuristics

Oprah Winfrey says she never set a goal. She intuitively knew
that the *heuristic*, or non-formulaic, experiential path, was as
valid as the very goal-oriented paths that her colleagues were
taking. A heuristic approach is one of discovery, experimenta-
tion, and ongoing evaluation. No one can argue that goal-setting is a legitimate means of operation. But Oprah and many
creatives and tech pioneers have proven that the "plan your
work and work your plan" strategy is not the only way to
go—that the heuristic path has its own merit.

A heuristic approach is one of moment-to-moment unfoldment. Heuristics is the yin to yang paths that are well planned,
with goals and benchmarks set according to yang-dominant

standards. Storytellers are especially aware of the differences. Whereas classic stories have well-established beginnings, middles, and endings, heuristic stories are started by storytellers who jump in with a theme and "spin the yarn" as they go. Classic storytellers preserve stories and the lessons they hold, while heuristic storytellers have faith in the creative process of unfolding a story that is almost as unknown to the teller, who is only a step or two ahead, as it is to the audience.

In both traditional and heuristic stories, a theme, or focus, is established. The difference is not in the subject matter, it is in the means used to develop it. In the classic approach, the means is a more linear process based on memory and history (yang). In heuristic storytelling, there is a nonlinear trust in creativity and in the ability to intuit meaning (yin). Actors and comedians also work both ways, either by memorizing scripts or counting on heuristics to improvise. Despite how many millennia humankind has been trying to figure it out, the creative force that brings the heuristic storyteller his or her words, or a comedian the next punch line, is still mostly mystery. It is a force of mojo.

It is easier to appreciate the role of heuristics in the arts than in offices. In Oprah's case, just like her colleagues, her focus was on making good television, but her pathway to success didn't conform with entertainment industry norms. She never met industry standards for weight or whiteness, which, especially as she was coming up, were extremely misogynistic and racist. The track that had been determined by history held little hope for her, and her own propensities didn't include a penchant for planning. She totally trusted where her heart and intuition led her.

Oprah appears to be more masterful than most with picking up on and following inner signals. Her legacy has not just validated the paths of those who are heuristically inclined, it has also provided a beacon for those who are not so heuristically inclined to trust the path of no foreknowing. Because we have been so steeped in the ontological assumption that goal-setting in accordance with established norms is the only way to success, most of us probably have a negatively skewed perception of the risk in trusting discovery-based, emergent decision-making.

Goals tend to be more concrete while heuristic approaches are more metaphysical. Especially given our cultural contextualization of metaphysicalities, very few of us can expect to have Oprah's deep-seated willingness to follow her inner voice. There is no doubt about it, that inner voice can be highly disruptive. Many people who have reached greatness have stories to tell of the havoc that they experienced by way of following their inner voices down heuristic pathways. At the same time, just like we hang on the edges of our seats when a storyteller or improviser is on a heuristic roll, there is a kind of charisma and attraction that emanates from people who are in heuristic mode that brings us into a kind of coherence with them. The fact that heuristics can both dramatically disrupt and strongly cohere means that heuristic capacity is an instrument of power.

The Heuristic Path

A heuristic path requires hyperpresence in the moment. It requires using on-the-spot discernment to discover the next right word or action, rather than relying on a set of predetermined rules or steps. Heuristics requires a kind of heartedness that is not for the faint of heart. While goal-setting requires its own kind of fortitude, heuristics requires trusting the cutting edge of discovery in the same way that a comedian trusts that a punchline will spontaneously emerge and a storyteller trusts that a worthwhile tale will be told. But taking a heuristic approach is a much bigger risk for leaders who directly impact the lives of others than it is for a storyteller or comedian.

Heuristics, a process that isn't standardized and predictable like goal-setting is, requires that we stay conscious of our moral, physical, emotional, and spiritual motivations. That's because heuristics relies more on internalized drivers than external benchmarks. Improvisational actors often work extra hard on personal homework because they know they need to trust that the inner workings they are tapping into are not so polluted by personal stuff that they stop the flow. It is no coincidence that Oprah puts so much focus on personal development, because it is such an important component of the heuristic path of her own success. Whereas in rule- and goals-driven processes the guide rails are specific external parameters, in the heuristic process the guide rails are internal.

The benefits of holding a narrow focus on specific goals are well documented, while the benefits of heuristic discovery are not because we tend to relegate them as flukes that come from "out of nowhere." And in one sense, that's true because heuristic impulses do unfold from a mysterious place. But in another sense, it is hard to make an argument that Oprah's success was a fluke because it was purposeful and not random. Goal-setting versus heuristics is not an either/or, but our familiarity with goal-setting so far exceeds our familiarity with heuristics that, generally, most of us could benefit from putting more attention on heuristics. Heuristic paths involve more organic and permeable parameters (yin), while the path of goal-setting has more rigid (yang) parameters. There is a time for each and a time for both—heuristic approaches and goal-setting are complimentary, not mutually exclusive.

Both approaches need to be held in dynamic equanimity with each other. However, we are so indoctrinated with beliefs in preplanned outcomes, it may behoove us to err on the yin side of trusting the heuristic urge more than we might think we should.

Heuristic endeavors are generally riskier in the short run. They are more likely to not only appear off track or to be headed nowhere, but they may well lead to what, on some levels, can only be construed as divergence or failure. It is an inherent danger on the heuristic path to lose sight of things and for the winds of change to scatter good intentions. That is just the deal—following heuristic urges can lead people down the proverbial rabbit hole. It can also lead to extraordinary heights. Sometimes it's only clear in far hindsight whether a heuristic path was productive or not.

In traditional work environments, the heuristic process can be squelched by yang-dominant norms. Too often, "nonlinear" is translated as "nonproductive," while getting trapped on the goals-only path can end up with goals being maintained at the expense of missing greater opportunities. When the dynamic tension between goal orientation and heuristics is not managed well, creativity and innovation can get disrupted and breakthrough discoveries can be missed. Our ontological framework of high valuation for yang-dominant goals and rules-driven pathways can mask the value of heuristic, yin-ward options.

With overemphasis on goal-setting, potential is sometimes truncated by the declaration of failure when a goal is not met. If potential is defined only by the limited parameters of a set goal, when something gets in the way of reaching that goal, it can be perceived as an end of a narrow, predetermined pathway. In an organizational ontology where goal-setting and rule following are the only "right" paths to success, false failures can be declared on the brink of true greatness. On a heuristic path, failure is understood as a resting place on a creative trajectory, a place to learn and develop from, a point of necessary change toward a more desirable outcome that could not be seen from the starting point. Heuristic approaches require infrastructures and measures for success that are more flexible, open-ended, and adaptable.

Alchemy entails having facility with causal principles such that rules and goals can be followed, amended, or transcended as needed with minimal drama and maximum gain. When there is equanimity between the yang of goal-setting and the yin of heuristics, as higher potential reveals itself, the path unfolds toward it.

Potential can be cut off by the perception of failure when valuation for predetermined paths overshadows valuation for heuristics. Potential can be compromised even in the face of reaching a goal when too narrow of a focus blinds us to revelations. Likewise with rule-setting. Like goals, rules can certainly be very helpful, but they can also limit innovation and impede relationship-building. There can never be a set of rules that can manage everything that comes up. Still, many organizations expect rule-setting to be a more comprehensive means for management than it actually is.

Predetermined paths and heuristics each have their merits and pitfalls. The heuristic path can lose focus and the predetermined path can lead to tunnel vision that restricts development. A healthy interplay between the two is like good electrical wiring for positive and negative charges. In the long run, when an organizational culture can maintain both its heuristic and its goal-centered footing, it has the creativity (yin) and the infrastructural strength (yang) for realizing full potential.

Alchemical leadership creates harmony between the get-it-done effectiveness of goals-driven systems and the heuristic means by which Oprah rose to success. Heuristic gains can sometimes be hard to measure by current standards, and the markers for heuristic paths can be subtle and easy to miss. Heuristic paths can be highly divergent from the norm; however, it is especially then that they lead to out-of-the-box great things.

Following a heuristic path requires tuning into a kind of inner knowing. There are plenty of resources available for effective path-mapping through goal-setting and reaching. But there is very little guidance on how to go where our inner voices lead us. In some ways, that's due to cultural biases. In other ways, the nature of the heuristic path can give us a sense of there being no guideposts until we practice it enough to have confidence in our inner guidance. Trusting that inner guidance is arguably the most important decision Oprah made on her journey to becoming one of the richest self-made women in the world.

A Different Kind of Data

Getting into the heuristic flow requires willingness to rely on intuitive input. Intuition provides us with a yin type of data that holds little to no valuation in yang-dominant systems, despite that pretty much everyone has had some experience of not knowing how they know something. Most of us experience our intuition on a spectrum somewhere between knowing the phone is going to ring or having an inkling to do something we couldn't have expected and finding out later that it was important, and the adeptness the yogi displayed on the top of the mountain.

There was a Counselor character in the TV series *Star Trek: The Next Generation*. She was a top-level, senior officer whose job was to advise in accordance with empathy, intuition, ethics, and compassion. She stood for the greatest good with no regard for politics. She represented the classic voice of wisdom, a timeless voice that permeates literature throughout all of history. Her moral authority made her a highly revered crew member within the closed system of a starship, where there is no escape valve for cultural toxicity and limited resources for restoking mojo once it's lost. The writers of the show recognized the need for a designated keeper of the culture who had high capacity for tuning into the intangibles. The culture valued her internal guidance in equanimity with the mechanical guidance offered by other officers. While her colleagues crunched numeric data, she relied on intuitive intelligence.

As an intuitive and empathic person, the *Star Trek* Counselor tapped into wavelengths that her cohorts were not as sensitive to. Yet they fully recognized and valued the power of the invisibilities that she accessed. She tapped into what we might think of as a voice of universal wisdom, an energetic flow of information that was not as readily available to the other characters.

Her job was to dive empathically into deeper truths that lay beneath the symptoms that the conflicted person or parties were reacting to. She also worked in a visionary capacity to see potentialities and to identify alignment/misalignment with positive future outcomes. She was able to move beyond her personal viewpoints and concerns to listen deeply for paths toward harmony and well-being. She had the capacity to instigate catharsis and epiphany, and to help people's mojo stay in alignment with each other and with Star Fleet success, where there was little margin for retrograde energy, or retro mojo. In effect, her job was Chief Mojo Officer.

Intuition

Jonas Salk, the inventor of vaccination science, said, "Intuition will tell the thinking mind where to look next." Just like the Global Positioning System (GPS) we use in our cars, we all have access to an inner GPS that offers invaluable intuitive guidance. Our inner guidance system is an information stream that functions like a metaphysical GPS—like a powerful data source that can be paid attention to or ignored. We all experience things like quiet voices in our heads, feelings, inklings, urges, gut sensations, dreams, visions, and other inner GPS signals. That's how we tap in to a kind of mysterious inner knowing that is intuition, a common metaphysical human trait. Our intuition gives us inner GPS data that can come through physical, spiritual, mental, and/or emotional channels. Even though it tends to be beneficial to self and others, few of us take the time to get still enough to track our internal GPS, and many have a hard time trusting the signals they receive.

Albert Einstein said, "The only real valuable thing is intuition." Oprah Winfrey, inventors, artists, politicians, and successful businesspeople all use intuition, some more consciously than others. Mothers are famous for their intuition! No matter how each one might conceptualize it, all are accessing an inner GPS guided by an inexplicable source that is not unlike the satellites that guide a mechanical GPS—always streaming and available for tuning in to. *The source of your inner GPS is operative 24/7.*

Some people have more proclivity toward tuning in than others, but everyone has access. While a mechanical GPS taps instantly into satellite transmissions when turned on, our inner one has a mysterious source to which accurate attunement needs to be honed over time. Personal homework, self-care, and yin time support that attunement.

According to Paula Underwood, the late oral history-keeper for the Iroquois tribe, during a mass relocation, her tribal ancestors witnessed highly developed intuition in a tribe they were migrating past. By communal deliberation, they agreed that it was a highly valuable trait to have, and they reached consensus on wanting to evolve tribal consciousness by seeding intuition into their own culture. Three squaws voluntarily agreed to immerse in the intuitive population and get pregnant. When all three confirmed their conditions, they gave the agreed-upon signal and their warriors raised a ruckus to get the women out with the seed of intuition consciously rooted in Iroquois culture. It was a radical, but effective, move toward breeding in propensity toward inner GPS acuity.

Star Trek: The Next Generation writers corroborated the valuable resource that the Iroquois recognized. The show's creators identified a leadership slot for aspects of consciousness that we know as empathy and intuition. Reality often follows science fiction. The writers were, in a sense, predicting that future generations would come to see higher value in intuition. The *Star Trek* Counselor character puts a face on a new impetus toward higher valuation for intuition, which is a yin factor that has been downplayed, even ridiculed, in yang-centric cultures. While its roles in innovation and decision-making are sometimes acknowledged, few organizations cultivate the personal and communal ground where intuition thrives and from which insight dawns.

No one would want a GPS in a car that only transmits north and south coordinates. Yet, by leaving intuition out of our deliberations, we have allowed pervasive yang dominance to limit the range of coordinates we use to determine our way forward. Carving out quality yin time will give you access to a larger range of internal coordinates because, even when yin time is not specifically focused on intuition, it can expand our inner beings such that intuition is more accessible.

Just like we have a choice as to whether or not we use our car's GPS, we have a choice as to whether or not we tune in to our inner GPS. Similar to how our car's GPS has to be tuned in to where the guidance is coming from, our role is to be receivers of our inner GPS signals. Our work is in managing our receptivity and in translating the data we receive. Buddhists teach that enlightenment is not something to strive for but rather something to wake up to. Likewise, just like there is no need to chase a GPS signal to access it in our cars, our intuitive guidance is something to expand into and turn on to, not chase after. Trying too hard can actually interfere with inner GPS receptivity and with accurate interpretation of inner GPS data.

Accessing intuition might take some radical personal and professional yin-ward swinging to counterbalance how drastically it has been devalued in the last several centuries. You can gain greater access to intuition through counseling, walks in nature, mentor or coach time, journaling, creative expression, self-reflection, prayer, and just taking time to "feel the love" or whatever makes you feel in the "zone." Everything from ten-minute walks to radical sabbaticals can improve the range and accuracy of your inner GPS.

Practice strengthens the intuitive "muscles" needed to access inner GPS data. Listen for the signals, feel for them, note them, speak about them, follow them, and they will get stronger. While there are no boundaries around the flow of intuition, insight, and mojo, that flow is influenced by place. The intuitive voice can be tougher to access at your desk than in the car, and harder to hear at the supermarket than when you are home alone. The ability to harness intuitive power at work requires sourcing that power outside of work by deliberately creating the time and aesthetics that are conducive to letting go and tuning in.

It is not uncommon for people who are more attuned to metaphysical data to be perceived as threatening by bosses and co-workers, whose more limited inner GPS access triggers fear-based reactions. Intuitives often find themselves being disparaged when, in actuality, they are bringing a very valuable A game to the table that is being overridden by people playing lesser hands—entropy. The trashing of intuitive data is a lose-lose scenario because not only does the alchemical adept lose his/her sense of coherence with the group, and therefore withhold mojo as well as intuitive information going forward, but the organization loses the advantage of the powerful asset of a well-tuned GPS. The cultural backlash further restricts development of that capacity in everyone—entropy all the way around.

Propensity

Some of us are naturally like the *Star Trek* Counselor in the sense of having greater than average propensity for tuning in to intuition. It is kind of like piano playing—not everyone who studies with the same teacher and practices the same amount of time will come out playing at the same level. Some people just have the propensity to be able to progress further faster.

Some have an innate sense of musicality that enables playing in ways that deeply touch listeners while others can play the exact same notes at the same speed and volume and not inspire anyone. Everyone can learn to play piano and some people just learn better than others because something in their personal makeup is more conducive to good piano playing. Likewise, there is greater and lesser propensity for tuning in to our internal guidance systems. But just like anyone can learn piano, anyone can tap in to inner GPS signals.

For those of us who do not have propensity for piano playing, we benefit when we hear those who do. Likewise, for those who have less propensity for tuning in to metaphysical information, there is great benefit to finding ways to work with those who have more. At the same time, just like recreational musicians with mediocre ability get personal benefit from playing instruments, despite having no great propensity for mastery, there is also tremendous benefit in practicing tuning in to your own intuitive voice, no matter how naturally it flows for you. And just like a mediocre piano player has a special understanding of the genius of great playing, working with your own internal GPS is a good way to recognize the validity of other people's. Not only does practice automatically make you more adept, but just like a recreational piano player has a unique appreciation for those who are masterful, attention to your own intuition will give you a better sense of who you can trust with interpreting metaphysical GPS coordinates for you and with you.

Valuation for the Intuitive Voice

While we do hold cultural value for great musical performances, we do not hold much valuation for the vision and insight that comes with intuition. Our devaluation of intuition compromises our access to a powerful information stream that exists for everybody and is especially strong for some. Quakerism is a good example of a culture that holds high valuation for the intuitive voice as evidenced by its heuristic approach to worship and to leadership. Quakers, who are Christians, usually have no minister because each member is invited to bring his/her own ministry to the community by nurturing and honoring "that of God within." They do not believe that a minister is necessary to mediate one's connection with that essential voice but rather that each person is responsible for presencing it for him- or herself and sharing it with others.

A Quaker service, called a "meeting for worship," is typically silent until a member of the congregation feels called to stand up and share something. The calling comes from an inner voice. Standing to deliver the message as it is coming through in the moment is pure heuristics. Many theistic, nontheistic, and atheistic belief systems tap in to the same internal guidance system that Quakers do, while the mystical paths within every spiritual tradition are dedicated to communion with our inner sources of deep knowing and timeless wisdom.

Quakers got their name because they traditionally experienced a sense of quaking in their bodies that signaled the call to a heuristic spiritual flow. An intuitive urge, or inner quaking, or mojo movement, causes someone to spontaneously stand and start speaking, and that is Quaker ministry. When no one is feeling the inner leading to share a message, the congregation sits in silent reflection. There is no problem if the entire hour of the meeting for worship is silent.

There are strong teachings against coming to a meeting for worship with a preplanned share or any kind of agenda about what people should hear or think. Elders will pull aside and have a serious chat with anyone who tends to speak from opinion/agenda rather than from present-moment, heuristic leadings. The difference is remarkably clear in Quaker meeting houses, where the inner voice has been held in the highest regard since the seventeenth century. Authentic leadings to speak somehow touch and inspire others in the meeting, while attempts at preplanned inspirational speaking ring hollow and tend to dampen the spiritual vibe.

Quakers practice silently waiting for, and setting aside everyday consciousness to make way for, the voice of inspiration. Worshipers trust that voice enough to stand and present it, much like mystical practices from most other faith traditions. Mystics, no matter what their religions, apprehend truths that lie beyond the intellect. Inner GPS signals come from the same place.

Quakerism is fully staked on that small voice that we gain facililty with every time we sit in silent expectation of connecting with it and every time we trust it enough to move or speak in accordance with it. For Quakers, just attending the meeting is demonstration of intention to connect with that mysterious source. They have a shared belief that each speaker is an instrument who brings wisdom forward in a way that will be valuable to the community. Hafiz, a twelfth-century Muslim mystic of the Sufi tradition, wrote about being the flute through which the metaphysical voice of divinity plays. The voice of intuition flows through us in much the same way that air flows through a wind instrument. Alchemical leaders attune their instruments to that flow, and if they recognize that they do not have great propensity for that attunement, they bring people who do into their inner circles.

Practicing Quakerism includes working on discerning the difference between the quality of voice that comes from earthly stuff and the quality of voice that is inspired by wisdom, a discernment that can be very tricky for those who are not practiced with the workings of inner knowing. Quakers, like all mystical aspirants, find strength in their weekly practice of tapping in to that source within, and in trusting what is brought forward through that mysterious voice whether it arises in self or others.

Whether you have religious or spiritual inclinations or not, it does not change the fact that the voice of wisdom is always available and that it is inherently resonant with truth. At some level, most, but not all, people know it when they hear it and they naturally align with it, except when fear blocks or scatters inner GPS signals.

Inner GPS Attunement

Inner GPS input comes from sub- and supra-logical sources that are invisible, mysterious, alluring, and unreasonably compelling. How well you capitalize on that input is determined by personal equanimity, by the quality of your attunement with your inner guidance, and by your ability to discern what to do with the information. Even if intuitive information is coming from someone with greater propensity than your own, tuning in to your internal GPS is still important in discerning whether that information is valid and what to do with it. Accessing your personal inner GPS always exposes a fuller range of options because it engages unique neurological and energetic pathways for problem-solving, negotiating, enrolling, and innovating.

Howard Behar, who took Starbucks international under his presidency, told me he hears seven distinct inner voices during a chat I had with him as part of my podcast series, *Masters of Profiting on Principles*. Howard named each voice and knows each one intimately as discrete personalities inside his head. More importantly, he holds high value for each of their unique perspectives, and calls on specific voices for specific types of input. He credits those voices with being an important factor in his success. Behar sought counsel with his voices as a means for accessing coordinates on Starbucks' map for the way forward.

The feeling of inner GPS attunement is deeply personal and unique for each of us. You can consciously attune your inner knowing mechanism, your inner GPS, by engaging with it like Behar consciously engages with his voices or like Quakers do by sitting in receptive expectation of it. Rather than words or personalities, your GPS mechanisms might include a variety of sensory and extrasensory sensations like dreamlike images, internal nudges, shivers, a sense of just knowing.... Your body can be a highly accurate GPS indicator when you pay attention to physiological sensations like tensing of your shoulders, a flip in the gut, a skip of the heart, tingling ears, a posture shift, itchy nose, emotional triggers, chills, mental images, a wave up your spine, a sense of serenity.... Notice how inner GPS information lands in you, because its subtle cues are highly accurate compass points for decision-making.

Get to know your personal GPS by noticing your inklings, the small-voiced inner truth-tellings that, when you first start paying attention to them, may only come clear after the fact. It is a lot like speaking in a new language where first you remember the right word hours later when you're lying in bed. If you keep speaking the language, the right words start coming sooner than later until they are just there when you need them. Likewise, the more you trust the expression of your inner GPS by acting and speaking in accordance with it, the more adept you will get at attuning to it.

Even though our inner GPS tends to reveal profoundly simple information, it does not always, maybe even doesn't usually, lead us onto the easiest paths. But it does tend to lead to fertile ground because our inner GPS never leads us to petty obstacles, but rather to clarity about exactly what needs surmounting and how. Along with making the time and space for tuning in to your inner GPS, it is well worth the effort to seek out people who may have an easier time tapping in to their intuition and/or who respect the data that comes from it.

Communities and organizations that are led by people who have a well-honed inner GPS tend to come out on the right side of history. That's because inner GPSs are partly moral compasses and so values are critical coordinates in the system. People who are service-oriented often enjoy a kind of ease in accessing and following their internal GPS, although it is unclear whether those geared toward service naturally have more propensity for accessing that inner guidance, or whether the ability to tune in more deeply to it leads people to serve.

Either way, Quakers are a great example of how inner GPSs lead to greater good because they are notorious for taking highly effective social justice actions that are in accordance with what they feel called to do or say. In other words, they walk their talk. It is not impossible for unethical, self-serving people to tune in to inner GPS guidance, it is just more rare. And more dangerous, because when such a powerful tool is applied to no good, bad things happen. In some kind of universal justice, though, it appears that those who use metaphysical guidance toward illicit ends tend to fall harder when they crash, which they inevitably do, because time wounds all heels and arrogance shatters like glass. The mechanism of our deepest inner knowing, our internal GPS, seems to prioritize coordinates for greatest good.

Tuning in to your inner GPS is the act of aligning with the formidable energy source that de Chardin called the rediscovery of fire, the source that makes Quakers quake and that provides highly reliable metaphysical data. The old computer term GIGO (Garbage In, Garbage Out) applies here. In the computer world, it means that if you put junk code in, you will get junk content out. In terms of inner GPS, if you have not cleared your inner circuits from the mental and emotional garbage we often carry around as part of our human journeys, the data you move forward on cannot be as reliable. Quality personal homework yields quality inner GPS data.

Our inner GPS urges us to check something out even when it does not make sense, to decide to say yes when all indicators say no or vice versa, or to take a risk despite the lack of good reasoning behind it. It is often only in retrospect that inner-GPS-based choices can be called wise, but part of how you know that you are truly tuned in is that, even when it makes no logical sense, there is a quality about that internal signal, a felt perception, that is undeniably compelling and unmistakably clear. The more you listen for it and act on it, the clearer it gets.

Wisdom's Whispers

Paula Underwood, the Iroquois oral history-holder, told me that, because they spoke so many different languages, Native Americans used to use a simple sign language among tribes so that they could trade and learn from one another.

She said that their limited universal language included a sign for wisdom. That they felt they needed to have a shared sign for wisdom demonstrates the high valuation that indigenous cultures typically hold for it. The sign she taught me was to put one hand to head and the other hand to heart and then bring them together, signifying a distinct intelligence that is made up of equanimity between heart and mind. Wisdom is where we bring inner GPS information together with our best knowledge.

Leaders often feel like they are running on empty as they function in a yang-dominant ontology that values mind development (yang) but has minimal valuation for cultivation of heart (yin). One result of that is that seemingly smart decisions often do not end up being wise. And wise eats smart for breakfast! For many leaders, traveling on the wisdom path does not feel like walking but more like whopping big leaping.

Intelligence and knowledge are two different things: having metaphysical command of information is not the same as knowing stuff. Wisdom includes intelligence, but it is much more than that because it also accesses information from sources that lie beyond intellect. Wisdom is situated more deeply in our bodies, minds, and spirits than intelligence and understanding are. Wisdom is an ever-evolving state of consciousness. It comes with time and experience, but it can also come in a flash or from the mouth of a child. Alchemical leaders cultivate the wisdom to comprehend and apply knowledge, and to bring it together with values, in ways that move hearts, minds, hands, and feet. *When the well of wisdom is tapped, power is sourced.*

Accessing wisdom comes not with working extra hard to hear it, but with relaxing into its subtleties. As disorienting and disempowering as it may seem, letting go of knowingness is the key to accurately attuning to the wisdom voice. Releasing what you think you know, no matter how good the evidence is for your knowledge, takes you to that beginner's-mind consciousness where wisdom's whispers can be fully heard. It is just like when someone is whispering in your ear. If it's happening in a noisy place, it is hard to hear. If it's happening in a settled atmosphere, it is audible. Dedicated reflection and/or meditation time helps you discern that "still, small voice" that is often whispering truth just below our proverbial radars.

The domain of wisdom can be tricky to navigate because when we get too attached to wanting it, we can push it away and because its individual components of heart and mind can seem contradictory at times. Our cultural conditioning tempts us to go with the mind every time while self-help teachers are telling us we should always go with the heart. Wisdom is where heart (yin) and mind (yang) sync up into a formidable power source. If and when we let the syncing happen. That is what makes this domain so tricky—the work is not in trying, it is in allowing.

Accessing wisdom requires allowing lots of leeway for not knowing, for the action of no action, and for the choice to not choose, because sometimes a void is the utmost fertile ground for the seeds of wisdom. It is not always apparent how the yang dots of logic connect with the yin dots of creativity and intuition. Alchemical leadership requires taking the time and making the space to find the wisdom that sits at the connecting points of those dots.

It is not always easy to stake ground for wisdom in systems that dismiss it as being too abstract, esoteric, fluffy, and woo-woo to matter. But history is quite clear that wisdom is an access route to ultimate power, and it is an absolute necessity for using power well. While unwise ones have undoubtedly won many battles, it is only the wise who are powerful enough to transcend battling.

The phenomenon of wisdom runs so deep and so steady that it provides a sort of anchoring for heuristic expression. The problem is that we have devaluated the voice of wisdom so much that the absence of it is rarely seen for the impediment that it is. But alchemical leaders recognize that *mojo flows as wisdom goes!* Wisdom can be accessed anywhere and at any time. However, it can't necessarily be cultivated that way. There is great advantage in building the aesthetics, the vibes, the time, the space, and the presence it takes for wisdom to flourish because wisdom is power.

No wise figure from history ever walked a predictable path. Likewise, the career trajectory for alchemical leadership often includes more uncertainty than the traditional leadership ladder does. The concept of risk sits in an entirely different conceptual framework when wisdom is cultivated and relied on as the touchstone for leadership. Wisdom makes the difference between foolish risks that fail and failed risks that lead to brilliant next steps.

When you let go into the present, into allowing heart and mind to guide in equanimity with each other, it may not always take you where you thought you were going, but it will always lead you to your wisest choices.

The Role of Wisdom in Organizations

The Counselor was a regular on the show because the *Star Trek* culture inherently valued the voice of wisdom in decision-making and advising, as well as in culture-building and peacekeeping. There are problems on the show that only she can solve because she is the only one who accesses the invisible drivers of behaviors, like emotions, needs, desires, hidden motives, values, and energetics. She alone was able to foster solutions that lay beyond the rights and wrongs of he-said-she-said and beyond hierarchies, Star Fleet rules, and social norms.

She was clearly very smart, but her counsel was more than intellectual, it was more empathic than psychological, more strategical than practical. Her input led to ending struggle and averting danger. It came in the form of intuitive insight, ethical reasoning, and connecting the dots between personal development, organizational well-being, and galactic harmony. In their leadership infrastructure, her wisdom held equanimous value with the more fact-based input of her colleagues. Her character provides a good role model for helping to distinguish metaphysical leadership strengths.

Collective Wisdom

Quakers rely on consensus-building as their decision-making process. Consensus is a shared sense of alignment. Quakers align around a shared sense of resonance with the wisdom voice they regularly practice tuning in to and trusting. Their belief in direct connection with divine wisdom, along with their continual exercise of their discernment "muscles," produce stable, almost corruption-free communities whose members have been, and continue to be, world leaders in social and environmental justice. The power of consensus-building around inner GPS wisdom knows no bounds.

Traditionally, many indigenous tribes have sought consensus by convening wisdom circles that deliberate on the greatest good for the whole tribe. The participants around the circle, which is often convened around a fire and/or altar, are chosen such that all are represented, including elders and youth, warriors, those who stand for animals and nature, tribal leaders, those who have vision, and those who caution. The healers and spiritual leaders around the circle sometimes go into prayer, ritual, and/or trance to facilitate sacred insight into the community's present concerns and to help discern their trajectory into the future.

Wisdom circles tend to stick with the process for however long it takes to come to consensus on the underlying wisdom of the situation they are deliberating about. One very big difference between the indigenous mind and Western thinking is how we perceive time. Our understanding of time is much more linear and finite than theirs is and it holds much more importance to us, and so when they are working things out, they don't stress about the amount of time it takes. They focus on coming to a clear and settled sense of consensus because they know that *if the quality of their deliberations is good, the outcome will be sound.*

Similar to Quakers, indigenous circles take no movement until there is aligned clarity, no matter how long it takes. In fact, the Quakers learned about consensus-building from the Native American tribes they encountered when they settled in America in search of religious freedom. The persecution they were fleeing from is a good example of how yang-itis can affect our inner GPS. The Church of England was extremely hierarchical and patriarchal and, as such, had no tolerance for individuals connecting directly with the divine because that connection was being used as a means of control that was only entrusted to church hierarchy.

Quakers were persecuted for their attunement and so they came to America to freely tap in to the mysterious source they still value so highly. The "good news" proclaimed by Jesus in the Bible was that we each have access to the same source that

He did, an idea that Quakers take very literally. Jesus' news was considered so dangerously radical that he had to be crucified. This stuff is subtle, but the impact is huge.

Yoda from *Star Wars* is another fictitious example of the link between wisdom and mojo. Yoda has a remarkable consciousness that is reflected in his deep, unwavering wisdom and unquestionable ethics. His extraordinary consciousness (big yin) is complimented by his formidable physical and mental powers (big yang). Just like yogis who accomplish the inner power to manifest unexpected outward results, and just like the Counselor who developed her inner wisdom as a means of providing transformative leadership, and just like Jedi warriors who dedicate their lives to positive expression of source energy, alchemical leaders develop a metaphysical rigor with the energy that starts at the center of our beings and extends infinitely beyond our bodies. That rigor avails you to wisdom that is always already there but not always apparent.

Because the intuitive voice typically does not have a meaningful place in our processes and procedures, those who have propensity for tapping in to the intuitive field are often left out of deliberations entirely. The Jedi and *Star Trek* characters exemplify recent cultural trends toward higher valuation for intuitive guidance and for its role in holding the high watch for best outcomes. The voice of wisdom has everything to do with the health of organizational cultures, and it is worth dedicating time and attention to bringing it forward.

Leadership Reflections

1. It is hard to fuel a great culture when your own spark is dwindling. Cut some of your doing time this week to free up the being who may not have been given due diligence. Do three things that spark your heart and soul, creative or inspiring things like playing music, getting out in nature, going to a religious or spiritual gathering, reading or writing poetry, dusting off art supplies.... The intention is not to accomplish, it is to nourish internal sparks.

2. On a scale of 1–10, with 1 being oblivious to subtle signals and 10 being highly psychic, rate yourself on your own intuition. Your current intuition rating does not necessarily reflect your actual capacity to intuit. What needs to change and/or happen for you to better pick up on your inner GPS signals?

3. Exercise for inner GPS development: For a couple of weeks, take mental, audio, and/or written notes of inklings, sensations, dreams, premonitions, and/or urges that come from within. Note all that comes up, especially what you are not sure about, and see what happens. Before you to go to sleep, take a few moments to explore the links between intuitive urges felt earlier in the day or week and a subsequent event. Note how it feels in your body and psyche. Start trusting your intuition by playing with being more heuristic in your speaking and in your choices. Wrestle with your intuition—allow and challenge it. Give it voice and give it value.

4. Consider meditating. Meditation creates access to intuition. A relatively small amount of sitting time can give rise to greater attunement to inner GPS signals. Not only do meditators "get the picture" faster than their contemporaries, they make more sound decisions, especially in difficult circumstances, are more resilient to burnout, and are more likely to have the personal capacity for building fertile cultures around themselves. Simple meditation: Sit in a safe and quiet place and make sure you will be undisturbed. Set a timer for ten minutes. Focus on your breath. When you lose that focus, bring it back. Add more time when ten minutes feels easy and look around for other meditation methods that feel right for you.

5. Look back on struggles you have had in the last few days and ask, "What would wisdom do?" The wisdom path typically follows the trail of values. Search for values words and then translate those words into wise action or into the wisdom not to act.

PART THREE

THE BIG PICTURE

CHAPTER 9

WHO ARE WE?

A Deeper Cut

Self-awareness is an important component in the practice of alchemy, but in and of itself, it's not enough. It needs to be contextualized in a more comprehensive inquiry into what it means to be human. While contemplation of one's own self and one's own context is important for accessing metaphysicalities, the realm of causality is much bigger than a person and his/her culture. Capacity for alchemy is commensurate with developing your consciousness of deeper ontological frameworks within which your tasks and responsibilities occur.

Beyond self, and beyond culture, lies the very essence of the human experience. Working from that level is what "magically" produces results "out of thin air." Three metaphysical factors to consider are:

1. That we are all interdependent with one another and with everything else on the planet.
2. That the deeper we go within ourselves, the more we realize that the concept of "self" is less personal and more universal than we can ever fully know.
3. While the devil might be in the details, the angels are in the ethers. Polls overwhelmingly show that most people believe in, and actively seek to connect with, consciousness that lies beyond our own. According to Pew research, about 75 percent of us petition the metaphysical realm, usually in the form of prayer to angels and deities, daily to request influence on our personal situations.

No matter what their personal beliefs might be, alchemical leaders must factor in that:

- there is an interwoven fabric of humanity
- we are much more than we know
- there are sources of consciousness that can be tuned in to, tapped in to, and turned on in such a way as to influence outcomes
- as physical beings, we exist at the frontier of nonphysical power sources.

Interdependence

The quantum physics principle, "If a butterfly flaps its wings in Hong Kong, there will be an effect in New York," is a way of saying that, beyond the shadow of a doubt, every action taken everywhere impacts everything on the planet. Life is essentially an interdependent co-arising—no being and no species would be the same if it were not for all others. This is a critical understanding for leaders because it is too easy to look at one person or one aspect of a struggling system and scapegoat that person or process as a lone culprit. But that kind of reductionist thinking leads to a whack-a-mole style of leadership wherein symptoms get chased while systems decline.

Alchemical capacity comes from the vantage point of seeing both the interdependencies inherent in your systems and the inherent interdependency of your system with the greater whole. Despite yang-dominant, dog-eat-dog cultural norms, cultural historians like Riane Eisler, evolutionary biologists like Elisabet Sahtouris, and many others have confirmed that the web of life is interwoven such that partnership always works better than competition. Rather than "survival of the fittest," a more accurate statement is, "survival of the cooperators." Because the most common factor for human happiness is connectedness, and, because we know that team coherence leads to better outcomes, we know that we are better off cooperating than competing. The old adage, "All for one and one for all," has faded in Western thinking, but leaders would be well served to revive it by building partnership-based systems.

We tend to think of partnership as a type of deal-making, but it is a much bigger word than that. Partnership does not just mean collaboration, it also implies deeper metaphysical connections, like dedication to a shared sense of unity and purpose. From the biochemical bath that is released by our brains and that cascades through our bodies when we connect positively with other people, to the neurological synapses (brain firings) that are triggered by interconnectivity, to the mental, emotional, and social strengthening that happens when people come together with common purpose, the data is unequivocal regarding bottom line impact: *"we" beats "me" every time.* Alchemy requires facility with the metaphysics of "we."

No matter what we consciously focus on, we are always functioning as an integral part of a world that changes with the flap of a butterfly's wings—and even more so with the flapping of mouths. Cooperation-based, values-driven systems build on the reality that we are an interdependently co-arising species among species, which is far more solid ground than the outmoded idea that domination is the path to success. The quality of your leadership depends on the skill with which you ride the inevitable ebbs and flows of that interdependency.

Domination-based, competition-oriented, hierarchical systems work in opposition to our natural inclination toward, and life-sustaining need for, cooperating with one another. Partnership-oriented systems capitalize on the natural human instinct to seek connectedness and on the complementarity that happens when diverse people cooperate. Connectedness and complementarity are mojo multipliers, while entropy results when mojo is drained by acts of domination because the people who are being dominated are highly likely to withhold mojo going forward and spending personal mojo on dominating other people yields low return mojo investment. *While we call domination-oriented leaders "big shots," there is no longer any question that they play a very small game.*

Ubuntu

Alchemical leaders recognize, accurately valuate, and effectively capitalize on humanity's inherent interconnectedness. The African Zulu tribe's philosophy of *ubuntu* is a good exemplar. It means that a person is a person only through other people. The translation of *ubuntu* is: *I am because we are.*

Ubuntu is the recognition that the happiness and well-being of any individual is inextricably linked with the happiness and well-being of the whole community. This story is thought by some to be how the West discovered *ubuntu*:

An anthropologist played an experimental game with Zulu children. He put a basket of sweets near a tree, placed the children about twenty feet away from the tree, and then announced that whoever got to the basket first would get all the sweets. After he gave the signal to go, he was surprised to watch all the children take hold of each other's shoulders, elbows, or hands before they ran together toward the tree. They arrived at the basket as one single group, divided the sweets equally among themselves, and sat down to enjoy them together. When they finished their treats, the anthropologist asked them why they didn't race against each other to get more for themselves. They answered, "*Ubuntu*," and then asked, "How can one be happy when the others are sad?" The Zulu ontology within which the children lived their lives simply did not accommodate greed. It was not an option because it just did not fit in with their version of reality, their paradigm.

In tribal settings, just like on a starship, small isolated groups live in such conspicuous interdependency that it is more immediately obvious to everyone that the well-being of each equates to higher survival rates and better quality of life for all. In such small, interwoven communities, no one is invisible or expendable and individual contribution, or lack of it, is felt by all. Indigenous people are acutely aware of the strand that each community member is in the weave of their culture. A remarkable similarity between indigenous cultures I embedded with in the African bush in Malawi, and in the Amazon Jungle in Ecuador, and among North American indigenous teachers that I've learned from, is that people are not judged or ridiculed for what they are not. Rather, there was an unspoken dignity of personhood that was assumed for one and all. The judgmentalism that I have experienced as rampant in our culture did not appear to be present in theirs.

From the bush to the jungle to the boardroom, it is clear that individuals and groups thrive when cultures are developed such that positive human values apply to everyone without discrimination. In the Shuar culture, from a very young age, every member understands his/her value in the interdependent weave that keeps the tribe alive. That is largely how they have remained resilient in the face of corporate invasions that have created horrific human rights and environmental violations in their territory.

Indigenous wisdom has always recognized that all of life, from the spiritual to the bacterial and everything in between, is part of our interdependent weave. That is a more common perspective for people who live close to the land. But most of us live in more complicated cultures where it is much harder to feel our sense of place in the universal weave. Nowhere is that more evident than in workplaces where, even though we now know it is counterproductive, there is still a common ethic for moving up by getting over on the next dude before s/he gets over on me.

Ubuntu encapsulates how the scope of "we," versus the myopia of "me," leads to sustainable success. We know that when co-workers are not clawing to get ahead of everyone else, when dignity prevails, and when they link their figurative arms such that they become a coherent unit, goals are better reached, there is more fertile ground for innovation, and greater profits are gained. (see Barrett) For the Zulu, *ubuntu* is baked into the culture—it is their ontological reality. For a twenty-first-century Western leader, who has been acculturated with beliefs that competition and domination are not just the way to the top but also the key to survival, building *ubuntu*-style ethics into the culture is not such an obvious part of the job.

Nobody ever gets to the top alone. But research is crystal clear that reaching the top by using the backs of other people as a means to get there is not a great strategy. In fact, it is a good way to stay stuck and/or to regress because backs can and do break. It is also an invitation for backlash, which can be a career crusher. And getting ahead by hurting others is a good way to get sick because, somewhere deep inside, everyone's body knows when it is being compromised by the expression of negative values, because the brain unleashes an unhealthy cascade of chemicals. In other words, somewhere deep inside, we all know when we are being jerks and, however conscious or unconscious we are about it, being a jerk degrades us on many levels.

Competition and Cooperation

Competition is a more yang dynamic, cooperation is more yin. We need yang as much as we need yin. Competition has its place. It can be a productive mojo mover. Healthy competition makes great sports experiences and is often a meaningful motivator, albeit a motivator that can easily backfire when it is not tempered by other values and when it is relied on too heavily as a modus operandi. An *ubuntu* approach is a yin dynamic. It has its place. We need yin as much as we need yang. *Ubuntu*-oriented consciousness is the ontological basis for win-win solutions. If competitive consciousness prevails, it means people are functioning within a win-lose ontological framework. When the way of being of an organization inherently makes people feel like losers on a regular basis, mojo naturally bleeds out as entropy.

Cooperation is a mojo multiplier. There are times to stir up mojo through competition. And there are times to multiply our mojo by investing it in cooperation. While there are undeniably times to compete and times to cooperate, the odds will fall in your favor if, when you hit a crossroad, you choose the path of cooperation. Ultimate outcomes are far better when people hold power with, not over, others. Cooperation beats domination in terms of results, even though it often takes longer and entails more chaotic processes. It can be challenging to get cooperative practices established because they differ so much from the dictates of the yang-dominant cultural ontology we are all steeped in.

Changing Dreams

Indigenous wisdom from all over the world is consistent in its recognition of the interdependency of the web of life. The Shuar invited outsiders like me in because they say it is the dreams of those of us in the Northern Hemisphere, particularly in the West, that are causing their suffering these days. Corporate encroachment, mostly for the sake of grazing cattle for fast food and tapping oil for Northern Hemisphere lifestyles, threatens them far more than losing warriors' heads to neighboring tribes ever did. They face devastation because people like me dream about bigger houses, unsustainable diets, faster cars, and more and more and more stuff, with little regard for how our dreams impact the rest of the planetary weave. And often, even those who are very conscious of making undue impact do not feel like we can do much about it because it is hard to see options that lie beyond our own ontological reality. Even though they had far less exposure to the rest of the world, the Shuar seemed to have a greater awareness of their place in it than I did.

The Shuar invited us into their world because they believed that, by immersing in their culture, we would gain the wisdom to start changing our highly consumptive dreams. They see that the things we want are driving the death and destruction that is collapsing their habitat and threatening their immediate existence while threatening our own survival in the long term. In their ontological framework, where interdependence is such a central factor, they believe that those whose choices would cause such physical suffering must necessarily be spiritually suffering themselves. For evidence, the tribal members who had traveled and been educated in other places cited our high noncommunicative disease and stress rates, our environmental degradation, our high capitalization of war and gun violence, our infant mortality rates, as well as incarceration rates of minors and adults. Because their survival depends on Westerners making different choices, and because their understanding of global interdependency was so deep, they felt that our healing was as important as their own. The Shuar felt that by experiencing their habitat, harmony, prayers, and rituals, we might change our dreams such that what we want doesn't keep destroying their habitat and endangering ourselves.

Their invitation to change our dreams was offered in the spirit of compassion for those of us who practice what they see as barbaric warfare, who feel disconnected from other people and from their own spirits, and who have been unable to commit to our own survival. The Shuar enticement to change my dreams helped me see how junk piles up as people sink down. Their "primitive" tribal wisdom is not so different from highly advanced cultures like Finland, Holland, Sweden, and

Japan, who share underlying values that not only produce robust economies and strong cultures, but also the world's most well and happy populations. Staying with the Shuar helped me understand why cultures that place high economic and social value on junky behaviors and trash-destined stuff are at higher risk than those that hold higher valuation for happiness, well-being, interconnectivity, and nature.

But there was something even more important that the Shuar wanted to impart. They also wanted us to have a direct experience of that spark of life, the *arutum* or mojo, that feels super present and accessible within the primal pulse of the jungle. Families invited us to meals and to sleep with them on the dirt floors of their thatched huts where there was much laughter, song, and dance, and where the log fire in the center of it was never allowed to go out. Shamans invited us to ancient ceremonies that celebrate our oneness with one another, with the rest of the planet, and with that primordial spark of life that animates it all. They wanted to help us heal by evoking our sense of place in the universal web of life. They knew that when we stepped into their primeval world, there would be no escaping the consciousness of our interdependency with the rest of the planet, and with the spark of life that is that which can never be adequately named.

Archetypes

The human spirit expresses through the particularity of each and every individual. At the same time, the human spirit is something that is universal because it transcends the individual experience. Archetypes are a means for identifying common expressions of the human spirit. An archetype embodies a collection of characteristics, for example, those of a typical caregiver, explorer, rebel, or lover. A cultural archetype is a model that is made up of the collective traits that the culture thinks a "normal" person should have.

Archetypal stories offer clues for how we can become who we want to be. They also serve as moorings, as common anchors that give us a sense of constancy of the human spirit. Over time, some archetypal norms have transcended cultural and historical boundaries to become more universal archetypes that embody quintessential human traits. Archetypes help us access our inner architecture. Universal archetypes get at who we are at our core and they function as prototypes for who we aspire to be.

The most common archetypes are heroes and villains who define what the culture considers good and what it considers bad. Interpretations of archetypes vary tremendously between different cultures. For example, in some cultures, someone is a hero if he kills his daughter for having sex out of wedlock. She is considered the villain, even if she was raped. Such an extreme yang cultural heroic archetype does not square with the universal hero archetype because universal archetypes tend to typify our most evolved ideals, like unconditional compassion and justice.

Universal archetypes are a way to identify idealized aspects of ourselves, and they help illuminate pathways for transcending our limitations. They provide models that serve as a backdrop for each generation to reinterpret. Reinterpretation of what it means to be a hero, for example, in matters like femicide, is how we evolve. As human beings, we cause things to happen all day, every day. Archetypes provide metaphysical and ontological insight into who causes what. The warrior, the noble person, and the hero are three universal archetypes of success.

The Warrior Archetype

The Samurai, who started cohering as a group in the 900s and were preeminent in Japanese culture between the 1600s and 1800s, exemplify a universal warrior archetype and provide insight into the differences between cultural and universal archetypes. The Samurai are a good illustration of the skills, mindset, wants, and needs of universal warrior consciousness. Whereas modern warrior archetypes tend to be defined more in terms of violence, the Samurai were expected to be exceptionally well-rounded, clear minded, and ethical public servants.

In all cultural interpretations of the warrior archetype, s/he is entrusted with high-level life and death decision-making. The Samurai version of the warrior archetype was heavily influenced by Buddhism and by Taoist teachings about yin and yang, and it characterizes warriors as masters of any given moment. While Samurai infamy has to do with the fact that they were fierce combatants, their success was also measured by how much they did not have to fight and violent digressions assured they would never advance in rank.

Unlike modern soldier prototypes that portray super yang-dominant attributes like toughness, lethality, and high capacity for violence, Samurais held high valuation for personal equanimity. They cultivated gentler yin practices along with their yang fight training. A Samurai was expected to master as many as possible of the Sixty-Four Arts, with only a handful of those being martial arts. Their warrior training routines included the arts of calligraphy, tea ceremony, poetry, meditation, and esoteric lovemaking. They trained in cultural arts like civility, discourse, and meting out justice. They are among the most ferocious warriors in human history and yet, at the same time, they prioritized engaging in arts like music, dancing, and painting.

Gambling was an especially interesting one of the Sixty-Four Arts that the Samurai were supposed to master. The philosophy behind including it was for the practice of maintaining equanimity while having a personal stake in an unknown outcome. Gambling was a way of reckoning with attachment issues. It enabled them to practice letting go into the unknown and accepting the outcome in full warrior consciousness, unshaken, and as ready to roll the next dice as they were to roll into battle. They believed that trusting their fate so completely as to be able to put their fortune on the line, and lose it but not lose composure, or win and not lose purpose, was good training for the presence they needed to have in tough situations. It is also possible that they used gambling as a way of practicing intuition.

Gambling is a good lens for looking at the ontological ground on which behaviors happen. In their cultural context, the Samurai used gambling as a way of developing qualities of consciousness like faith in the future, precognition, discernment, non-attachment, and inner strength. We use gambling today as an entertaining escape that's often sought to the point of addiction. Although gambling is gambling, the difference between the experience of a Samurai and that of an addict is pretty stark. That difference is warrior consciousness.

Wounded Warriorship

By cultivating the full spectrum of their own humanity, the Samurai knew they would be more equanimous in their presence—that is, able to face the world with inner fortitude and outer confidence. Arts for armies may seem preposterous to

us, but the valuation that the Samurai held for self-actualiza-
tion is a key to the universal warrior archetype. Compared to
Samurai times, there has been a yang-ward ontological shift in
what it means to be a warrior.

Over time, the warrior archetype has shifted away from the
equanimous Samurai model of a highly developed, full-spectrum human being, and toward a model wherein ever-esca-
lating yang is understood as the path to winning. But the
universal warrior archetype first does no harm and, if harm
needs to happen, it is done with discernment and respect for
life such that there is no such thing as collateral damage. The
modern warrior prototype is based on individualistic identity,
as opposed to the universal warrior archetype who identifies more communally. The plight of today's warrior is often
myopic in its notions of what constitutes a win, as evidenced
by the millions of veterans who fight battles they struggle to
understand and then return home to find themselves hurting
so much that they are unable to live in peace and well-being in
their own communities. The plight of traumatized American
veterans who have inadequate access to the services they need
to become whole again is a particularly wretched symptom of
yang-itis. The more equanimous style of the universal warrior
archetype depicts a kind of well-being that is carried through,
on and off the battlefield.

An extremely yin approach to establishing equanimity in
warriorship was practiced in ancient Crete, a matriarchal culture. When men came back from battle, they reentered the
community through a temple and they stayed there until their
bodies and spirits were whole again. Along with medicinal
and nutritional attention, they were given the spiritual space
to heal from the horrors of battle. The temple had different
kinds of healing and spiritual practitioners including sacred

prostitutes who lovingly served to help traumatized fighters heal the pain of post-traumatic stress, regain their equanimity with the excess yang that is a natural part of warfare, and restore any lost aspects of the universal archetypal warrior. The ontology of Crete society was such that sexual healing was not contextualized as adultery or promiscuity. Wives would likely have been grateful that husbands were fully prepared to reenter the marriage bed as restored men who were over the worst of their nightmares and fully reoriented from fighting to loving, and communities happy that strong and whole citizens were returning ready, willing, and able to move forward. (see Eisler)

Just like gambling was something else entirely for the Samurai than it would be for a modern-day soldier, lovemaking, in this case, was used as a sacred healing modality that could help restore the warrior such that he could most easily retake his place in civil society. The practice exemplifies a kind of wisdom that many ancient cultures had about the importance of people feeling whole. Sexual healing was just one of many modalities the temple offered so that warriors could transition in a way that gave them, their families, and the community confidence that they would reenter their lives without bringing the inevitable wounds of battle with them. Pretty remarkable valuation for yin-ing out!

While sacred prostitution is a misfit for our ontological reality, it is an interesting example of ancient understanding of the need for establishing equanimity, especially after extreme experiences. More and more companies are recognizing that, just like the universal warrior archetype, the more holistically a leader (and everyone else) develops him/herself, the more likely s/he is to succeed. The universal warrior archetype provides insight into leadership by way of how it connects the metaphysics of being-ness with the responsibility for getting hard things done. It offers clues for alleviating the chronic yang-itis that drives the day-in, day-out grind of systems that obfuscate our most powerful drivers. *The universal warrior archetype depicts full personhood as a critical aspect of power that requires time and attention to cultivate.*

The warrior archetype also helps demonstrate how, when an organizational culture supports power mongering, that is, when odious, unchecked yang manifestations of power are the norm, that culture is more vulnerable. On the other hand, when they have Samurai-like discernment in their capacity for managing both the yin and the yang, our defenders are far less likely to become offenders.

Both the warrior and nobleman/woman archetypes are in service to strong communities of happy and well stakeholders living together peacefully. Both noble and warrior archetypes are powerful in their discernment of when to build on what's so (yang) and when to destroy what isn't working (yin).

The Noble Archetype

The meaning of "noble" has been bastardized such that it has come to denote excess and dominance. But long before nobility meant gluttony, it was understood as compassionate and just leadership. Before it was distorted by modern ontologies, the noble archetype was understood as a wise being who walks as easily with peasants as with kings, and whose dedication to being a good leader cannot be changed by fame, fortune, or lack thereof. Universally archetypal nobles combined yin inclinations toward compassion and justice, with the yang power to lead and protect citizens. Like warriors, they were expected to swing yin-ward or yang-ward, a little or a lot, depending on what was best for the most people—just like alchemical leaders.

Nobility and royalty have come to mean excessiveness, power-mongering, posturing, conspicuous consumption, and hoarding. By definition, though, nobility really means having excellent morals and taking principled action. Nobility, in the sense of being ethical and wise, is one of the most time-honored human aspirations and, at the same time, a common birthright for all. It is a prerequisite for alchemical leadership.

Long ago, noble lineages were traditionally thought of as God's direct messengers or descendants on earth and, as such, were assumed to have a metaphysical, god-like adeptness for consciously causing things to happen. Some cultures relegated nobility to the work of a vengeful God while others understood their nobles to represent a God of Greatest Good who would never violate the human spirit. True nobility is benevolent, that is, noble people are expected to make choices and take actions with the intention of benefiting all. The archetypal noble person resolves situations in accordance with their best understanding of creating the greatest good in the present moment and for generations to come.

Native American traditions provide a great example of nobility in how they consider the impact of a particular decision on the seventh generation ahead. The noble archetype concerns him- or herself with being a better and better servant, with supporting their constituents in continually upgrading their lots in life, and with ensuring that the world is a better place for those yet to be born.

"Noble" is also a concept in the field of chemistry where a noble state of being means that elements and gases are non-reactive, or stable. The principle of stability applies to the archetype for nobility in that true nobility is un-corruptible.

It is also nonreactive, and so more ably responsive. When a chemical is noble, it means that it can be counted on as a constant. Just like a noble chemical is constant in all conditions, the archetypal noble person embodies the constancy of personal equanimity along with constant commitment to common good.

The stability of chemical nobility is a good metaphor for an alchemical leader. In accordance with chemistry's definition of noble being a substance that is inactive or inert, *the noble archetype has unwavering integrity and an unshakable ethic for being in service to well and happy constituents.* Equanimity is the first step toward nobility. Equanimity means that emotional triggers won't dictate circumstances or decisions. When a leader is not reactive, when s/he maintains the noble presence of personal equanimity, of holding the high watch, and of staying ethical, s/he gains greater agency with collective mojo.

Nobles usually have the duty of managing the common treasury, which is not just made up of money, but also of cultural capital. Whether it be ancient lords, kings, and queens, or CEOs today, we always want our leaders to be prudent in their management of our collective treasury such that there is abundance—plenty for everyone and enough for helping those with extra need. We want our leaders to be prudent in terms of getting the best return on investment of our financial and cultural treasuries. Prudence dictates that a leader be economical with the primal energy, the mojo, of each citizen. The noble archetype recognizes that it does not serve any population to squander its very essence, the mojo that fuels joy, satisfaction, and sound decision-making.

We want our leaders to empower us in our own nobility. We want to know that leaders have got our backs in terms of basic human needs. And we want to know that our time and talents will be valued, and our work dignified and aptly rewarded. Alchemical leaders are noble in their humble service to unseen forces for good (yin). They also build systems (yang) that value all stakeholders' nobility. Alchemical leaders build cultures where everyone can express their noble best because noble leaders support the nobility of all stakeholders. They borrow from *ubuntu* in their understanding that "I am noble because you are noble."

Noble Seed, Royal Soil

Throughout cultures and over time, wise ones have taught us to honor each and every person's nobility, or the human dignity and spirit in each. Twelfth-century Christian mystic Meister Eckhart used the metaphor of a noble seed to get at the very essence of who we are as human beings. He said, "A noble seed requires a noble soil to grow in." Eckhart uses the soil metaphor to refer to the conditions in our personal, organizational, social, and universal worlds—the ontological soils in which we are planted. Eckhart's idea that everyone is a noble seed was a radical political statement about everybody having the right to live and work in dignity, peace, and in accordance with universal values. His preaching was considered so radical that it got him ex-communicated from the Catholic Church.

What the Catholic hierarchy failed to recognize was that when everyone shows up for work at their noble best, good things happen for leaders. Not their best in the bastardized sense of the word "royal," not overdressed and self-possessed, but in the universal archetypal sense of being open-minded, ethical, respectful, respectable, engaged, and dedicated to doing good so everyone can do well. A leader's job is to develop the personal and cultural ground for nurturing the seeds they are in charge of to their fullest and juiciest fruition. Alchemical leaders tend to the metaphysical "soil" of organizational culture such that the seeds of all stakeholders thrive.

Unlike the bags of uniform, sterile potting soil that most of us are familiar with, the kind of royal soil that holds the noble seed reflects the constancy of change. Fertile soil is always composting—it is always in a simultaneous cycle of breaking down and building up. Generating best results requires that leaders develop the personal equanimity to manage both the building up (yang), and the breaking down (yin) that is part of every cycle everywhere. *The art of alchemy includes discerning when to build and when to allow for breaking down.*

Evolution mirrors the transformative plight of the seed as it disintegrates either as a shell that falls away from a sprout, or as the composted matter of a seed that rots instead of germinating. Whether it becomes a plant or soil, life evolves as the seed changes form. A leader needs to build collective soil that is developed with recognition of the inevitability that everyone, and every culture, does indeed cycle through ups and downs. Also, what is fertile for some seeds is deadly for others and so leaders need to know where and when to build what kind of soil.

Eckhart's words about noble soil reflect a leader's need to create circumstances that will help everyone bear their best fruit. Personal and systemic self-reflection on fears, needs, gifts, vision, and values creates fertile cultural soil. Even though there are excellent tools available for doing so, noble traits are rarely accounted for, and, especially given how much they impact the bottom line, are often grossly disregarded. *Simply raising your consciousness of your personal nobility, and that of every stakeholder you work with, will give you enormous metaphys-*

ical leverage in managing the treasury of cultural capital that you are accountable for.

Inanna and the Hero's Journey

The Sumerian goddess, Inanna, fulfills the archetypal model of a noble person. She was a benevolent and wise leader who was adept with the laws of the universe. Part of her story follows what Joseph Campbell identified as the three-part hero's journey. First, there is a departure from the ordinary world that is brought on by an inner leading. This stage usually includes angst and reluctance but there is either a mentor or compelling calling that cannot be ignored. Callings are heuristic urges.

The second stage of the hero's journey is the venturing into the unknown, where the tasks and trials can be brutal, and where there is sometimes help and sometimes not. This part of the journey spirals deeper and deeper until the hero reaches "the innermost cave" where s/he is completely alone and fully immersed in the central crisis, the ordeal, the obstacle—the point where s/he is tangling with the enemy and/or challenge to the point of being existentially threatened.

The third stage of the hero's journey is returning to the world with the reward, usually wisdom, which is gained either voluntarily or by coercion. Having been to the point of no return, the hero is newly born back into the world as a transformed person with new gifts for the world. The hero often returns with a new level of metaphysical power, a power gained through the wisdom that develops from having walked the hero's walk. Like any good hero's journey, the alchemical leader's path includes exploring the land of the soul and making discoveries that are ultimately not only personal but that also lead to greater good.

The hero's journey is well illustrated by the ancient story of Inanna, the Middle Eastern goddess of love, beauty, sex, desire, fertility, war, justice, and political power, who was worshipped in Sumer between 4000 and 3100 BC. Two to three thousand years later in Babylonia, Inanna became known as Ishtar, the goddess of Heaven, who had been given the gift of knowing all the laws of the universe. Because they are often universal archetypes, many god and goddess figures appear with different names throughout different cultures.

Inanna was living a good life and was adored by her people. She risked everything for a hero's journey into the Underworld where she was only permitted to enter "naked and bowed low." Humility is a common theme in heroic journeys for the same reason that it is an essential trait in both the noble archetype and the alchemical leader. Humility signifies capacity for evolution.

Inanna decided to visit her ferocious sister, who was the goddess of the Underworld, in response to an inner calling to gain greater understanding of the universe. In order to access the realm that her sister ruled, Inanna consciously embarked on a downward spiraling journey through seven stages of releasing her identity, starting with losing her jewelry and ending with hanging lifeless, in pieces, strung on meat hooks, in the deepest, darkest part of what some might call Hell. She was eventually rescued by two cherub-type angels. One concentrated on resurrecting, feeding, and healing Inanna, while the other provided empathy and care for her sister captor, who was either in grief or labor or both, according to different translations of the original Sumerian text.

Inanna's sister captor, whose ontological reality was that of the Underworld, was so disarmed by the compassion of the cherub that her power over Inanna relinquished, allowing her to arise back to her heavenly throne with renewed vitality, deeper wisdom, and even higher authority with her people than she had as a beloved goddess/queen before her hero's journey. Inanna arrived back at her starting place with new strengths, new insight, and as a literally renewed being. Throughout the entire story, despite her super-human capabilities, Inanna maintained the equanimity to never question her journey, never flinch in honoring her calling, and never stop her journey by stooping to fight her sister's negativity with negativity. Even though her supernatural powers were some of the best in the pantheon, she did not use her power to override her sister because, on a hero's journey, the only way out of it is through it. And the way of a hero's journey always includes tunnels, pitfalls, frightening leaps, failed efforts, shattering consequences, and/or dark turns.

One lesson that an alchemical leader can take from Inanna's journey is that, even in the face of absolute devastation, transformation comes by surrendering to the process. It also comes by way of choosing values-driven paths, like having compassion for the one who appears to be the destroyer. Inanna was freed because her sister captor was overcome by acts of compassion and that lesson is echoed by sages ever since her time, most especially Jesus, Mohammed, and Buddha.

Inanna's story is one of how falling into darkness is sometimes the only way to know the full spectrum of light, even when you are the queen of heaven. She literally re-membered her cut-up corpse, a metaphor for how we sometimes need to fall apart so that we can remember our greater selves. Inanna's story also illustrates how endings often turn out to be new beginnings, a subplot of all heroes' journeys.

Heeding the Call

Inanna's story demonstrates the power of listening to the small voice that makes no sense. She was doing as well as anyone could possibly be doing at the time she consciously chose to take her deep dive. She would have been fine staying where she was. Still, she followed an inner knowing, even as it took her through disorientation and, eventually, to devastation. *No matter how challenging the journey of a hero might be, after you dare to dive deep, when you rise, you will find your roots are better anchored for reaching higher than before.* Deep diving is yin. Given the degree of yin repression that we have tolerated for many generations, finding our center requires a walk on what, from a yang-itis perspective, feels like the wild side. It is risky to allow the yin to rise. It requires venturing into uncomfortable conversations, making timetable compromises, letting some things fall apart, creating more permeable boundaries, and/or negotiating unknowns.

The intuitive voice, the one that calls to us from our depths, is yin, while the voice of solid reason is yang. The yin call toward incomprehensible action often gets shouted down by a yang-dominant cultural ontology that values reason over intuition. Howard Behar listened to, more than that, honored, the same yin-intoned voice that Inanna followed. The voices that Howard credits as critical to Starbucks' success could be construed as mental illness by today's norms. Yet, timeless teachings like the tale of Inanna tell us that nothing could be further from the truth. In her time, Inanna was pretty much the CEO of all things relevant to the mortals who depended on her reign to keep them well and happy. She knew that she could not best exercise her role without venturing beyond it, without listening to the same kind of voice that Behar followed through the kinds of ins and outs that every leader faces. Inanna and Behar are examples of having a hero's faith in their inner GPSs and of having the courage to step onto the heuristic path of a hero.

The nature of a hero's journey is that people rarely have the insight Inanna had before she consciously set out on hers. Most often, there is just a strong signal from an inner GPS that feels like an inexplicable calling toward unknown territory. Heuristically following it can feel as simple as having the faith to put one foot in front of the other, or as dramatic as stepping off a proverbial cliff. Heroes always follow a path that they cannot fully fathom when they take their first steps. There are reasons that those who take hero's journeys are often known for decades, even millennia, after they lived. One of those reasons is that there is always something gained for the greater good. Another is that the remarkable courage and fortitude that it takes to even start out on, let alone complete, the journey of a hero is the stuff of legends.

The Leadership Journey

Alchemical leadership consciousness and practice come with the ability to follow the heuristic journey that is revealed moment by moment by our inner GPSs. Following heuristic urges does not always mean walking the path of a hero's journey but heuristic capacity is a part of the hero archetype. The heuristic path is an emergent, self-evident path that keeps you at your personal edge.

The hero's journey inspires us because it resonates with that special spark that drives us, especially the best of us, the ones who end up having roads and schools named after them, and whose stories are still told long after they lived. We find the travelers of the hero's journey so remarkable because it takes some awesome mojo to complete one. The hero's journey is so universal because, at some level, we have all felt the compelling force that called Inanna, that drove her to her demise, and then to her consequent resurrection as a more powerful being. Some have more propensity than others toward journeying, but life always presents opportunities for embarkation. Especially a leader's life.

Just like lack of propensity is not a reason to forego enjoying playing the piano, it is also no excuse for hitting the brakes when your inner GPS is signaling you toward the hero's path. In fact, lack of propensity for heroics is a great starting place because it probably means the path will be followed with humility, an important attribute for going the hero's distance. Many heroes' journeys start out just the opposite of Inanna's, where the main character is arrogant or fear-centered, and a great lesson of the journey is a resetting of such personality constraints. No matter how it starts, there are always good reasons to turn back, but heroes don't. In fact, even their best reasons to turn back are stripped away, just like Inanna's jewelry, clothing, and identity, as they keep on journeying toward where their inner GPSs are leading them. The leadership journey includes the stripping away of reasons because *reasons kill mojo*. Heroes live legendary lives because they transcend good reasons for turning back.

Alchemical leaders choose to step off the proverbial cliff from time to time, not knowing if they will fall or fly. They have the discernment to follow that inner voice that compels them to take a step, even when there is no apparent reason to do so and there is every reason not to. Sometimes heroes fly, sometimes they walk, limp, or run, and sometimes they crash. Heroes' journeys are not about how the transportation is going, they are about keeping going in accordance with our inner GPS, even in the face of devastating failure. Heroes, like alchemical leaders, listen to metaphysical voices, they risk, they learn from what came before them, they put their whole selves on the line, and they are malleable enough to learn the lessons from journeys taken on infrequently travelled roads.

Alchemy has a lot to do with contentment as well as equanimity. The noble archetype is a content person. The warrior represents the willingness to manage discontent head on. The hero represents the courage to move through discontent in such a way as to gain even greater levels of contentment. The warrior, noble, and hero archetypes offer insight into the ways and means of becoming a leader whose contentment supports tapping in to the transformative power of alchemy.

Leadership Reflections

1. How does your workplace soil need to be fed, tilled, discarded, or otherwise managed so that it can grow the most noble seeds?

2. Do any seeds under your supervision need replanting in more fertile ground? How can you till the cultural soil so that people under your leadership are working on more fertile ground?

3. Are you processing breakdowns more like compost or more like endgames?

4. Take some time to dialog with, and seek wise counsel from, people who stand out to you because they embody noble, warrior, and/or heroic consciousness in that they are curious, intuitive, compassionate, content, equanimous, heuristic, wise, courageous, ethical, and/or seem to live a deeply spirited life.

   It may feel weird to share deep thoughts and/or to ask unusual questions but don't be concerned, because wise ones tend not to judge, and they do not get caught up in mundane nonsense like gossip. Their ability to cut to the core of what's up will save you enormous amounts of time, and just dialoging with them will tonify your own inner wisdom.

5. Where could you use more nobility? What would it take to evolve your inner warrior to the next level?

6. Is there anything that has been nagging you, maybe way in the back of your mind, to take a risk into the unknown? If you were to take a hero's journey, what might be the first step?

CHAPTER 10

PARADIGM SHIFTING

Changing Times

Not one of today's pressing work and/or world problems is a result of too much kindness and caring, nor of too much accommodation of differences. Yet, despite a plethora of evidence to the contrary, the leadership genre has been saturated with yang messages that people, especially women, value those kinds of yin things too much and that there is no place for such fluff at work. But an undeniable international call is arising for revaluating what we value and how we value it. It is coming from a highly diverse and growing demographic that is increasingly adamant about creating cultural norms for better work in a better world. That emergent demographic, first identified in a longitudinal study on Cultural Creatives (see Anderson and Ray), is a cross-sector of men and women who recognize that there are pervasive problems in the systems of business-as-usual.

As the world comes to terms with the problem that current ontological assumptions about economics are not a plan for human survival, pioneers like Oprah Winfrey, Tony Hsieh, and thousands of civic leaders, executives, business owners, managers, farmers, artists, spiritual leaders, and concerned citizens are forging more life-affirming ways of defining success while they soar through financial ceilings. There is a global trend toward values-centered economics, policies, and practices that is reflected in part by the increasing market share for personal well-being products and services, for all things eco-friendly, for fair and transparent systems, and for ecologically and socially responsible companies.

Across the planet, there is growing alignment around the call for systemic, values-driven transformation and that collective urge is already big enough to impact everyone's work everywhere. It is a worldwide wave that is gathering momentum as it heads toward a new shore, a new normal, a new paradigm, where our common aspirations for dignity and vitality take their rightful places in our economic and social systems. There is growing recognition that conventional metrics, like gross national product (GNP), stock prices, and standard spreadsheets, only measure an extremely narrow spectrum of what people value. Despite that limitation, economic indicators are often assumed to be social indicators and that leads us to conflate indicators like a high GNP with the notion that all things are good. Increasing numbers of people are concluding that common economic standards are unacceptable because they lack valuation for the things people value most.

Gross National Happiness

In 2008, the country of Bhutan took a new approach. As their young king, Jigme Singye Wangchuck, was taking the throne after his father's death, he recognized that Bhutan needed to evolve from its historical isolationist policies. Although he wanted his country to be a player on the world stage, he was not willing to use the standard international metrics for success. Wangchuck said, "Gross national happiness (GNH) is more important than gross national product." He commissioned his officers to find new ways to gauge the vitality of his people and the viability of his culture. Nine GNH indicators were established:

- Psychological
- Material well-being/Standard of living
- Good governance
- Health
- Education
- Community vitality
- Cultural diversity and resilience
- Balanced time use
- Ecological diversity

Standards for GNH were instituted in Bhutan similarly to how instruments like GNP were being used elsewhere. It was immediately clear that they were doing something right. It was not a panacea. Bhutan still has its issues. However, by way of consciously measuring and managing the things people value most, Bhutan moved into being a significantly more robust economy in a relatively short amount of time, and the world took notice. At the same time, other indices based on full-spectrum, values-driven norms were being developed by governments including Canada, Japan, Jordan, and Finland, and in universities including Yale and Berkeley in the US, and Cumbria in the UK.

An Emergent Paradigm

There is growing backlash to yang-dominant norms that have resulted in imbalances of power and inequities in the distribution of resources. It appears that a yin-ward worldwide wave is emerging as more and more groups are cohering around values like happiness and well-being, and as more and more businesses adopt a quintuple bottom line that includes people, prosperity, planet, partnership, and peace. Many people believe that the emergent wave is nothing less than an international ontological leap toward a new paradigm, meaning a new basic model, a new set of fundamental assumptions about the way the world is. Our paradigm is our shared reality. A paradigmatic change is a fundamental ground shift, an ontological transfiguration, of our basic assumptions about personal, financial and social power. A paradigm shift means that the basic meaning of leadership power is morphing dramatically.

The demographic of new paradigm early adapters comprises a mix that crosses almost all sectors, including race, gender, age, occupation, ethnicity, education, geography, and class. Its constituents are at every level of rank in organizations and they represent a critical mass of all organizational stakeholders. They share a resonance with what their hearts and souls are telling them about their work and about the world. As this book goes to press in 2019, hate mongering and reactions to it are dominating the airwaves while there is a distinct lack of representation of the ever-widening circles of people who are establishing new levels of accountability for the value of values. Although they are still a somewhat incoherent demographic, which is partly why they are under-represented by media, new paradigm early adapters are a force to contend with. Whether you identify with that demographic, find yourself deeply suspicious of it, or choose to ignore it completely, as a leader you are necessarily contending with the reality of its depth and breadth, consciously or not.

Small and large businesses, schools, governmental, nongovernmental, and civic organizations are demonstrating what decades of studies bear out: operationalizing values is the best insurance for living and working with robust people, within robust economies, on a robust planet. We know that there is enough for everyone on the planet to be well and happy, but the problem is that our systems are geared toward other priorities. In other words, we have enough to cover everyone's needs but not to cover everyone's greed. The term "new paradigm' designates an emergent global ethic for creating workplace and civic cultures that are organized around personal, organizational, and social greatest good. You could argue that exactly the opposite is happening and site the news as evidence. Big front, big back.

The UN's Vote for a New Economic Paradigm

A significant indicator of a paradigmatic shift was the April 2012 United Nations General Assembly's vote to start convening toward a *"New Economic Paradigm Based on Happiness and Well-being."* The motion was put forward by Bhutan, and the vote was unanimous—a watershed moment in and of itself since the General Assembly is a body that often seems like it cannot agree that the sky is blue. But the evidence behind the motion was compelling enough to support unanimity in recognizing that values-driven economics create strong societies. The UN's vote exemplifies how the very basis from which leaders make day-to-day decisions is being transformed by a critical mass of diverse people worldwide who make up a growing sector of common moral suasion.

The UN is an organization of nations, a place where the well-being of whole populations is at stake, where the weight of the whole world's well-being is literally on their shoulders, and where rigid protocols are deeply entrenched. On the one hand, the UN vote to start convening toward values-driven systems seems like a radical, 180-degree shift. On the other hand, the reason that the UN General Assembly members were unanimous was because they were well aware that data from around the world, including the Bhutanese report to the United Nations, is clear: *what's most valuable to people are things like relationships, freedom, happiness, and wellness. When those values are fulfilled, almost all social and economic indices go up significantly, no matter how large or small the sample group is, and whether it be a nonprofit organization, a business, a school, a community, a whole country, or entire region.*

The reason the UN General Assembly was so united in their vote is that the countries and municipalities that are already practicing values accountancy have better economic numbers, stronger children, and fewer needs for spending money on alleviating human suffering. The UN's declaration of intent to move toward creating a new paradigm reflected an international appeal for more inclusive valuation of what people actually consider valuable—things like being able to put their kids to bed safe, fed, and warm.

A new paradigmatic framework is emerging as the world comes to grips with understanding that economics-as-usual is not a viable long-term strategy for even surviving, let alone thriving. While they may not use these terms, many people around the world are realizing that unhealthy ontological assumptions are at the root of pandemic short-term consciousness, horrific organizational and civic values digressions, and a lot of burnout—pandemic yang-itis. The paradigmatic shift is not about discounting old paradigm success metrics. Financial indices have their place, just not such an overblown place in our social priorities. The 2012 UN initiative coalesced an emergent worldwide call for more accurate valuation of values.

New paradigm theory expresses more of a journey than a destination; an unfoldment more than a goal; an emergence more than a line of demarcation. It recognizes a worldwide wave of people who are standing for a new cross-cultural Ground Zero, a new paradigm where personal and global well-being are the central organizing principles. A new paradigm is not an attempt at merely fixing the old one, it is an ontological breakthrough. History will ultimately name what the United Nations General Assembly called a "new paradigm," but there is undeniably something to be named. The UN vote reflected an emergent global coherence of consciousness that is focused on setting new ontological ground where the right for all people to be happy and well is established as a fundamental norm.

Only time will tell, but we may well be at a paradigmatic tipping point. A growing mass of people is saying no to old paradigmatic norms and saying yes to a completely different set of cultural expectations that do not yet have an official name but are nonetheless cohering across borders, and within and throughout organizations, in every sector, on every continent. What is emerging, as the old profit-at-any-cost paradigm appears to be on a collision course with humanity, is an increasing call for new assumptions about what we consider to be normal. The call is for new ontological ground that builds on the good that we've got and "composts" what is not working. The call is for building a more royal soil for everyone everywhere, that is, for all global citizens. As organizations, governments, families, and individuals all over the globe are revaluating what we value and how we value it, that impacts every leader's work regardless of whether they buy into the idea of a paradigm shift.

The fact that the UN vote was unanimous between all countries, an uncommon occurrence even when they are voting on much less extreme matters, reflects an international urge toward reinventing our social reality. That's the macro lens. The micro picture is that every leader has to accommodate seismic cultural transformation at the same time that they are juggling the complexities of just getting their jobs done, all while business-as-usual is making less and less sense to more and more stakeholders. As a leader, consciously or not, *you are managing both the shifting market as well as the rising tide that is happening in, around, and through your organization.*

The pedal might be to the metal at the level of governments and the UN, but the rubber hits the road on your desktop. The new paradigm concept captures an ontological shift going on in our ideas about leadership, meaning that the world is going through a change in the very ground of being used to define leadership. We are facing a fundamental change in what it means to be in charge. For example, Sheryl Sandberg, now COO of Facebook, wrote a book called *Lean In,* in which she advised women to essentially be more yang, to push through issues rather than to follow their natural inclinations to sometimes take more yin approaches.

That kind of old paradigmatic thinking, that leaning in to profit making is always the best strategy, played a part in leading Facebook, which had historically been a relatively strong and principled culture, to make questionable decisions on privacy issues, election meddling, and hate mongering. Sandberg's message, geared mostly to women, that essentially that they need to be more yang, has not reflected well in Facebook profits. While "yang up, gals" has been standard messaging from leaders like Sandberg and even more so from her male counterparts, it appears that heeding the new paradigm's call to "yin out, folks" might have done more for Facebook's profits and public trust.

Today's leaders stand at a precipice of consciousness. Unfortunately, cultural conditioning, outdated grad school programs, and standard practices have left many standing blindfolded at the edge. *A paradigmatic tidal shift means leaders are surfing monumental waves of change and that even the most aware leaders are doing it in uncharted waters.*

A growing mass of people across the demographic spectrum are resonating and aligning, some more consciously than others, around new fundamental priorities. It is not like we are flipping a switch between one paradigm and another, it is more like a worldwide urge toward readjusting dangerously dramatic imbalances by establishing new civic set points. In a sense, a paradigmatic shift is like a complete systemic rewiring. Just like rewiring a house, things can go haywire in the process, depending on the consciousness of those in charge. And just like the wiring in your house has everything to do with how your television works, there is significant overlap between the emerging macro trends and the relatively micro concerns that fall under your leadership.

The UN vote epitomized an emergent global call for leaders to take new accountability for building measurably better lives by creating better work in a better world. From the United Nations, to thousands of private, educational, and nonprofit organizations worldwide, to local and national governments, leaders are realizing what studies confirm: that values-driven leaders and cultures produce better numbers whether we are measuring profits, share prices, innovation, stakeholder loyalty, or personal well-being. The international demand is for a more compassionate, healthy, and just world by way of creating more compassionate, healthy, and just workplaces. Leaders who are early adapters of these new paradigmatic norms are already reaping the rewards from just how big the global call is and from just how well it pays to heed it.

Whether history proves that an ontological shift was or wasn't made, there is a clear global trend and it is unwise to ignore it. *Leaders risk being blindsided by their own irrelevance as the world's metrics move beyond the limited valuations represented on ordinary spreadsheets, in MBA texts and case studies, by standard economic indicators, and by common systems of work rewards.* Millions of people worldwide are consciously and unconsciously evolving away from old paradigmatic principles that do not factor in the value of values while, at the same time, visionary leaders are overwhelmingly proving the value of valuing values.

Old and New Paradigms

Critics say that the new paradigm concept is too esoteric, too idealistic, too radical, and/or unrealistic. Paradigm shift theory is a conceptual model and so it is helpful to remember the great twentieth-century statistician George Box's warning that "all models are wrong but some are useful." Part of the usefulness of the old/new paradigm concept is that it helps unpack the underlying reasons for the extraordinary numbers attained by the producers, consumers, civil servants, and whole countries who practice values-driven development. Paradigm change theory also helps to articulate a pathway forward toward a better world and it defines a leadership frontier.

The UN's 2012 vote reflected an emergent calculus that attempts to set a new cultural zero point, a new ontological basis of common good centered fundamentals. The proposition of a new paradigm is a way of conceptualizing a new framework for the next stage of our evolution, one that holds more accurate valuation for the metaphysicalities that make up our lives. In our current paradigm, cultural and economic norms hold extremely high valuation for yang criteria, like profit, growth, patriarchy, and political power. Yin criteria, like wisdom, well-being, peace, happiness, and connectedness, have been obscured by a yang-dominant worldview that prevails in global markets and governments.

Millennia of cultural yang dominance has resulted in a yin deficit that is reflected by the lack of women in religious, political, and civic leadership, by compromised human rights, and by deflation of valuation for the interconnectedness that people value most. While old paradigm leadership models allowed for unchecked values digressions, new paradigm norms are such that you can lose ground, lose opportunities, and lose money in accordance with lack of values accountability.

The black-and-white nature of new/old terminology is a bit misleading because it is not like we could go to bed one day and wake up in a new paradigm the next. The emergent global movement toward new fundamental cultural assumptions will take generations to establish and even more generations to stabilize. The comprehensiveness of the word "paradigm" is useful in helping to identify just how big a change is being called for. The truth is, though, there is nothing new under the sun. Ancient wisdom is well reflected in what we are calling new. The ageless principles of metaphysics are helpful in figuring out how to integrate what's on your desk right now with something so amorphous as a paradigm shift.

Our place on the human timeline seems to demarcate a swing away from a paradigm that is crippled in some ways by its inherent injustices, for example, endemic poverty. It appears we may be in a yin-ward swing toward a paradigm that is better rigged to deliver on a world of liberty and justice for all. Yin inclinations, like respecting human rights and the environment, are aspired to but not supported by old paradigm economic valuations. The emerging paradigm seeks to establish more parity between yin values for caring and yang values for productivity.

Old paradigm norms include ideas like "war is the way to peace" and "we can only afford to talk about creating a better world after we know that profits are strong." But such ideations are slowly losing their grip as new paradigm leaders are establishing beliefs like "peace is the way to peace" along with new norms for a robust quintuple bottom line that accounts for people, planet, prosperity, partnership, and peace. *New paradigm ontology restores the noble archetype by asserting new fundamental assumptions about leadership being an incorruptible channel for greatest good.*

A paradigm shift is not a leap from yang overbearingness to a kinder, gentler yin predominance. It is a striving for equanimity between all the important aspects of our lives. A paradigmatic shift means that we are not just transforming cultural norms, but rather transfiguring them. We are not just remaking old paradigmatic systems, we are redefining the ontological basis on which we build our systems.

The Paradigmatic Pendulum and the Problems on Your Desk

If you think of the timespan of humanity like a pendulum, you could think of paradigmatic changes as epochs, or distinctive periods in history, when we swing more in yang-ward directions and those when we swing more yin-wardly. For example, epochs of large-scale war are more yang, while those of more peace and prosperity are more yin; epochs known for high productivity, like the industrial revolution, are more yang, while those known for creativity, like the Renaissance, are more yin.

It is important to be conscious of macro swings because everyone is affected by them no matter how aware they are of the changes. That is not always easy because it's kind of like the old science experiments where frogs were put in pans of water that were heated up very slowly. The frogs acclimated to each new degree of heat such that they didn't discern the moment they needed to jump out to save themselves from being scalded to death. Paradigm shifts happen mostly gradually and indicators can be overlooked or mistaken as isolated issues.

It is a critical time for rethinking how you measure success. Because financial metrics have been established on extremely shallow definitions of success, old paradigmatic norms have left a lot of "successful" bosses and their employees sick and tired and living with their families in toxic conditions. The new paradigmatic yin-ward swing of our cultural pendulum is a move away from success metrics that do not include human

and environmental factors. The paradigmatic shift is quick-
ening as millennials and subsequent generations demonstrate
decreasing tolerance for many old paradigm norms.

The yin-ward swing toward higher valuations for happiness and well-being, as well as for cultural and ecological
vitality, is a swing toward more accurate accountancy for how
much people really value those things in comparison to how
much they actually value things like quarterly reports, stock
prices, and burnout. While the swing is toward higher valuation for intangibles, the new paradigm concept does not
advocate foregoing all earthly comforts. To the contrary, it
appears that, by becoming more conscious of the intangibles,
we have better quality experiences with our tangibles, including greater satisfaction and less stress about having them.

Yin tendencies toward joy, empathy, and pleasure
have been suppressed, ridiculed, and otherwise trashed by
yang-dominant paradigmatic norms that have been determining what's worth what. Old paradigm leadership was cast in
the model of militia leaders heading the charge of a brigade.
Consequently, we have understood leadership as the dominant position over a team that has been assembled for the
purpose of dominating other groups of people and/or market
forces. Being in charge has been understood as the act of having power over allies, colleagues, team members, competitors,
products, and/or services. But the framing of leaders as the
masters of the place and of everyone in it and around it is
fading, as cooperative models are proving to be not just more
effective, but also a lot easier to live with.

Old paradigmatic workplace cultures ignore even the primal equanimity between the yin of a good night's sleep and
the yang exhilaration of a jam-packed, use-you-up-in-a-good-
way day. People who compromise health, family, and well-be-

ing for the sake of logging work hours are well rewarded by old paradigm standards—until they crash and burn. It is not hard to see why mojo gets crushed by old paradigm systems where exploitation and degradation are common means of achievement. Getting beyond the pervasiveness of old and dysfunctional paradigmatic principles requires diligence with the personal, civic, and spiritual homework necessary to nurture the noble seed in self and others.

Having swung heavily yang-ward for so many millennia, a shift in direction seems inevitable at this point in history. The nature of an ontological, paradigmatic shift is that it is a move toward something radically different from current norms. Ushering in a new paradigm means building a new box—not just fixing the old one. A paradigmatic shift means that leaders must reorient to a much broader definition of success, and that means that leaders' roles are being reframed while at the same time they find themselves tasked in accordance with regressive and narrow definitions of leadership.

Old Paradigm

Subsequent to the 2012 UN vote to start convening toward a "new economic paradigm based on happiness and well-being," the work has been reframed not just as economic change but as deep systemic transformation. The word "economic" was dropped within months, as experts re-factored its place in their calculations to more accurately depict economics as just one important strand of a comprehensive reweaving of global assumptions. At its core, the UN's decision to convene toward establishing a new paradigm is a call for resetting the world's organizing principles to be human-rights-centric and values-driven as opposed to economics-centric and money-driven.

The old/new paradigm theory contextualizes how we might shift away from accepting economic indicators as the central organizing factors around which most other policies and practices are determined. Whereas the old paradigm held economics as core, new paradigmatic structures hold economics as an integral part of a much broader field of priorities. Instead of letting financial profits run every show, we now have the evidence and wherewithal for, and a cross-cultural, multi-sectoral demographic will toward, switching to values-driven operating principles.

Old paradigm hyper-valuation of materialism goes hand-in-hand with questionable ethics. Old paradigm socioeconomics overlooks the costs, and greatly inflates the value, of questionable moral behaviors like exploitation of people and resources, values digressions, and the mismanagement of mojo. The old paradigmatic, yang-dominant systems are based in reductionist ideas like, for example, that a particular gizmo is the result of a "complete" system that does not factor in stakeholder well-being or degradation of the air, water, and earth—the so-called "collateral" or "externalities."

As old paradigmatic systems struggle to reconcile quarterly growth expectations with the ebb and flow of reality, leaders end up in various vestiges of enslaving themselves and those around them because they keep trying to fulfill on the fantastical belief in a yang-dominant, growth-only model. Of course, growth and profits are fundamentally important. *But nothing anywhere only grows. There is no precedence for the growth-only model in nature nor in systems functionality.* The idea that the only measure of success is growth, yang, is arguably the old paradigm's most fundamental flaw.

The theory of perpetual dramatic growth violates human nature as well as natural law. It is an artifact of an unsubstantiated old paradigmatic marketplace mythology that still defines most of our workplaces. The old paradigmatic growth-only mentality, which is both a symptom and a cause of our pandemic yang-itis, has produced unfathomable economic and social deficits along with some of humanity's greatest glories. Big back, big front. Big yang, big yin. Hyper-valuation for yang drivers, like productivity and profitability, has yielded some amazing innovations and contributions to humanity. However, the insufficient valuation for yin drivers, like joy and freedom, has meant that progress has come at a huge cost to humanity in terms of war, greed, poverty, violence, massive migration due to political and environmental devastation, and widespread injustice.

Gatekeepers of the airwaves keep the yang trumpet sounding with incessant tales of violence, not enough-ness, and promises that the next pharmaceutical or cosmetic product holds the answer. Part of the paradigmatic shift is a recognition that we are all compromised when the yang message to buy eclipses the yin inclination to be. Yang dominance in religious, commercial, and political theory and practice has suppressed the quiet yin voice within. Ubiquitous screens and speakers saturate us with a pervasive cultural static of yang-dominant messages like "Buy, buy, buy," "Be afraid," and "Money is more important than dignity." Such old paradigmatic values can overwhelm the noble voice within—so much so that it sometimes feels like our most noble ideas get sucked into a cultural stream that's running the other way. Nonetheless, the cultural wave that's rolling away from old paradigmatic norms is formidable and cannot be ignored.

As a new paradigm is emerging, the old one is imploding. The drama of that implosion explodes on our screens everyday as we watch the news and think that things cannot sink any lower, and then they do. We are witnessing extraordinary values-compromises, many made by people claiming to be on a nonsensical moral high ground that somehow gives them license to stoop to low-level behaviors. The endemic lack of accountability for basic human values is resulting in serious personal, spiritual, systemic, and ecological depletion. Old paradigm ideations about success are based on a limited spectrum of humanity. That deficiency of scope ends up truncating the field of possibility, and that is why alchemical leadership requires having a sense of the bigger picture.

History may or may not show that our times fall in a crack between paradigms. But it is likely that our children's children will read and watch stories of wobbling systems that practiced poor accountancy for how badly people were hurting and for how tired the planet was. Depletion of our natural resources along with horrific compromises to the human spirit are raising increasingly prominent calls to recalibrate success metrics.

We are beginning to recall and implement the wisdom of indigenous people who, for example, never bought into the myth that something can be thrown away. Their ontological realities do not include an "away" to throw something into. Part of what defines the new paradigm is a growing international aspiration toward the verdant and just world we could live in if economic standards accounted for the delusion of "away."

As our environmental abuse is threatening our very existence, Americans have also developed an ethic that accepts the idea of throwaway people—elders who are essentially warehoused, one of the highest imprisonment rates in the world, impoverished kids with crummy odds for having a functional family life and worse odds for realizing their potential, and a country full of workers who find less and less meaning in their lives as the fruits of their labors reap diminishing rewards. While the fading paradigm has certainly brought us great strides in every area of our lives, there is growing awareness of how it, in too many ways, contrasts with our deeper aspirations. That contrast is helping us see our way to a new epoch where more people do better.

The old paradigm's ontology, its ground of being, is mostly silent on the value of values, even when values are purported to be central organizing factors like, for example, American ideals for "liberty and justice for all." In old paradigmatic systems, obstructing someone else's liberty can actually pay off extremely well. The movement toward a new paradigm is a global call for establishing core valuation for liberty and justice such that they cannot be usurped for economic or political gain.

New Paradigm

The new paradigm valuates values more accurately than the old one does. For example, the new paradigm defines "liberty and justice for all" much more literally than the old one does and holds both liberty and justice as core pillars, not aspirations to be reached after economic metrics are met. The new paradigm locates "life, liberty, and the pursuit of happiness" more to the center of the cultural spectrum, whereas the old one allows those ideals to only be lived by some and only after artificial conditions are met. New paradigm leadership understands freedom and the right to pursue happiness as starting, not ending points for all global citizens; as basis points rather than as things to be hoped for against odds. *A new paradigm comes with new odds, ones that are stacked in favor of all people being well, free, and happy.*

The emerging paradigm's higher valuation for more yin values is evidenced by how much its early adapters invest in robustness of body, mind, spirit, and nature, and by their prioritization for values like purpose and connectivity. The chasm between valuing and devaluing wisdom is a big gap between new and old paradigms. Alchemical leaders understand that the path of wisdom is a path of power and new paradigmatic systems cultivate and capitalize on wisdom. New paradigm principles not only align with ancient wisdom, but they also reflect our best political, business, and scientific thought leadership as well as our most heartfelt desires.

Respect for the dignity of every stakeholder is a new paradigmatic norm, as is the integration of compassion with economics. In the old paradigm, calling someone a "do-gooder" was often seen as derogatory. In the new one, it is an expectation. *New paradigm holds high valuation for social partnerships between people who are all deemed worthy of winning, partnerships aimed at experiencing and delivering goodness.* The new paradigm recognizes that all beings are global citizens who are entitled to be happy and well and to live in dignity and peace.

New paradigm socioeconomics takes more accurate accountancy of the link between work and well-being. New paradigm early adapters are proving that it pays to create workplaces that engage the whole person and that do not compromise the noble seed in anybody. The language of the new paradigm is partnership-based, values-driven, and fair-minded. As it turns out, that is also the language for success. New paradigmatic thinking is an awakening to the opportunity to develop our work and our world in accordance with our deepest drivers and highest aspirations.

The new paradigm dispenses with the myth of externality, which is the old paradigmatic theory that collateral damage, for example, water and air pollution from manufacturing, is external to the company and so does not need accounting for. The world is coming to terms with the reality that there is no such thing as "away" while, at the same time, we are also learning that there is no such place as "nowhere" when it comes to practicing the art of causality. The call for new paradigmatic norms reflects renewed and evolved consciousness of how we fit into the circle of life.

New paradigm ontology holds high valuation for inner-GPS wisdom on how to invest time, talent, and treasure into what works best for people, profits, and the planet. New paradigm leaders understand that organizations, and the people who make them up, are always evolving and that evolution does not only happen in forward linear motion but rather unfolds through the inevitable ebbs and flows of the human condition. That's why new paradigm early adapters heuristically follow inner inklings as much or more than predetermined paths.

While growth and consumption were cultural set points of the old paradigm, values for inclusive and fair economics are new paradigmatic set points. *The new paradigmatic model holds high valuation for values themselves, and it aligns around common good as a core value.* New paradigm early adapters appear to share a sense of interconnectedness of hearts, minds, bodies, souls, and universe. They often resonate with indigenous spiritual teachings and with a new—and ancient—kind of spirituality that is not necessarily reserved for organized religion. *The new paradigm holds valuation for the human spiritedness that shows up in the workplace as a powerful element of power—supercharged mojo.*

Leadership Reflections

1. What aspects of paradigm change theory do you find easiest/hardest to swallow? Are there ways that you might be caught in the gap between paradigms?

2. What is the difference between new paradigm operating principles and how your workplace operates?

3. What steps can be taken to evolve your workplace such that it syncs more with new paradigm principles? Are there old paradigmatic habits that need to change?

4. Consider having a dialog with peers about the idea of paradigmatic change and how it might inform leadership in your world.

CHAPTER 11

NEW PARADIGM LEADERSHIP

Alchemical Leadership in the New Paradigm

Emergent norms reflect many of the same pillars that alchemical leadership is built on. The paradigmatic tide is turning as a critical mass of people throughout the world are not only recovering the noble promise of humanity, but are being transformative in how they fulfill on it. New paradigm early adapters have become an increasingly mainstreaming demographic that is rarely addressed as the driving force that it is. It barely recognizes itself as a demographic, so people do not necessarily self-identify as being part of a new paradigm group, but they are unquestionably a market force that is obviously driving sectors like proactive health care, green alternatives, and socially conscious businesses, and not-so-obviously driving subsectors of people who desperately need to move beyond business as usual. New paradigm early adapters are driving markets, and because they are embedded in organizations everywhere at every level, they are also driving internal systems toward new paradigmatic policies and practices.

Even though millions of new paradigm early adapters are in leadership positions in every type of organization, they often feel isolated and unfulfilled. Not only do they struggle to relate to common business standards, they are often fearful of letting co-workers in on how much they love the fluffy stuff. And justifiably so, because the pushback can be brutal. New paradigm adapters appear to address situations at more subtle levels than their counterparts do. Consequently, co-workers can end up reacting out of fear due to lack of understanding about what is being said or done by someone who is more adept with the intangibles than they are.

The truth is: alchemists truly are threatening to the status quo because their input can impact the very ground of being, the ontology, of what is going on around themselves. *Many of the most adept alchemists are the walking wounded because the cultures they work and live in either overlook the value of, or negatively value, their propensities.* The persecution of people with alchemical proclivity is legendary. So is their contribution to evolution, which is why they're legendary. Alchemy and persecution do not necessarily go together, but when they do, it is a sign of fear-based decision-making and also an indicator that leadership is functioning in accordance with old paradigm values.

Having had the privilege of consulting with many of them over the last few decades, I know that, for quite a few years, new paradigm-leaning leaders have been whispering among those who "get it" and feeling alone the rest of the time. Many of their colleagues don't see that there is an "it" to get. But leaders who do not "get it" risk being swept away by the shifting tide of market forces and stakeholder desires. Even leaders who really "get it" still often feel trapped because they fear, and often face, disrespect and/or loss of position if they fully commit to making a better world through a better workplace. Despite the mounting evidence that following their instincts would lead to stronger organizational metrics all the way around, even those who totally "get it" cannot always figure out how to translate their understandings into their jobs. But it is not that hard. The paradigmatic leap we may be in is, at its core, a values leap. So assessing your organization's current and aspired-to values is a good first step toward making a smooth paradigmatic transition.

All Win

One of the differences between paradigms is the old one is hardwired for wins/losses, whereas new paradigmatic systems are set up for all to win. Power-mongering is a natural part of old paradigm win-lose ontology, even though we know that it is a mojo-zapper. The underlying logic goes something like: "I can only be powerful if I somehow overcome your power." We are subconsciously acculturated to suspect that "win-win" must be fantasy. New paradigm, on the other hand, is based in an all-win ontology that says: "I'm only powerful to the degree that you are"—*ubuntu*. It is hard to transcend win-lose ontology because we are immersed in it. Even so, the win-lose premise that success comes with inevitable "collateral" damage is being transformed by an emerging vision of a world that is fundamentally geared toward all global citizens doing well.

New paradigm thinking is dialectical, meaning that it sees seemingly opposing things as manifestations of wholeness, that fronts and backs, wins and losses are all part of the same whole. A dialectical viewpoint is a both/and versus either/or, a holistic worldview versus more silo-oriented thinking. The yin-yang lens helps to expose the full spectrum of a situation and that helps us identify dialectical solutions.

All-win cultures account for the inevitability of breakdowns, whereas in old paradigm win-lose cultures breakdowns are often framed as failures that can pull people further down. That's why there is a growing trend for companies to keep professional mediators on retainer so that differences get resolved on a win-win basis—a great investment in retaining talent, in efficiently and effectively overcoming problems, and in recapturing the mojo that gets drained by unresolved disagreements. In win-lose cultures, it is not unusual to be shocked by someone resigning over losses that s/he feels deeply but that you may not even have been aware of, even though you probably already paid for them by way of unseen entropy. Even when they are aware that losses are too endemic in their systems, leaders who are functioning within win-lose cultures do not have a solid ontological platform from which to intervene.

Zappos is a good example of how high valuation for personal and organizational energetics can create a culture where everybody wins. And thousands of organizations with far less progressive practices than Zappos' are also demonstrating that it is no longer realistic to ignore mojo management and still believe you are going to do your best. Zappos is radically different from how most companies its size operate, and its practices are situated squarely in new paradigm territory. What old paradigm leaders and their accountants consider to be frivolous costs, new paradigm leaders, like former Zappos CEO Tony Hsieh, understand to be capital investments.

Zappos is also a great example of how new paradigm values manifest in everyday practices and how fulfilling on those values leads to exponential growth. When I visited in 2009, one of Zappos' stairways held an employee art gallery and the other was for positive graffiti, because management had found that when it honored creativity, it got improved problem-solving, more innovation, and greater employee satisfaction. Every team had a budget and time allocation for playing together in whatever way they chose. Some chose to play board games for a few months in a row so they could save the money to see a show together in their hometown, Las Vegas. Other teams volunteered in the community, had dinner and happy hours, took group lessons, did service projects, threw parties, or went on outings with their families.

Zappos employees regularly moved around departmental work areas and redecorated with every move, so they literally refreshed their workspace on a continual basis. There were party decorations hanging from every drop-ceiling rail, and those decorations changed with every move. As goofy and time-consuming as that might seem, and as uninterested as many of us might be in cheap decorations, mojo moves when space is changed, no matter what prompts the refreshing of the atmosphere. The moves brought new neighbors, and so they heightened relationships between departments. The moving around also meant fresh beginnings were made from new digs on a regular basis, which was psychologically renewing. Zappos employees did an inordinate amount of moving of desks, but it worked for them at that time, and the lessons can be applied in many different ways. If you want to change a situation, think about changing the literal space it is showing up in—even in a small way, like cleaning a drawer.

Zappos bases its systems, policies, and practices on the fact that better people make better workers. It invests heavily in making sure that whole people come to work and that, when they get there, their collective mojo is pumped and aligned. At the entrance of the Zappos building, there was a bulletin board with messages for employees about when they could take advantage of on-site services like car washing, oil changes, dry-cleaning pickup, tailoring, and pet grooming. The company saw those as good investments in human resources because, when employees can manage errands during the workweek, it frees them from mundane chores over the weekend so that they can do recreational, restorative, and creative things that amp up their mojo for Monday morning. Zappos' return on investments in mojo was a vitalized, productive, coherent, and committed workforce that operated in a high-functioning workplace that Amazon bought for a billion bucks.

As part of its ongoing investments in fertilizing its corporate culture, Zappos had in-house cultural-upliftment programs, like fun and creative team contests, and a life coach on staff who would work with anyone in the company on just about anything except career progress. She was only there to support personal transformation—because *organizations don't transform, people do.* Some employees coached to accomplish something for charity, some for support for creative pursuits, some for physical achievements, and others for personal growth and lifestyle shifts like losing weight or improving social life. Some did not coach at all, and that was fine too. Zappos held high valuation for mojo enhancement, and it reaped the benefit of employees who were more than happy to reinvest a good bit of that mojo back into their work.

Another unique Zappos practice was that, no matter what position someone was hired for, s/he always started out in the customer service department. That way everyone began by working on the number-one priority of the company and by connecting personally with who was being served. The initial customer service orientation helped new hires understand how the company supported them to be happy and well so that they would be best positioned to best serve the customer. Connecting the dots between mojo and success was part of the onboarding process. And so was orientation to functioning in a win-win system, which was a foreign concept for most new hires.

As a very early new paradigm adapter, Zappos founder Tony Hsieh took a huge risk in investing in the kind of chaotic, limit-pushing, people-centered, yin-ward thinking that is required for the kind of breakthrough innovation, extraordinary profits, exemplary customer service, and stakeholder loyalty that companies like Zappos enjoy.

Whereas the old paradigm's set points are based on how to get the most value out of people, emergent economic valuations are based on creating value with and for people. The distinction between getting value out of people and creating value with them is subtle but profoundly important in terms of alchemical capacity. Zappos is a great example of how *new paradigm norms are predicated on empowering people to naturally manage situations such that benchmarks are not just more reliably met but are, more often, exceeded.*

Where Is the Center?

A fulcrum is the point on which a lever rests and from which it tilts or pivots. A fulcrum is a balance point, a central point. A cultural fulcrum is the central point where values converge. A new paradigm is not just a rebalancing on the same old center, it is the movement of the center itself. The paradigm shift we may be experiencing is like our cultural fulcrum is being resituated—like we are doing macro recompensation for how far to the yang side our fulcrum has been situated.

For example, the gender gap is a worthy enough cause given the state of women in the world, but the gap itself, which usually rewards men and hurts women, is a symptom of systemic yang-centric norms. Despite new laws, greater public awareness, and sincere efforts to correct it, the gender gap is still a major problem because it can only be fully remedied at the causal level by establishment of new cultural set points that just do not accommodate the dysfunction of sexual discrimination. When gender issues are a problem, they are indicative of deeper cultural imbalances. Many of those imbalances may be larger cultural issues that may not fall under your purview, but, managing your internal culture such that it cannot support gender bias is not only possible, it is crucial to creating a less discriminating world. If there is any degree of gender imbalance in positions, pay, or respect, there is cultural transformation to be done.

Old paradigm yin-yang inequities are especially glaring in the messages to women leaders who have been getting relentless advice to, "Get tough, lean in, play like the guys, and leave your feminine sensibilities at home, because there is no place for that fluffy stuff at work." Many old paradigm workplace cultures simply cannot accommodate the full range of women's contributions because femininity is yin and the cultures are so yang-centric that the yin gets choked out, one way or another, no matter how civil the discourse may be. If yours is one of those types of culture, you are not likely to fix it by being more evenhanded with women, although that's a good start. But if you are not dealing with the more systemic causes of discrimination, meaning cultural fundamentals, you are not likely to be able to harness the full mojo of half the population.

A paradigm shift is a shift in mass consciousness. A paradigm change is not just a transformational correction. It is a transfigurational resetting of our cultural pendulum's center point. The emerging paradigm is establishing a new set point that more accurately accommodates the yin drivers that have been devalued by millennia of yang-dominant leadership consciousness. A paradigmatic shift would be a reorientation of our cultural fulcrum—a relocation of what we consider to be center.

A Yin-ward Tilt

Imagine that there is a cosmological pendulum that spirals between equal and opposite poles. The emerging paradigmatic shift is a macro spin to the yin. A global paradigmatic shift would mean that the whole world would be tipping yin-ward in search of a new equilibrium that might liberate us from dysfunctional yang-dominant norms. A yin-ward tilt looks like more investment in, and higher valuation for, things like personal, professional, and communal renewal, personal and systemic self-reflection, shared vision development, falling apart and letting go, risking, contentment, relationships, inspiration, creativity, vitality, and happiness.

When organizations yin up by investing in greater kindness and caring, they are necessarily doing their part in creating the world we want. The paradigmatic reorientation toward a well and happy world is a metaphysical gearshift and that requires that we negotiate the metaphysical aspects of our reality on their own terms. We can be good without a radical yin-ward shift, but it is getting harder and harder to be great without adequately valuing the ever-deepening and ever-emerging wisdom of yin. *When in doubt, yin out.*

Paradigmatic changes do not have to fit into your work, but your work will need to fit with them because, recognized or not, they are, by definition, ubiquitous. The macro reality of paradigm shifts, and the micro reality of getting things done, sync up at the level of leadership.

The UN's Own Paradigm Shift

I started working with UN departmental and UN-based Non-Governmental Organization leaders in 2007 to support fulfillment of the UN Charter, a values-rich document. People were frustrated because organizational cultural dysfunctions were hindering their reasons for leaving their homes and families, for making less money than their private-sector colleagues, and for managing the mind-boggling, and often dangerous, frontiers where cultures of nation states collide.

In a Visionary Dialog series I led over five years, high-level UN leaders shared their fears that, in the hierarchical, protocol-driven UN culture, career trajectories could be derailed by conversations that included metaphysical distinctions, despite the fact that the UN Charter is one of the world's greatest values statements. It often struck me that, if it was that hard to build alignment at the UN, where values are so primary to its mission, no wonder it is so hard for other kinds of organizations to build and maintain their cultural capital.

One UN country leader told me that people who were operating on new paradigm-oriented principles were part of a "secret society." I saw letting the secret out (without compromising the individuals who were sharing to the point of tears in our sessions) as part of my job description, so I experienced the 2012 vote for a new paradigm as a watershed moment. It felt like a roller-coaster swoop from fearful dialogs about career damage for making transformational, values-driven choices to the unanimous vote to convene toward a new paradigm based on universal values for happiness and well-being.

What, for me, started as discrete dialogs among a narrow band of progressive UN leaders had evolved into a unanimous vote for a paradigmatic swing toward exactly what the visionary leaders I was working with were unwittingly gearing up for. The UN, as an organization, has begun translating new paradigm distinctions into its own system by prioritizing its own transformation.

Sustainable Development Goals

Between the years 2015 and 2030, the UN has unanimously agreed to work on a seventeen-item to-do list for the world, the Sustainable Development Goals (SDGs). It is the first time that such comprehensive goals and targets have been so clearly articulated and committed to as a transformative agenda that the whole world has signed on to. The unanimity on the SDGs is profound because it was reached after a few years of an extraordinarily inclusive, worldwide process for determining exactly what the goals would be and what the specific targets are for meeting each of those goals. The process was done cooperatively, over time, with respect and common purposefulness—a good setup for the alchemy it will take to realize the goals. The seventeen Sustainable Development Goals are:

GOAL 1: No Poverty
GOAL 2: Zero Hunger

GOAL 3: Good Health and Well-being

GOAL 4: Quality Education

GOAL 5: Gender Equalities

GOAL 6: Clean Water and Sanitation

GOAL 7: Affordable and Clean Energy

GOAL 8: Decent Work and Economic Growth

GOAL 9: Industry, Innovation and Infrastructure

GOAL 10: Reduced Inequality

GOAL 11: Sustainable Cities and Communities

GOAL 12: Responsible Consumption and Production

GOAL 13: Climate Action

GOAL 14: Life Below Water

GOAL 15: Life on Land

GOAL 16: Peace and Justice and Strong Institutions

GOAL 17: Partnerships to achieve the Goals

The SDGs are an important step in terms of identifying tangible outcomes, like clean water and air. It was a breakthrough to break down such a comprehensive agenda into such clear and distinct bullets. However, as the work has gone forward, people are increasingly recognizing the interdependencies between the goals—that we cannot accomplish one goal without accomplishing them all. The UN has a motto: "No one left behind." Similar to the realization that no goal exists independently of the others, there is increasing clarity that, as long as one person is behind, we are all living beneath our potential—*ubuntu*.

UN actors appear to be getting more resolute about how old paradigm hierarchies and protocols must transfigure into new values-driven structures because the SDGs cannot be fulfilled on from within the same systems that created the problems that the SDGs address. The UN, along with many others, appears to be recognizing that ultimate power comes with honoring the interdependencies of our co-existence. At the UN and elsewhere, there is a growing movement toward establishing a global citizenship ethic that is based on the fundamental premise that all beings have the right to live their best lives and that the well-being of all depends on the well-being of each. Global citizenship refers to the policy and practice of creating royal cultural soil so that each and every noble seed can thrive. (see Carley, Kosmos Journal)

A New Story

Many people miscategorize the transformative work that is happening all over the planet as the work of sustainability, but that word is seriously deficient. Sustainability has been a good concept for helping to transition our thinking, but it does not make the paradigmatic leap. Paradigm change is a change of boxes, so, by definition, if we are trying to sustain one box, we necessarily are not developing a different one.

The consciousness-raising that has been done by the movement toward sustainability has been important, but the problem is that sustainability is a very low benchmark. Extraordinary work is absolutely being done by good people in the name of sustainability. But sustainability consciousness limits vision and possibility because it literally means prolonging and upholding what is already so, which is not a great plan since we are well into the danger zone in terms of climate and pollution problems. Also, sustaining is impossible because the nature of reality is that it is always changing.

Imagine if you met an old friend on the street and asked, "How ya doing?" and s/he replied, "I'm sustainable." You would probably be concerned, maybe even worried, since that would indicate some stuck mojo at the very least. Although sustainability is a well-accepted concept, it is rarely examined for what it actually means. To begin with, compared to thriving, sustaining is a low bar and so not all that compelling of an aspiration. Organizations and situations that seek to merely sustain are more likely declining because the goal of sustaining is not much of a mojo-mover. As a leader, if you are playing to sustain, you are playing to keep the status quo going—an extremely weak leadership platform that has high probability for going retrograde.

Despite it not being a very inspiring cultural aspiration, sustainability is compelling enough that many of us rally around it without stopping to ask, "Sustain what?" Sustain systems that are fundamentally flawed by making those systems a little greener? Work done in the name of sustainability too often amounts to greenwashing the fact that *a cleaner version of business-as-usual is a nonsensical aspiration in terms of planetary survival.* There is no possible way to sustain the natural world from within a paradigm that inherently trashes it.

Sustainability is an idea that takes us to the ontological divide between paradigms. Without a leap onto a new ontological platform, that is, without inventing a new story about who we are, what we do, and how we do it, we will be stuck chasing never-ending symptoms of an outmoded ontology. While the rallying around sustainability has been effective in moving us forward, it cannot get us to where we need to go because sustaining is not a plan for basic survival, let alone for thriving.

A paradigm change is a story change and, as technology and trade are shrinking our world, we now have the unprecedented capacity to consciously evolve ourselves toward a common-good-driven story of how our world works. Ronald

Reagan said, "There are no great limits to growth because there are no limits of human intelligence, imagination, and wonder." Growth is limited when intelligence, imagination, and wonder are limited by the stories we are thinking, imagining, and wondering about.

There is an increasingly coherent population whose inner GPSs are leading them to create new stories, ones that are far more expansive in their inclusivity of the full range of human potential. Our shifting priorities along with our e-interconnectedness are shaping a new values-driven narrative that is not just yielding extraordinary numbers, but is also creating a global citizenship-centered ontology that cannot accommodate many old paradigmatic problems.

Leadership Reflections

1. Language is the key to how well you negotiate the paradigmatic divide. Do the words you choose align with the emergent global will to alleviate yang-itis?

2. How does the idea of a yin-ward cultural wave resonate for you? How do you see that affecting you and your organization? Are there team members who seem particularly in/out of touch with new paradigmatic principles?

   Is there someone around you who probably "gets it"? Find out what s/he is thinking.

3. Are there small (or big) changes that need to be made in your physical space? There may be other people on your team who have more propensity for recognizing

and creating quality of space. Ask their opinions and
take their advice.

- Is there a small change, even one that is hardly
  noticeable, that you could make in a workspace?
  Is there one drawer, one pile, one vase, one shelf,
  one desktop configuration that could be changed,
  cleaned, or cleared? Do it. Because mojo moves
  when space is changed.
- What physical changes would make your workplace more vibrant? When you look around, do
  you notice any areas where things tend to pile up,
  get dark, or seem to be unapproachable? How can
  you move the mojo in those places?

4. Where are there win-lose dynamics playing out in your
   workplace systems? How can you start to transform
   them to win-win? What would it take for all of your
   stakeholders to win?

5. Appendix 2 is the United Nations Global Compact, a
   document that outlines business principles. How does
   it apply to your leadership situation?

- In what ways are you compliant/noncompliant
  with the UN Global Compact?
- How can you enhance your organization in accordance with Global Compact principles?

CHAPTER 12

THE REINVENTION OF WORK

Dawn of a New Fire

Mystics and philosophers have forever grappled with the spark of life that generates intentions and makes them real. The only thing we know for sure about the spark that animates us is that words can never describe it. The most cross-culturally consistent word seems to be "love." *A Course in Miracles* (see Schucman) says there are only two emotions: love and fear. That pretty much captures the metaphysical difference between old and new paradigms. You could say that the old one is fear-based and the new one is love-based. Not romantic love. Not on-again, off-again gushy stuff—but the most powerful driving force in the universe because it has the capacity to transform what it touches. *When people love their work, they deliver!*

Metaphysical influences have always been, and will always be, pervasive and operative in the human experience.

New paradigm thinking is both a renewal of our availability to metaphysical realities, as well as higher prioritization of our facility with them. With so many leaders already making the transition to values-driven leadership, we are seeing the dawn of the new fire that de Chardin wrote about—a common-good-centered fire, one that cannot be fueled by fear or through the pain of others, but rather by humanity's greatest force: love. Old paradigm leaders have spent billions of dollars, and far too many lives, to intervene between populations and their direct connection to that inner fire because it can be so threatening to the status quo. But alchemical leaders catalyze those sparks of causality and then fan the flames.

As "softer," more yin indicators and practices are becoming more and more operative in our workplaces and our world, we're seeing higher prioritization of, and greater valuation for, well-being, dignity, compassion, harmony, and justice for all global citizens. A new fire is dawning with an emerging clarity that we are the hearts, we are the hands, we are the feet, we are the voices, we are the minds, and we are the souls who can and must co-create our peaceful co-arising with one another and with the planet.

Reinventing Work

Most adults put the highest percentage of their time and energy into the workplace, and the practices and outputs of workplaces have the biggest impact on the world. So uplifting workplaces is key to having the world we all want to live in. New paradigmatic norms are geared not just toward increased organizational strength, but also toward better quality of life for all stakeholders. *You can train dogs, but you have to develop people. And people develop best when their leaders create fertile cul-*

tures for their most noble instincts. It is now clear that no matter what the organizational situation, it pays to support the very primal human drive toward happiness and well-being.

Many organizations have broken free from yang-dominant norms to create thriving workplace cultures that place more equitable valuation on the intangible (yin) aspects of their success. Jay Wilkinson, CEO of Firespring, installed a huge sliding board between floors when he remodeled the building that houses his marketing company. He told me he was surprised that it was not only used more often and by more people than he expected, but that so much mojo got stoked by it. Accountability for invisible factors continues to rise as leaders are finding new ways to shift energetics. New paradigm way-finders are also aspiring toward more horizontal, and less hierarchical, structures because *organizational mojo hangs in the balance of how well-distributed power is.*

New paradigmatic leaders have to work deeper than their predecessors because they are expected to account for their organizations' primordial power, their mojo. The more that values are operationalized, the greater the mojo that is available. *New paradigm accountancy factors in the fact that mojo rises when basic human needs and values are met—when the noble seed is rooted in rich royal soil.*

New Paradigmatic Leadership

Alchemical leadership comes down to the capacity for catalyzing, harnessing, and unleashing mojo. A leader's personal consciousness determines whether s/he effectively manages mojo or suppresses it. The former is alchemy, the latter is mojo mismanagement. While old paradigm leadership behaviors often result in mojo-mucking, new paradigm leadership focuses on mojo-making. Many organizations are either creating new positions, like Chief Happiness Officer, or Head of Culture, or including similar distinctions in more traditional job descriptions. As increasing numbers of organizations are consciously slotting mojo-management duties into positions of power, there is mounting evidence of high returns on investments in those positions.

Every organization needs a designated Chief Mojo Officer, a CMO, who is in charge of fueling sparks. It could be taken on by a CEO, a current team member who works that job maybe for only an hour a week, or it could be filled by an outsourced consultancy contract. Designating CMO accountabilities signifies valuation for culture, happiness, and well-being. Creating that valuation in your systems puts the odds in your favor for successes that exceed expectations.

Leading-edge leadership experts are echoing the guidance that philosophers, moral leaders, and clergy offer for maintaining equanimity while walking the ever-changing landscape of life. Just like champion martial artists develop their inner fire and outer moves, alchemical leadership requires continually evolving your internal personal power along with your effectiveness with wielding it. Advanced martial artists, just like all other elite athletes and many masterful organizational leaders, always have coaches. In the same way that high-stakes athletes work with professionals to facilitate physical and professional gain, alchemical leaders often do their deep-diving with seasoned counsel. *If the quality of your deliberations is sound, the results of those deliberations are more likely to be successful.* Deliberating in a vacuum is not likely to be a sound process.

As the old paradigm premise that power is located in a position is eroding, new paradigm leaders are capitalizing on our natural tendency to grant authority to those who take on responsibility and manage it wisely and nobly.

Conscientization

The most successful leaders produce a spectrum of success that ranges from strong financials, to best practices, to contributing toward greater good. To do that, they need to be conscientious of the big picture. Twentieth-century Brazilian philosopher and educator Paulo Freire coined the principle of "conscientization" to describe the call for each person to achieve in-depth understanding of the world, particularly through contemplation of social and political contradictions. Conscientization is a helpful concept in terms of alchemical leadership because it defines a spectrum of consciousness that supports leaders in producing more than the sum of parts.

The three-stage process of conscientization moves from magical thinking, to naivety, to critical social examination. Interestingly, indigenous wisdom often holds value for each of those stages, but the indigenous approach tends to be more circular, while the modern Western approach to the three stages tends to be more linear.

Indigenous wisdom values magical thinking for its own sake, whereas more Western thinking can treat it as a waste of time or a phase to rise above and leave behind. Western ontology holds deflated valuation for that which the rational mind can find hard to make sense of. The devaluation of the magical-thinking stage can end up diminishing creativity and vision. Step two, naivety, is another way of saying "beginner's mind" or looking without prejudice and seeing without bias. Step three is the vantage point of high-level awareness of social context, an invaluable leadership perspective. It is the point of understanding self as a global citizen.

The alchemical leadership conscientization process moves from unconventional ideas about what's possible, to open-mindedness about feasibility, to a more universal consciousness of cultural, ontological, and spiritual scaffolding. *The three stages of alchemical conscientization are out-of-the-paradigm thinking, beginner's mind, and focus on the cultural context within the organization as well as the larger cultural context within which the organization exists.* Having a sense of the larger picture is important because your work is necessarily influenced by the paradigm it is happening in. At the same time, *paying attention to the larger cultural context helps sharpen the lens of global citizenship, a lens that helps us see how we want to play our parts in co-creating the world we all want.*

Setting your Leadership GPS

Alchemical leadership requires an inner GPS with coordinates that are set for what lies beyond what is known. It requires the bodacious-ness to walk the path of wisdom toward territory that is beyond a world still largely defined by yang-dominant worldviews. The wisdom path is not just the knowing path, or the feeling path, or the path of vision and truth seeking. It is all of those combined and more. It is a path of infinite inquiry.

Alchemical leadership requires making the ontological leap from framing a leader as someone who merely has the right answers to someone who more often has the next best question. Having good questions necessarily means you have had the bodacious-ness to ask dumb ones. Comes with the territory. In fact, the nature of the metaphysical domain is often that what looks like a brilliant question one day turns out to be ridiculous the next, and vice versa. What might seem like an absurd question based on magical thinking can turn out to expose the next greatest frontier. What appears to be naive can reveal new ways of thinking. What appears to be social criticism can lead toward more compassionate and just norms.

Just like an electrical charge must be sourced, sparked, and directed, so must a leader charge the invisible currents in themselves and their organizations. As a leader, it is not enough to work on your own mojo, because the greatest wins happen when everybody's mojo is fully fueled. Empowering everyone else's sense of personal equanimity, and their acuity with their inner GPSs, is a key factor in the practice of alchemy. Where there is a front, there is a back, though. When everyone is empowered, leaders sometimes find themselves feeling like they are herding cats. That is a genuine concern for new paradigm leaders that is best managed by consciously developing cultural coherence and staying accountable for cultural capital.

Wise ones have taught that empowering others is the best way to empower yourself. It seems counterintuitive to think that empowering others necessarily empowers me, but new paradigm norms define leadership to mean being empowered by the whole to represent the whole. Building on that definition, it is logical that when those who make up the whole are empowered, so is the leader. More empowerment equals more mojo to work with. But there is undeniable risk in stepping back so that others might step up, which is why it can be a questionable step within old paradigm ontology. Alchemical leadership surmounts that fear-based acculturation by capitalizing on the fact that all boats rise when the water level does.

Organizational Mojo

Yang-itis is losing its death grip on people's spirits while they are at work with the emerging understanding that a spirited workplace is a sign of abundant cultural capital. Spiritedness is a metaphysical spark. Generating, harnessing, and unleashing that spark is a matter of leadership consciousness.

Oprah's off-the-charts success exemplifies how well it works to invest in people's spirits and in the spiritedness of the collective. Spirited leaders like Oprah can be accredited as paradigmatic pioneers who have established common good as the central organizing factor so that whole people put their whole selves into what needs to get done. *Common-good-centered cultures support common-good-driven behavior.*

One reason that values-driven approaches pay off so well is that the more stress bio-chemicals that are released in the body, the less focus and wellness an employee has. *Stress happens when values are threatened.* A stress-inherent cultural ontology reflects unconsciousness of metaphysical drivers like creativity, emotional stability, and vitality, which release feel-good bio-chemicals that make people happy, productive, and energetic. While we cannot go around doing blood tests to check on how bio-chemicals are flowing, it is not that hard to tell if people are in the mojo flow zone. The more content they are, the more likely that they are in it. *The emerging leadership paradigm holds high valuation for the internal zone people need to be in to produce their best work.*

Alchemical leaders create the conditions for a strong mojo zone most of the time. Personal and inter-relational spiritedness, or mojo, is cultural capital and it is worth consciously investing in because it costs a lot less than the unconscious mojo crushing that happens in so many workplaces. You could say that if you want to stoke mojo, stroke it. *Since mojo has the alchemical effect of multiplying your power, subsidizing mojo-raising cultural development is not an expense. It is a capital investment.* Alchemical leaders recognize the power of individual mojo, they recognize the enhanced power of collective mojo, and they recognize the value of creating alignment and coherence among the collective so that mojo movement is in sync.

Interconnectivity

Whether we look at it from the vantage point of indigenous wisdom, physics, philosophy, ecology, or biology, it is clear that we can no longer ignore the reality that all things everywhere are interdependent—especially work teams. At the same time, international happiness studies, including Barrett's "National Values Assessment Resource Guide" as well as the collaborative BRAINPOoL Project, confirm that, across cultures and demographics, the thing that most people value most is feeling a sense of interconnectedness. Accordingly, organizational mojo is fueled by investment in interconnectivity.

New paradigm organizations account for interdependencies by taking a more horizontal, partnership-based, and co-creative approach to leadership than the old, more hierarchical, paradigm does. Co-creativity is the currency of interconnectedness. It is a mindset, a cooperative state of being that underlies the doing of things. Co-creativity is an alchemical process that transcends vicious cycles of rule-making, -following, -breaking, and -enforcing because, by definition, it builds co-ownership and cooperation, both of which are strong metaphysical forces.

The benefits of managing the interconnectivity within an organization are pretty obvious, while the benefits of managing it with everything and everyone else on the planet are not so apparent. Alchemical leaders factor in our interdependencies by attending to a quintuple bottom line–*people, planet, prosperity, partnership, and peace.*

Emergent Development

A common complaint about new paradigm-oriented practices is that they take too much time. By old paradigm standards, that's true. But sometimes you have to go slow to go fast, that is, go for big yin to produce big yang. Even though most leaders do not feel like they have the latitude to slow down enough to focus on it, conscious cultural development cannot be an afterthought because, when you take the time to do it right, it gives you a solid launching pad for everything else. Alchemical leadership depends on cultural development, and that just takes time and other resources.

Cultural development is an emergent process that is ever unfolding and so it is never-ending. Going back to the seed analogy, when something new is emerging from a seed, the hard shell gets broken open by the expansion of life from within. The emerging plant is a heuristic unfoldment in that, although its genetic makeup determines a lot, it, like every other life form, will be a unique expression of a common gene pool. Alchemical leadership makes way for heuristic unfoldment as one of its core strategies because producing more than the sum of parts is reliant on unique expression.

Organizational expansion happens within a framework of leadership that may/may not have the capacity to support what is emerging, and that may/may not be able to find equanimity between pressing deadlines and a shell that may be breaking apart. Some organizations don't even have enough mojo for shells to be cracking and may not recognize that their dormancy is hurting productivity. And sometimes so much focus goes to a cracked seed that what is emergent goes un-nurtured. *Alchemical leaders have the courage to allow for breaking down, the fortitude to hold steady when things unexpectedly break, and the clarity to recognize when breakthroughs are emerging from seeds that appear to be falling apart.*

Leadership Reflections

1. How do you account for culture? What values are operative in your workplace? Which ones are compromised? What values could be better operationalized? The values list in Appendix 3 may be helpful.

2. Are you a quintuple-bottom-line company? Of the five—people, planet, prosperity, partnership and peace—which is the strongest? Weakest? Which one feels like it is most ready for transformation?

3. How can you subsidize mojo? Mojo investments might reflect Zappos' bulletin board for services like car washing, dry cleaning, animal grooming, and other errands so that employees are free to live a fuller life on weekends; or team connection budgets that they get to allocate; or subsidies for arts lessons, meditation classes.... It might be something much bigger, like installing an exercise or meditation room or setting up a care program for babies or elders.

4. Consider convening wisdom circles, either within your organization, with peers and/or with community

representatives. They might look like quarterly opportunities for systemic self-reflection, creating feedback loops, or holding meetings for discernment when there are issues to be worked out, or they could be meetings for blue-sky thinking.

5. Walk yourself through the three steps of conscientization:

   - Do some magical thinking.
   - Release into beginner's mind.
   - Explore the cultural context you are imagining into.

   Keep in mind that this is both a linear and a non-linear process—skip around.

6. What does being a global citizen mean to you?

CHAPTER 13

CONCLUSION

Universal Transformation

Alchemical leaders realize that people at the top of the responsibility chain play especially critical roles in creating the work we want to do and the world we all want to live in.

The vast concept of a global paradigm shift is a way of:

- conceptualizing the larger context in which your organization is situated
- contextualizing your leadership role in transformational times
- revealing the roles of those with strong propensity for ushering it in.

Thanks to the great minds and hearts that contributed to the amazing world we've got, there are solid historical yin and yang pillars to build on as we formulate new paradigmatic understanding of what power is and what we want to do with it. After living in a yang-dominant ontology for millennia, we are witnessing the dawning of a new ontology that holds universal well-being as an anchoring principle. The conscientization process is a way to think about how to utilize the momentum of this evolutionary moment to catapult your organization to new heights.

Whatever it ends up being named by history, leaders and business schools risk irrelevance if they choose to ignore the leap of economic and social consciousness that is represented by the concept of a new paradigm. There are many choices yet to be made between where we are and where a new paradigmatic reality might take us. But wherever we end up, it is clear that it no longer works to equate power with control or success with just financial growth. Workplace parameters are evolving, and leaders must evolve themselves and their cultures to keep up.

A paradigmatic resetting of cultural coordinates demands a resetting of every leader's personal, professional, internal, and external compass points such that the role of mojo is no longer considered extraneous but is squarely located at the center of decision-making. However, alchemical leaders go beyond developing personal and collective mojo alignment. They take a global citizen approach by aligning their organizations with universal ethics and values, which, in turn, sends signals to workers that automatically raise individual and collective mojo because that's what happens when people feel part of something that is bigger than themselves.

Reinventing Success

We are living through a reestablishment of just what the equanimity needs to be between yin factors like intentionality, civility, relationship, inner strength, and wisdom; and yang factors like financial data, methodology, physical strength, and rationalism. Paradigmatic shifting is not about valuing the yin more than the yang, it is about creating a dialectic ontology based on both/and, rather than either/or, consciousness. *A dialectic ontology frames power as yang best practices, expertise, and competence being in dynamic equanimity with yin morals, shared vision, and aligned consciousness.*

Since we have had yang-dominant norms for so long, the emergent paradigmatic correction needs to be yin-ward leaning. The world is demanding that the yin voice be brought into full-fledged harmony—not muted, not retuned, and no longer kept at a hum. As the paradigmatic pendulum swings away from the yang-ward spiral we have been in, the emerging yin-ward cultural swing is toward the whispers of wisdom's voice. The acknowledgment of metaphysical influences along with heightened consciousness of our interdependence with one another constitute a cultural epiphany. And now that a critical mass of people is experiencing that epiphany, there is no going back. Leaders must abide or step aside.

In such a rapidly changing world, it is becoming clearer than ever that the dynamics of success are far more fluid and far less tangible than we have been believing. Metaphysics, which is the study of the fundamental nature of things, is the domain for addressing the dire need to reinvent success in accordance with our universally desired common ground of interconnectivity, happiness, and well-being. We are each a factor in the evolution of billions of factors that make up life on Planet Earth. Our consciousness is a mega-factor, all the more so when it is aligned with others. The shift away from values-suppressive norms and toward a world that works for everybody reflects, above all else, a global shift in consciousness.

Going Forward toward the World We Want

As we enjoy unprecedented communications connectivity, we are waking up to newfound capacity for evolutionary leaping toward living out our highest ideals. The United Nations' 2012 vote to start convening toward a new paradigm based on happiness and well-being, and the world's agreement on the seventeen Sustainable Development Goals, reflects a growing number of people whose consciousness is aligning toward new ways of operating.

Though the mystery of our cosmic unfolding can never fully be known, we do know that time is a continuum of changes. *The capacity to demonstrate causality in the matter of change is alchemical power.* Alchemical leaders are adept with causing what is happening under their watch by way of consciously working with the metaphysical forces that flow through and around each one of us. Alchemical leaders catalyze the sparks of new, bold, bodacious visions of a workplace and a world that works for all global citizens.

Leadership Reflections

1. Consider how you might develop your workplace metaphysically. How can you cultivate causality?

2. Consider some group "being" time for your team. Create some out-of-the-box opportunities to laugh, play, or co-create together. Schedule and announce them.

3. Think of yourself as a global citizen. Using the lenses of interconnectivity and *ubuntu*, how could you see things changing?

4. How might your workplace become a bigger player in your community, your state, your country, and/or the world?

5. If you were to hire a Chief Mojo Officer, what would the job description be? What would you want CMO deliverables to be? What would you want her/him to fix or change in your current situation? What difference would s/he make?

6. Are there sparks in the air? Where? How can you and your co-workers play a bigger game?

7. The L.O.V.E. formula that follows is a framework for ongoing inquiry into having the life you love, the work you desire, and the world we all want to live in:

L—Look at an issue that touches you, that triggers something inside of you—something in the news, at work, in your neighborhood, or in the world. Learn about it. Be curious, open, willing to suspend what you "know" (beginner's mind) so you can broaden your range of understanding. Do some research, talk to others about their understanding, and/or just sit with the issue to get present with it.

O—Own it. Why does it matter to you? Drill down into the passion that makes this a concern for you. What is it about this issue that resonates with something in you? How does the issue impact your life? What difference does it make to you?

V—Valuate it. What are two or three underlying values that feel challenged, violated, or reinforced by your concern? What is the most important, most fundamental aspect of the issue? In what way does it reach the level of a values conflict or compromise? What core concerns does it raise for you? How does it fit in with your vision or desires for something better?

E—Evolve it. Evolving an issue can happen by doing things as small as changing your mind or saying a prayer, or as big as running for office or starting a nonprofit. Evolution of an issue can happen by posting online, by creating new conversations, working with or giving to an organization or a movement, or by just paying attention to a little nudge in the space of your own heart and soul.

What is not said and done can evolve things as much as what is. Evolution happens not just with action but with every decision not to proliferate the issue by telling an old story about it. It can happen by just being quiet when we might have complained or told a fear-based story.

Evolving an issue involves consciously changing the stories we tell about it as well as being more discerning about which stories we participate in. Consciously changing your language about an issue evolves it because changing stories creates ontological shift. Raising your awareness and purposefulness with the words you choose is a transformative act.

Whether you want to change your work or change the world, L.O.V.E. is always a good starting place!

GLOSSARY

Accountability—justification of actions or decisions; responsibility.

Acculturation—assimilation of a dominant culture; the process of normalizing a particular worldview.

Alchemy—the art of consciously using metaphysical principles to cause unexpected things to happen; the medieval forerunner of chemistry, based on the supposed transformation of matter; a seemingly magical process of transformation, creation, or combination. A transfiguration of resources into something more than the sum of parts which takes place in a way that is not obvious.

Alchemical leadership—the capacity to produce unexpected outcomes by being intentional with primal, metaphysical drivers, like values and volition; the art of recognizing, developing, harnessing, and consciously unleashing the richness of the metaphysical reality around and within self and others.

Arutum—the Amazonian Shuar tribe's word for life-giving energy that can be derived from nature and from personal and spiritual development. It is understood as critical to personal and communal well-being as well as to the ability to transform situations. Mojo.

Authenticity—relating to or denoting an emotionally appropriate, significant, purposive, and responsible mode of human life; a concept from existentialist philosophy.

Authority—the power or right to make decisions and give orders. Studies demonstrate that whoever accomplishes the highest level of personal development holds the most authority in a group—regardless of rank. That means that any leader's authority is superseded by anyone on the team who is further along in his/her personal development—regardless of job titles.

Bosons—a type of atomic particles that carry force versus their better-understood counterparts, fermion particles, which comprise matter.

Catharsis—the process of releasing, and thereby providing relief from, strong or repressed feelings.

Chi (ki)—Chinese and Japanese word for vital energetic life force that determines health and personal power for making things happen; similar to *arutum* and mojo.

Commons—the cultural and natural resources that are not privately owned and are accessible to all members of a society, including natural materials such as air, water, and earth, as well as intellectual property and civic space; shared informal norms and values.

Conscientization—the call for each person to achieve in-depth understanding of the world, particularly through expanding personal viewpoint and exposure to perceived social and political contradictions.

Consciousness—awareness by the mind of itself and the world; being awake to and aware of surroundings; perceptivity to intangibles; awareness with a purpose.

Culture—the values, beliefs, and behaviors of an organization and its leaders.

Cultural capital—a measure of the value that can be placed on the way of being, or the collective "personality" of a collective; the time, talent, and goodwill of a collective; the energy and alignment of an organization.

Cultural Transformation Tools (CTTs)—data-based, values-driven platform for multilateral coherence developed by Barrett Values Centre; inclusive, transparent assessment tools for developing shared sense of identity, purpose and vision; CTTs have been used to transform cultures of over seven thousand organizations in over eighty countries, twenty-four nations, and hundreds of governmental agencies.

Epiphany—revelatory insight.

Fluffy myth—the belief that intangibles are inconsequential; a fear-based cultural mythology that disregards evidence that intangibles have a far greater impact on success than tangibles.

Heuristics—enabling a person to discover something for themselves; proceeding to a solution by trial and error or by rules that are only loosely defined; following intuitive guidance; the opposite of preplanned.

Integrity—the quality of being honest and having strong moral principles; moral uprightness; the state of being whole and undivided; the condition of being unified, unimpaired, or sound in construction; internal consistency or lack of corruption.

Metaphysics—the study of causality, being, knowing, identity, time, and space; the field in which philosophy and science meet.

Mojo—a mysterious component of life that is both energy and power. Mojo represents the capacity for making things happen (energy) and, at the same time, determines whether and how energy gets converted from one form into another (power):

Mojo as Energy—a life-throb that pulses through living beings as zest, dynamism, drive, passion, zeal, zip, zing, pizzazz, bounce, spirit, oomph, moxie, get-up-and-go, pep, and feistiness; a visceral experience of a metaphysical charge. Compiling the elements that make up a grape into a lab dish cannot make a grape because there is a metaphysical charge that makes life live. Mojo is that energetic spark of life.

Mojo as Power—having the mojo to transform one type of energy into another; management of personal and collective mojo. A leader's power comes with the capacity to convert collective energies into actions that fulfill on mission.

Nonviolent communication—an approach to nonviolent living based on the belief that all human beings have the capacity for compassion and empathy. The four steps of nonviolent communication are: 1) observe without blame or criticism; 2) feel into feelings of self and other; 3) express needs and values of self and other; and 4) request a change and concrete action that will enrich self and other.

Ontology—the set of concepts, categories, and domains that make up a worldview. A shared ontology is the subconscious, intangible scaffolding of language, norms, customs, and expressions.

Paradigm—basic model, a set of fundamental assumptions about the way the world is; our shared reality. A paradigmatic change is a fundamental ground shift, an ontological transfiguration, of basic assumptions.

Power—the capacity to change one type of energy into another; a cohesive and/or disruptive force. The quality, direction, and force of energetic flow leads to power.

Prana—Sanskrit word for life force or vital principle, similar to mojo.

Quintuple Bottom Line—people, planet, prosperity, partnership, and peace.

Shakti—Hindu concept of cosmic energy; a mysterious psycho-spiritual force that animates creation and causes change; mojo.

Taoism—an ancient Chinese religion that does not believe in a deity but rather in the "tao" being the way that life unfolds. In Taoism, there is no good and no bad; everything is required to make the world.

Values—what we consider to be most important in life; primal drivers of behaviors. What we value determines what life means to us and what actions we take. Honoring our values on a consistent basis creates satisfaction and fulfillment.

Woundology—a word coined by author Caroline Myss to pinpoint the language of attachment to stories about past physical and emotional hurts, victimization, and upsets; indicates stagnation; a disempowered language of being stuck in pain and fear cycles.

Yang—Chinese philosophical concept for the active male principle of the universe, associated with tangibles, fullness, activity, mental activity, contraction, fragmentation, finite.

Yang-itis—excessive yang. Symptoms include overwork, uninspired action, burnout, numbness, unhealthy behaviors, overwhelm, frustration, values compromises, physical and/or emotional pain, over-emphasis on materiality, tunnel vision, and undignified communications. Leaders who are afflicted with yang-itis are more likely to be perceived as domineering, privileged, arrogant, judgmental, forceful, audacious, disconnected, out of touch, and/or inhumane.

Yang-ward—contractive, reductionist, compartmentalized, mind-led, productivity-oriented.

Yin—Chinese philosophical concept for the passive female principle of the universe; life-sustaining force associated with feelings, emptiness, intangibles, expansion, holism, infinity.

Yin-ward—expansive, holistic, inclusive, heart-led, universalist, feeling-oriented.

REFERENCES

Anderson, Sherry Ruth, and Paul H. Ray. 2001. *The Cultural Creatives: How 50 Million People Are Changing the World.* New York: Three Rivers Press.

Anderson, Merrill. 2001. *Case Study on the Return on Investment in Executive Coaching.* MetrixGlobal. http://ottawa-coaches.ca/pdf_files/CoachingROI-Merrill.pdf

Barrett, Richard, et al. 2008. *Best Companies to Work For in the USA.* www.valuescentre.com. Accessed 5 April 2012.

Barrett, Richard. 2010. *Cultural Capital: A Fundamental Driver of Financial Performance.* www.valuescentre.com. Accessed 4 June 2011.

Barrett, Richard. 2011. *National Values Assessment Resource Guide.* http://www.valuescentre.com/uploads/2012-01-05/NVA%20Resource%20Guide2.pdf. Accessed 7 September 2012.

Besheer, Margaret. 2012. *UN Admits Failures in Protecting Sri Lankan Civilians.* Voice of America. http://www.voanews.com/content/un-sri-lanka-rights-abuses/1546356.html

Box, George, and Norman R. Draper. 1987. *Empirical Model-Building and Response Surfaces*, p. 424. Hoboken, NJ: Wiley.

Brown, Michael. 2010. *The Presence Process.* Vancouver, BC: Namaste Publishing.

Carley, Joni. 2019. "We Are All Global Citizens." *Kosmos Journal*, Winter Quarterly, 2018/19. https://www.kosmos-journal.org/winter-2018/?message=subs

Carley, Joni. 2013. *The Case for a Values-Driven United Nations.* http://www.academia.edu/6284502/The_Case_for_a_ Systems_based_Values_driven_United_Nations

Carley, Joni, and Howard Behar. 2010. *Masters of Profiting on Principle.* https://jonicarley.com/product/masters-of-profiting-on-principle/

Carreira, Jeff. 2017. *The Practice of No Problem.* Philadelphia: Emergence Education Press.

Collins, Jim, and Jerry I. Porras. 2002. *Built to Last: Successful Habits of Visionary Companies.* New York: Harper Collins.

De Chardin, Pierre Teilhard. 1955. *The Phenomenon of Men.* Toronto: The Great Library Collection.

Desbordes, Gaelle, et al. 2015. *Moving Beyond Mindfulness: Defining Equanimity as an Outcome Measure in Meditation and Contemplative Research.* https://doi.org/10.1007/ s12671-013-0269-8

Eisenstein, Charles. 2011. *Sacred Economics.* Berkeley, CA: North Atlantic Books.

Eisler, Riane. 1988. *The Chalice and the Blade: Our History, Our Future.* New York: Harper Collins.

Flamholtz, Eric. 2001. "Corporate Culture and the Bottom Line." *European Management Journal*, 19 (3), 268-275.

Freire, Paulo. 1970. *Pedagogy of the Oppressed.* New York: Bloomsbury Publishing.

Gross National Happiness USA. 2018. http://gnhusa.org/ gross-national-happiness/

Hall, Brian. 2004. *The Omega Factor: A Values-Based Approach for Developing Organizations and Leadership.* Unpublished manuscript, Santa Cruz, CA: Values Technology. http:// www.valuestech.com/gui/OmegaFactor4.pdf

Henderson, Shar. 2004. *A Business Case for Working with Values.* https://www.minessence.net/articles/A%20Business%20 case%20for%20values%20_3_.pdf.

Hicks, Esther and Jerry. 2004. *Ask and It is Given.* United States: Hay House.

Hicks, L. E. 1970. "Some Properties of Ipsative, Normative, and Forced-choice Normative Measures." *Psychological Bulletin*, 74: 167-184.

Hsieh, Tony. 2013. *Delivering Happiness: A Path to Profits, Passion, and Purpose.* New York: Hachette Book Group.

Inglehart, Ronald, and Chris Welzel. 2010. *The World Values Survey Cultural Map of the World.* http://www.worldvaluessurvey.org/wvs/articles/folder_published/article_base_54

Joy, Leonard. 2011. *How Does Societal Transformation Happen? Values Development, Collective Wisdom, and Decision Making for the Common Good.* Quaker Institute for the Future, 4.

Koivula, Nina. 2008. "Basic Human Values in the Workplace." *Social Psychology*, University of Helsinki. https://www.doria.fi/bitstream/handle/10024/37972/basichum.pdf

Kotter, John, and James L. Heskett. *Corporate Culture and Performance.* 2011. New York: The Free Press (Simon & Schuster).

Kushi, Michio, and Alex Jack. 2013. *The Book of Macrobiotics: The Universal Way of Health, Happiness & Peace.* New York: Square One Publishers.

Kushi, Michio, and Alex Jack. 1987. *One Peaceful World.* New York: Square One Publishers.

Light, Donald. 2014. *New Prescription Drugs: A Major Health Risk with Few Offsetting Advantages.* Harvard University. https://ethics.harvard.edu/blog/new-prescription-drugs-major-health-risk-few-offsetting-advantages

Liu, Chun-hong, Zi-you Yu, and Dean Tjosvold. 2002. "Production and People Values: Their Impact on Relationships and Leader Effectiveness in China." *Leadership & Organization Development Journal,* 23 (3), 134-44.

McGovern, Joy, et al. 2001. "Maximizing the Impact of Executive Coaching: Behavioral Change, Organizational Outcomes, and Return on Investment." *The Manchester Review,* Vol. 6, No. 1. https://www.performanceconsultants.com/wp-content/uploads/maximizing-the-impact-of-executive-coaching.pdf

Meglino, Bruce, and Elizabeth Ravlin. 1998. "Individual Values in Organizations: Concepts, Controversies, and Research." *Journal of Management*, 24, (3): 199.

Metrix Global LLC. 2004. *ROI and Learning Evaluation, Leadership Coaching and Consulting.*

Miethe, Terance D. 1985. "The Validity & Reliability of Value Measurements." *Journal of Psychology* 119: 441-53.

Ohsawa, George. 1960. *Zen Macrobiotics.* Chico, CA: George Oshawa Macrobiotic Foundation and East/West Center for Macrobiotics.

Perkins, John, and Shakaim Mariano Shakai Ijisam Chumpi. 2001. *Spirit of the Shuar: Wisdom from the Last Unconquered People of the Amazon.* Rochester, VT: Destiny Books.

Pew Research Center. 2012. *American Values Survey: Prayer Is an Important Part of My Daily Life.* http://www.people-press.org/values-questions/q41a/prayer-is-an-important-part-of-my-daily-life/#total

Posner, Barry Z., and Warren H. Schmidt. 1993. "Values Congruence and Differences Between the Interplay of Personal and Organizational Value Systems." *Journal of Business Ethics*, Vol. 12, No. 5.

"'Pursuit of happiness is fundamental human goal,' Minister of Bhutan tells UN Assembly." 2015. UN News. https://news.un.org/en/story/2015/10/511502-pursuit-happiness-fundamental-human-goal-minister-bhutan-tells-un-assembly

Reucroft, Stephen, Howard Haber, and Michael Dine. 1999. "What Exactly Is the Higgs Boson?" *Scientific American.*

https://www.scientificamerican.com/article/what-exactly-is-the-higgs/

Ruedy, Nicole, and Maurice Schweitzer. 2010. "In the Moment: The Effect of Mindfulness on Ethical Decision Making." *Journal of Business Ethics.* https://doi.org/10.1007/s10551-011-0796-y

Rankin, William L., and Joel W. Grube. 1980. "A Comparison of Ranking and Rationing Procedures for Values System Measurement." *European Journal of Social Psychology* 10: 233-247.

Royal Government of Bhutan (2012). *The Report of the High-Level Meeting on Well-being and Happiness: Defining a New Economic Paradigm.* New York: The Permanent Mission of the Kingdom of Bhutan to the United Nations.

Sahtouris, Elisabet. 2014. *Gaia's Dance: The Story of the Earth and Us.* Self-published.

Schedler, Andreas. 2004. *Political Culture and Democratization.* Notre Dame University. http://www.nd.edu/~mcoppedg/crd/Ch8IDS.pdf, Chapter 8. Accessed 5 September 2012.

Scheeres, Hermine. 2002. *Producing Core Values in the Workplace: Learning New Identities.* AVETRA, University of Technology Sydney. http://www.avetra.org.au/abstracts_and_papers_2002/scheeres.pdf

Schmidt, Jennifer, Shankar Vedantam, and Parth Shah. 2018. "The Edge Effect." *Hidden Brain.* National Public Radio. https://www.npr.org/2018/07/02/625426015/the-edge-effect

Schucman, Helen. 1975. *A Course in Miracles.* New York: The Foundation for Inner Peace.

Schwartz, Shalom. 2012. *An Overview of the Schwartz Theory of Basic Values.* Jerusalem: International Association for Cross-Cultural Psychology. https://scholarworks.gvsu.edu/cgi/viewcontent.cgi?article=1116&context=orpc

Schwartz, Shalom, and Tammy Rubel. 2005. "Sex Differences in Value Priorities: Cross-Cultural and Multimethod Studies." *Journal of Personality and Social Psychology* 89(6):1010-1028.

Swimme, Brian. 1999. *The Hidden Heart of the Cosmos.* New York: Orbis Books.

The Ten Principles of the UN Global Compact. 2000. New York: United Nations. unglobalcompact.org

Thompson, Nick. 2013. *What Is the Higgs Boson and Why Is It So Important?* CNN. https://www.cnn.com/2011/12/13/world/europe/higgs-boson-q-and-a/index.html

Underwood, Paula. 1993. *The Walking People: A Native American Oral History.* San Anselmo, CA: Tribe of Two Press (Institute of Noetic Sciences).

Veltman, Martinus. 2015. *Discovery of the Higgs Particle.* 65th Lindau Nobel Laureate Meeting. https://www.media-theque.lindau-nobel.org/videos/34703/martinus-veltman-discovery-higgs-particle/meeting-2015

Weiss, Thomas. 2009. *What's Wrong with the UN and How to Fix It.* Malden, MA: Polity.

Wheatley, Margaret. 1999. *Leadership and the New Science.* San Francisco, CA: Berrett-Koehler.

Whitby, Alistair. 2014. *Beyond GDP: From Measurement to Politics and Policy.* BRAINPOoL Collaborative Project.

Whitney, David. J., and Neil Schmitt. 1997. "Relationship Between Culture and Responses to Biodata Employment Items." *Journal of Applied Psychology* 82 (1).

Zaidel, Dahlia. 2014. "Creativity, Brain, and Art: Biological and Neurological Considerations." *Frontiers in Human Neuroscience,* 8 (289). https://www.ncbi.nlm.nih.gov/pmc/articles/PMC4041074/

BARRETT LEADERSHIP SELF-ASSESSMENT TOOL

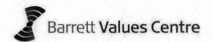
Barrett **Values Centre**

Leadership Self-Assessment

COMPETENCY	Strongly Disagree	Disagree	Average	Agree	Strongly Agree	Score
	0	1	2	3	4	
LEVEL 7						
Promotes ethical standards throughout the organisation.						
Actively promotes social responsibility throughout the organisation.						
Concerned about global issues and future generations.						
At ease with uncertainty.						
Compassionate, forgiving, displays humility.						
					Total Level 7	
LEVEL 6						
Builds mutually beneficial partnerships and strategic alliances across boundaries.						
Actively mentors and coaches subordinates.						
Active in the local community creating relationships that promote goodwill.						
Promotes environmental awareness and stewardship.						
Empathetic, intuitive and inclusive.						
					Total Level 6	

COMPETENCY	Strongly Disagree	Disagree	Average	Agree	Strongly Agree	Score
	0	1	2	3	4	
LEVEL 5						
Develops and consistently communicates company's vision and mission.						
Develops and consistently communicates company's espoused values.						
A living example of values-based leadership. Walks the talk.						
Builds an environment of trust among direct reports that brings out the best in people.						
Creative, passionate, committed and generous.						
Total Level 5						
LEVEL 4						
Seeks advice. Builds consensus. Creates positive spirit.						
Strong focus on continuous learning, continuous renewal and innovation.						
Actively engaged in own personal development, and supports personal development of direct reports.						
Empowers staff to make decisions. Resists the temptation to micro manage the work of others.						
Adaptable, courageous and enjoys challenges.						
Total Level 4						

COMPETENCY	Strongly Disagree	Disagree	Average	Agree	Strongly Agree	Score
	0	1	2	3	4	
LEVEL 3						
Uses metrics in some form of balanced scorecard to measure and manage performance.						
Displays strong analytical skills in evaluating systems and processes.						
Consistently evaluates risks before embarking on new ventures.						
Thinks strategically and moves quickly to capitalize on opportunities.						
Promotes order, efficiency, productivity, quality and excellence.						
Total Level 3						
LEVEL 2						
Regularly communicates both good news and bad news with all staff.						
Resolves conflicts with others and among direct reports quickly before relationships sour.						
Actively involved with customers, and gives priority to customer satisfaction.						
Regularly acknowledges and praises direct reports and staff for a job well done.						
Easily accessible to direct reports and all key staff.						
Total Level 2						

COMPETENCY	Strongly Disagree	Disagree	Average	Agree	Strongly Agree	Score
	0	1	2	3	4	
LEVEL 1						
Calm in the midst of chaos. Decisive in the midst of danger.						
Maintains long-term perspective while dealing with short-term issues and goals.						
Creates, manages and controls budgets effectively.						
Appropriately cautious in complex situations.						
Constantly seeks to improve the health and safety of staff.						
Total Level 1						

Scoring: Take the scores from each of the 7 sections and plot them on the histogram area between 0 and 20.

Leadership Style		0-5	6-10	11-15	16-20
7 Wisdom/Visionary					
6 Mentor/Partner					
5 Motivator/Inspirer					
4 Facilitator/Influencer					
3 Manager/Organiser					
2 Communicator					
1 Financial Manager					

Printed with permission from Richard Barrett,
Chairman of the Barrett Values Center

How to Plot: If, for example, all your Level 1 scores add up to 12, put 3 dots on the Level 1 chart and on the bottom row of the Plot. Repeat for all 7 levels. The resulting histogram offers graphic insight into your leadership. For more information on interpretation: www.valuescentre.com

Printed with permission from Richard Barrett, Chairman of the Barrett Values Center.

THE TEN PRINCIPLES OF THE UNITED NATIONS GLOBAL COMPACT

Corporate sustainability starts with a company's value system and a principles-based approach to doing business. This means operating in ways that, at a minimum, meet fundamental responsibilities in the areas of human rights, labour, environment and anti-corruption. Responsible businesses enact the same values and principles wherever they have a presence and know that good practices in one area do not offset harm in another. By incorporating the Ten Principles of the UN Global Compact into strategies, policies, and procedures, and establishing a culture of integrity, companies are not only upholding their basic responsibilities to people and planet, but also setting the stage for long-term success.

The Ten Principles of the United Nations Global Compact are derived from: The Universal Declaration of Human Rights, the International Labour Organization's Declaration on Fundamental Principles and Rights at Work, the Rio Declaration on Environment and Development, and the United Nations Convention Against Corruption. You can access more information at unglobalcompact.org regarding these principles.

Human Rights

Principle 1: Businesses should support and respect the protection of internationally proclaimed human rights; and

Principle 2: make sure that they are not complicit in human rights abuses.

Labour

Principle 3: Businesses should uphold the freedom of association and the effective recognition of the right to collective bargaining;

Principle 4: the elimination of all forms of forced and compulsory labour;

Principle 5: the effective abolition of child labour; and

Principle 6: the elimination of discrimination in respect of employment and occupation.